**Discover how to combine the phenomenal power
of the New Moon with astrological signs to
make your deepest dreams come true!**

IF YOU ARE . . .

LOOKING FOR LOVE

Let Jan Spiller show you what to wish for when the Moon is
in *Libra*. That time of the year is the best period to attract
and recognize the right marriage partner and begin a
happy relationship with that person.

LONGING TO CHANGE BAD HABITS

A *Sagittarius* Moon will give your carefully worded plea a
tremendous boost in eliminating such negative traits as the
tendency to excess and overdoing things.

SEARCHING FOR INNER PEACE

Focus your desire for serenity and control of your destiny in
a lovely affirmation when the New Moon is transiting *Pisces*.
During this fertile time, all feelings of panic can dissolve
and you will experience the bliss of being protected
by a Higher Power.

WISHING FOR FAME AND FORTUNE

The strong pull of the *Capricorn* Moon will help you find and
take those actions that lead to an enhanced social status, a
promotion at work, or financial windfalls.

Now is the time to work with the natural powers of the
universe to make your dreams come true! The key is . . .
NEW MOON
ASTROLOGY

Praise for Jan Spiller and *Astrology for the Soul*

"Jan Spiller is a brilliant, accurate, remarkable astrologer. . . . This is must reading for anyone on the spiritual path to fulfilling their soul's destiny."
—Harold Bloomfield, M.D., *New York Times* bestselling author of *How to Be Safe in an Unsafe World*

"I'm grateful to Ms. Spiller for presenting us with such a lucid, spiritually focused, accessible, and thought-provoking book. . . . [It] will illuminate minds, enrich relationships, enlighten souls, and change lives."
—Ronnie Grishman, editor in chief,
Dell Horoscope Magazine

"A fine contribution to modern astrological literature . . . Jan Spiller takes the nodal axis and points it directly at our hearts, opening and expanding our creative possibilities in the process!"
—Alan Oken, author of *Alan Oken's Complete Astrology*

"Jan Spiller has made it possible for the general public to go beyond sun signs . . . and for the spiritual seeker to find growth and self-awareness in practical yet uplifting terms."
—Donna Cunningham, author of *Moon Signs* and
The Moon in Your Life

"Illuminating . . . You'll find yourself in these pages: your personality, your relationships, your fears and hopes, what you really want and how you keep yourself from getting it!"
—Gloria Star, professional astrologer and editor of
Astrology for Women

✧ ALSO BY JAN SPILLER ✧

Astrology for the Soul
Spiritual Astrology

NEW MOON ASTROLOGY

Using New Moon Power Days to Change and Revitalize Your Life

JAN SPILLER

BANTAM BOOKS

NEW MOON ASTROLOGY: USING NEW MOON POWER DAYS
TO CHANGE AND REVITALIZE YOUR LIFE

PUBLISHING HISTORY
Bantam trade paperback / November 2001

Book design by Sabrina Bowers

LIBRARY OF CONGRESS CATALOGING-IN-PUBLICATION DATA
Spiller, Jan.
    New moon astrology : using new moon power days to
change and revitalize your life / Jan Spiller.
        p. cm.
    ISBN 0-553-38086-9
    1. Astrology. 2. Moon—Miscellanea. I. Title.
BF1723 .S655 2001
133.5—dc21   2001029519

PUBLISHED SIMULTANEOUSLY IN THE UNITED STATES AND CANADA

Bantam Books are published by Bantam Books, a division of
Random House, Inc. Its trademark, consisting of the words
"Bantam Books" and the portrayal of a rooster, is Registered in
U.S. Patent and Trademark Office and in other countries.
Marca Registrada. Bantam Books, 1540 Broadway, New York,
New York 10036.

PRINTED IN THE UNITED STATES OF AMERICA

FFG 10 9 8 7 6 5 4 3 2 1

Contents

Part III

Part IV

Contents ✧ xii

Part V

Acknowledgments

I would like to acknowledge my friend and editor throughout the years, Judith Horton, for her help with this book. Thanks also go to my editor at Bantam, Danielle Perez.

The initial stimulus prompting my research into combining astrological timing with the power of making wishes came from *The Book of Houses* by Robert Cole. Special thanks go to my father, Bill Nunn, for his consistent encouragement and motivation to "finish the book!" . . . and his business insights in the ongoing wishes section. Also thanks to D. J. Smalley for his awareness of the larger picture of the mission and for stimulating me to fulfill my potential.

The source of inspiration that evoked this work is the human spirit itself that is ever seeking to grow and expand to attain new heights and have new experiences. Grateful recognition is due the Guides and Angels who are so close to the human spirit at this point in history, totally supporting us in manifesting the dreams of our hearts.

JAN SPILLER

NEW MOON
ASTROLOGY

Introduction:
Why Wishing Works

The knowledge that there is power in wishing has been handed down through the ages. Children know to make a wish on a falling star or a passing hay truck. They instinctively see that this is a planet where dreams can come true, and that the power of wishing—focusing the mind at a "magic moment"—can transform the desires of the heart into material reality.

This book contains secrets for using the powerful astrological timing cycles of the NEW MOON to obtain your true heart's desires. I have been experimenting with using these basic Power Periods to make my own dreams come true for the past twenty-one years. As a result, my life has become different from the way I used to live. I have watched myself "magically" overcome troubling inhibitions, establish healthy new physical routines, and manifest success in areas of my life that were important to me. Many of these things seemed impossible to create, but working with Astrological Power Periods attuned me to a new energy that brought the people, situations, and shifts in my habitual ways of viewing life that were necessary in order for my dreams to come true.

Now I seem to operate in a whole different dimension. I travel in the "fast lane" in that my desires seem to manifest very quickly. Yet my inner experience is less stressful and more peaceful because I am not using the force of my will to obtain these results. When I use the natural power of astrological cycles and make my wishes known at the appropriate times, Universal forces automatically create opportunities for my dreams to manifest.

Without a dream, a conscious goal, or a strong intention to go in a specific direction, life is like being in a boat without a rudder—we are thrown around capriciously by the waves. Many live life this way, in reaction to other people and events. But life *can* be lived as a series of opportunities that we use to make our dreams come true. On more than one occasion I have asked myself: "If I were ninety-five years old, on my deathbed, and looking back over my life, how would I wish I had used this body, this intelligence, and this system of energy? What did I want to do with this lifetime?" These moments make me aware of the importance of using time to consciously accomplish what I feel is valuable, and to experience those things that I am deeply curious about.

Wishing is really a matter of deciding what we WANT to create and getting clear on our intention. It is more than a process of "thinking," however; it involves feeling *all the way through ourselves* that something is correct for us and accepting it fully, with all of our heart. When we take the extra step of writing that wish down and declaring it at a "magical moment," it will come true. One of astrology's greatest aids to the process of wishing is that it can alert us to these "magical moments" in advance.

For centuries farmers the world over have known to plant their crops by the cycles of the Moon. The Moon moves rapidly through the constellations of the zodiac, and aligns with the Sun (conjoins) once approximately every twenty-nine and a half days. This is called the New Moon, and is that period of time when we cannot see the Moon in the night sky. In America, farmers consult the annual *Farmer's*

Almanac, which supplies the dates and phases of the Moon to determine the best time to plant their crops in order to insure the greatest yield. The New Moon is a time that promotes all forms of growth. For example, if you want your hair to grow more quickly and fully, have it cut on the day of the New Moon. If you want your fingernails to grow long and strong, have manicures on the days of the New Moon. Anything initiated on those days will be met with rapid growth: a business venture, a relationship, a creative project. The New Moon is fruitful for strong new beginnings.

Timing is everything. When we plant seeds in the springtime, the laws of nature bring about a bountiful crop in the fall. The same seeds planted in a winter snowstorm will likely not yield results, or the results may require much more hard work and be scraggly compared to seeds planted at the appropriate time. Likewise, being aware of timing when making wishes is also important. Just as the New Moon is fruitful for starting material ventures, it is also a potent time for making wishes that stimulate new beginnings in our lives.

I began experimenting with Astrological Power Periods using only myself as the guinea pig because I wanted to find out what the rules were to best utilize the power of the specific timing, and to discover any potential problems. Later I began recommending the use of these Power Periods to my clients, and found that they experienced similar success. I coined the term *New Moon Power Days* to describe the days of the monthly New Moon and their strength for making wishes, and the term *Grandaddy Power Period* to denote the one month each year in the individual astrological chart when the power of wishing is the most potent. Over time, the formulas for maximizing the benefits of these time periods—and the most potent way to word the wishes—began to emerge. Now I am delighted to be able to bring you this road map for using astrological timing in your own life to obtain your heart's desires!

Part I

Rules of the Road

Timing

This is a planet where we reap what we sow. By knowing what we want to harvest in our lives (the dreams we want to see come true) and by planting the seeds at the appropriate time, we can manifest the dreams of our heart. This book teaches you how to determine the most powerful timing for making wishes using the magic released during potent astrological cycles. By looking up the New Moon for each month, you will be able to see the exact date and time, as well as the sign it's in (see the "What to Wish for When the New Moon Is in Each Sign" section, page 47). New Moon tables through the year 2050 begin on page 35.

Wishes don't always come to full fruition in the approximate twenty-nine-and-a-half-day cycle between New Moons, but once the seeds are planted, they will come true in the months ahead. Experience has shown me that wishes can be made up to forty-eight hours after the exact time of the New Moon; however, the most potent time is within the first eight hours.

DO write down your wish list within eight hours following the exact time of the New Moon, whenever possible.

Format

For New Moon Power Wishes to come true they must be handwritten on paper, not typed on a typewriter or a computer. I have no idea *why* this is important, but years of experience with wishes have shown me what does and doesn't work.

The *wording* of the wishes is also very important—they must be clearly stated so that the "feeling" behind the wishes comes through the words. Use your intuition. If, after you have written a wish, it feels "right" to you and evokes feelings of harmony and happiness, your wish is "on target." However, if it doesn't "feel right," I would suggest changing the wording or even waiting until a different time to make that particular wish.

You may make a maximum of ten wishes on each Power Day. You may make less than ten, but it is important not to exceed this number, as it would disperse the energy too much for your individual wishes to have the power they need to come true. The more wishes, the more dispersed the energy becomes. It is, however, important to make more than one wish to activate the energy of the day, even if your second and third wishes involve the same issue. Perhaps the most potent method is to make several wishes in one or two areas where you want to see some major shifts and progress, approaching each issue from several different directions (see the "Ongoing Wishes" section for more explanation, page 213).

As the energy of each month changes, and as your own life progresses and your areas of focus change, you may find that on some Power Days you are inclined to focus on shifting one or two areas very strongly. In other months it may seem more appropriate to wish for changes and improvement in diverse areas of your life.

Another important factor is to use every New Moon Power Day to make wishes. Depending on your individual astrology chart, some Power Days will be extremely potent for you personally, and others will operate to a lesser extent. This is because your specific astrology chart isn't mathematically duplicated for over twenty-five thousand years, due to the planets' traveling at different speeds around the Sun. Sometimes, due to the changing planetary alignment, the monthly Moon cycle will more vigorously trigger your individual wiring than at other times. Therefore, it is critical to use *every* Power Day, so as not to miss those that are the most powerful for you.

Clients often ask me what to do with their wish lists after writing them down, and I tell them to do whatever they like, short of throwing them away. I have one client who puts her wish list under her mattress—I don't know why, but if it feels right to her, it can't hurt. Wishes don't operate like affirmations, so after you've written them down you never have to see the list again—the outcome will still occur. But some people like to read their wish lists every morning. Do whatever makes you feel comfortable.

Personally, at the end of each Power Period I date my list and put it away and don't look at it again unless a series of things begins to unfold that seems strange to me ("What's that all about? That's not a normal pattern in my life . . ."), and then I'll go back to my wish list and realize: "Aha! That had to happen in order for wish number eight to come true!" You don't have to do anything special with your list for your wishes to come true, but don't resist the new you that begins to emerge and express itself in response to the wishes you have made!

DO write your wishes down by hand each month.
DO NOT write more than ten wishes on any one Power Day.
DO write more than one wish on each Power Day.
DO date and keep your wish lists.

Intuition

On each of the New Moon days listed, not only do you have the power to make wishes that will come true in the days or months ahead, but also the *wisdom* to make "proper" wishes: wishes that, when they come true, will bring you true joy. So pay attention to your inner feelings and trust them. After writing down each wish, check to see how you feel inside. If you feel happy and peaceful, then you're on the right track. If you feel troubled or uncertain, it would be best to erase that wish until a later time.

The ideas that come to you on these days will not be based on linear thinking, the past, your subconscious, or what others say you should have in order to be happy. The Angels hover close to the Earth during these time periods, and if you listen to your intuitive feelings with an open and innocent mind, on this day ideas about what will truly make you happy will come to you. It's an extraordinary day!

DO trust yourself in writing down those wishes that truly make you feel harmonious on the exact day of the New Moon.

The Role of Destiny

All wishes, when made repeatedly over an extended period of time, will come true—unless a wish is in direct conflict with your destiny. What you yearn for in your heart IS your destiny and worthy of pursuit. If a wish blatantly doesn't come true, then it may be because it was a wish that didn't take into account the good of everyone involved, perhaps including your own best overall interests.

The impulse to ardently wish for something that goes against one's destiny is extremely rare, and I have seen it occur only one time.

I had a client who was writing a book on working with juveniles to increase their self-confidence in saying no to drugs. The book was an outgrowth of a successful program he had developed in the local schools. We made wishes together on a very potent Power Day: that the book be published by a reputable publisher, that it receive national acclaim, and that it lead to seminars and public-speaking opportunities for him to promote his ideas. All of the wishes came true; his ideas for helping kids spread into other school systems and he became a public figure in his field. This client, who was initially a skeptic, became an ardent believer in the power of wishing!

The same man returned to me some months later for wishes involving a new book he wanted to write on male/female relationships. This time his motive was different—now he wanted to be famous with the general public, become rich, and be on national talk shows. We made all of the appropriate wishes, and this time none of it came true. Perhaps a different slant would have been more productive: i.e., that he be filled with right ideas about male/female relationships that would truly benefit others and effectively answer a public need. Or perhaps the book itself went against his destiny.

As it happened, he was called to help reorganize a rape prevention program, which was a huge success and had a major impact. He is currently developing a national training program for therapists on treating domestic violence, and again, his work is being hailed and he is influencing a large number of people in a very crucial area. Perhaps in the universal scheme of things, his talents were needed in this specific area and the book on relationships would have kept him from doing this important work.

DO trust your own process. The Universe wants you to be happy. If a wish doesn't come true immediately, keep repeating it, or watch to see what unexpected benefit comes in its place.

Wishes Involving Others

You can't make wishes that will affect the behavior or self-determination of another—experience has shown me that it simply doesn't work. However, you *can* make wishes for changes in your own behavior relative to that person that will open the way for a change in them. For example, wishes like: "I want Steve to fall in love with me" are not likely to come true. However, you can say: "I want to easily find myself saying the right words to Steve that evoke feelings of love in our relationship"; or "I want total clarity in my relationship with Steve, leading to my taking those steps that result in a happy, loving relationship"; or "I want all inner resistance to experiencing happiness and love in my relationship with Steve easily lifted from me."

If the other person is unavailable due to an involvement in another relationship, then it would be more appropriate to take a deeper look at what it is you actually want, rather than limiting your focus to that particular person. Are you looking for a romance, a life partner, a marriage? Are you looking for a person you are intensely attracted to for a fling . . . or for the purposes of building a stable family base? Once you are clear about what it is you would actually like to experience, then you can make wishes drawing a person to you who is available and wants the same kind of relationship. For example: "I want to easily attract, recognize, and begin a happy, healthy romantic relationship with the right man (woman) for me"; or "I want to easily attract the right marriage partner for me, someone who also wants a home and children, with whom I can build a stable, happy relationship." (For more wishes dealing with romance and marriage, see the sample wishes in the "Ongoing Wishes" section, pages 277 and 257).

If you want to make wishes pertaining to a child or a family member whom you want to help, the rule remains the same. Regardless of how altruistic your motive, it doesn't work to make wishes for other people. However, you can make wishes to alter your own behavior in order to affect in a positive way the person you are concerned about. For example, the wish "I want Johnny to do his homework and get good grades" will not work. But the wishes "I want to easily find myself saying the right words to Johnny that result in his doing his homework and improving his grades in a happy way," or "I want total clarity, correctly seeing how I can best support Johnny in getting better grades," *will* work because they are wishes for altering your own behavior and perspective.

The wishes "I want my children to be happy" or "I want my daughter's marriage to improve" will not work. Instead make wishes like "I want to easily find myself saying the right words to my children that help to increase their happiness"; or "I want to be an open channel, providing fresh, workable ideas to my daughter that will help her improve her marriage"; or "I want right ideas to occur to me to share with my daughter that will result in her improving her marriage."

If you are interested in helping a loved one with their health, you might make wishes like "I want to easily find myself being a channel through which information is provided that will help Betty with her health"; or "I want to act as a vehicle for healing energy for my son, Kenneth." The idea is to open yourself to be a channel for the goodness you seek for others.

DO NOT make wishes for other people. It won't work.
DO make wishes shifting YOUR approach to other people whom you want to influence.

Spring Equinox Treasure Maps

Another exciting way to use the power of astrological timing to help make our wishes come true was pioneered by fellow astrologer Buzz

Meyers. His idea was to use the visual potency of a Treasure Map (a collage) in combination with the Spring Equinox—the first day of Spring—a traditional time of new beginnings! Use the time of the New Moon following the Spring Equinox for creating your Map. You can determine that special day each year by locating the date of the New Moon in Aries (New Moon tables are on pages 35–44.

For your Treasure Map, you will need to have the following materials ready in advance: *magazines* containing pictures of the kinds of events or experiences you would like to have in your life; *scissors; glue sticks* (paste or rubber cement); and a *poster board* (the standard 22" x 28" is recommended). Have your materials ready, but for maximum success, the process of creating your Treasure Map (including the selection of the pictures) must not begin until the New Moon in Aries actually occurs.

At the appropriate time, leaf through the magazines and cut out all pictures, photos, or headlines that attract you and set them aside. When you are ready, begin to paste the images and headlines onto the poster board. There are no "rules" for how your Map should be laid out, only that it be filled with images and headlines that feel happy to you and are in alignment with what you would like to manifest in the year ahead. You may find it natural to put different areas of life on different parts of the board. For example: the pictures of what you would like to occur in your love life on the upper left section; your work desires on the upper right corner, etc. OR, you may prefer to paste the images in a less structured, more flowing way on your Map. Let your subconscious mind, your intuition, and your heart guide you.

As you are creating your Treasure Map, it's fine to return to the magazines for more images or headlines. In the moment of creative choice, you may find you select images that you hadn't anticipated as particularly important to you. Of course, the dreams you have wanted for a long time should also be represented on your Map. Feel free to type out your own headlines or draw your own images on your Treasure Map.

The window of opportunity for completing your Spring Equinox Treasure Map is within the first two days after the New Moon in Aries occurs. After that point, simply put your Treasure Map aside and watch the magic of the dreams you have put on the Map manifest as the year unfolds!

DO combine the visual power of a Treasure Map during the New Moon in Aries each year.

Grandaddy Power Periods

Each of us has an individual astrological time period lasting from three to five weeks each year (depending on your individual birth chart) when we have access to a Grandaddy Power Period, and writing down wishes during this time is phenomenally potent! I call this the Grandaddy Power Period because the timing is absolutely unsurpassed in magically empowering your wishes to come true. To maximize results, it's not necessary to make wishes on every day of this time period. Personally, I am very aware during the days of my individual Grandaddy Power Period, and make it a priority to write down wishes as they occur to me during this time.

To find the date of your Grandaddy Power Period, you will need to have your full birth chart (including time of birth). This magical period occurs when the transiting Sun is in your 11th House. I use Placidus house cusps. If you do not yet have a full copy of your birth chart and would like one, you can access www.cosmicpath.com on the Internet and download a free copy of your birth chart. This is my Web site, in partnership with my astrologer colleague and friend, Stephanie Azaria. Of course, if you remember to use EVERY ONE of the New Moon Power Days each year, one of the months you will hit your Grandaddy Power Period!

During the Grandaddy Power Period, the "rules of the road" remain the same, except that you are allowed up to forty wishes! And you can make wishes during the entire time the Sun is transiting through your 11th House. This time is so potent that I have clients who regularly check in for readings once a year during this time, as the results have been so dramatically successful for them. Since discovering it, I have never missed using the Grandaddy Power Period in my own life.

When you use the Grandaddy Power Period, I would definitely suggest you include the following wish on your list: "I want to easily cut through any fears or negativity that may arise in the month following my Power Period, and emerge with flying colors." I can best explain this suggestion by way of a personal example. The first couple of years that I experimented with my Grandaddy Power Period, indeed, my wishes began coming true. But in the month *following* my Power Period (when the Sun was in my 12th House), the anxieties that arose from such rapid changes were so intense that, even though my dreams were coming true, it almost didn't seem worth it during that month!

Beginning with the third year, *during* my Power Period I put the above wish on my list, and I never again had those anxieties arise with such intensity. So even though it takes up a wish, I strongly suggest that it be included on your list. Even with this wish, during the first year you use your Grandaddy Power Period you may experience some anxiety the following month when the Sun is in the 12th House. This is because there is a whole lifetime of garbage in the subconscious— negative conditioning from childhood, society, relatives, past lives, etc.—that is being uprooted and released, so it is natural to experience some discomfort.

If this occurs, one option is to write down a "worry list" of all your concerns and fears, and at the end of the day tear it up and throw it away. This is a symbolic way of discarding the negativity of the subconscious mind. It isn't necessary, but we all have different temperaments, and this may be very helpful for some people.

DO experiment with making wishes during your Grandaddy Power Period. It REALLY works at a super potent level!
DO include a wish on your Grandaddy list to release any intense anxiety that might arise during the following month.

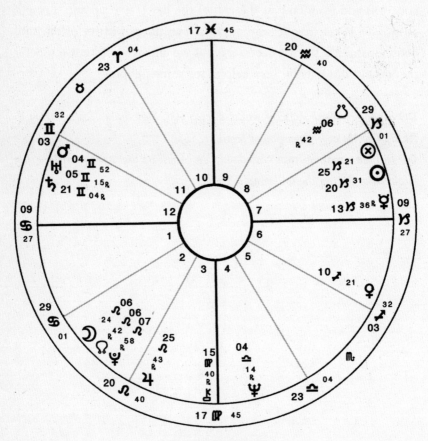

Helen Thomas-Williams
Born: 1/11/44, New York, NY, 4:50 pm

♦ Reading the Chart ♦

To find your personal Grandaddy Power Period, first determine the degrees and sign of the 11th House of your birth chart. Use the sign/date table that follows to translate the zodiac degrees into the dates during the year when the Sun is traveling through your 11th House and you are in your most *potent* astrological period for wishing.

For example, in the above chart Helen's 11th House begins with 23 degrees Aries 04 minutes (= 23 degrees. Use the degrees only). On the table showing the translation of zodiac degrees to calendar days, 23 degrees Aries is equivalent to April 13. Thus her Grandaddy Power Period *begins* on April 13. Her 11th House *ends* at 3 degrees Gemini, 32 minutes (= 3 degrees). On the translation table, 3 degrees Gemini = May 24. Thus her Grandaddy Power Period *ends* on May 24. To adjust for leap year and other complex shifts, subtract a day from each end to make the timing of the Grandaddy Power Period more accurate. So, Helen's Grandaddy Power Period falls between April 14 and May 23 each year.

The time period of your Grandaddy Power Period is so potent, it's *definitely* worth putting on your calendar each year!

11♏ ♐

Begins   Cap 4°   ⸫   12/26
          49 min.   } here

Evd   Cap 27°   1/18

TABLE TO DETERMINE GRANDADDY POWER PERIOD

ARIES

0 Aries = Mar 21
1 Aries = Mar 22
2 Aries = Mar 23
3 Aries = Mar 24
4 Aries = Mar 25
5 Aries = Mar 26
6 Aries = Mar 27
7 Aries = Mar 28
8 Aries = Mar 29
9 Aries = Mar 30
10 Aries = Mar 31
11 Aries = Apr 1
12 Aries = Apr 2
13 Aries = Apr 3
14 Aries = Apr 4
15 Aries = Apr 5
16 Aries = Apr 6
17 Aries = Apr 7
18 Aries = Apr 8
19 Aries = Apr 9
20 Aries = Apr 10
21 Aries = Apr 11
22 Aries = Apr 12
23 Aries = Apr 13
24 Aries = Apr 14
25 Aries = Apr 15
26 Aries = Apr 16
27 Aries = Apr 17
28 Aries = Apr 18
29 Aries = Apr 19

TAURUS

0 Taur. = Apr 20
1 Taur. = Apr 21
2 Taur. = Apr 22
3 Taur. = Apr 23
4 Taur. = Apr 24
5 Taur. = Apr 25
6 Taur. = Apr 26
7 Taur. = Apr 27
8 Taur. = Apr 28
9 Taur. = Apr 29
10 Taur. = Apr 30
11 Taur. = May 2
12 Taur. = May 3
13 Taur. = May 4
14 Taur. = May 5
15 Taur. = May 6
16 Taur. = May 7
17 Taur. = May 8
18 Taur. = May 9
19 Taur. = May 10
20 Taur. = May 11
21 Taur. = May 12
22 Taur. = May 13
23 Taur. = May 14
24 Taur. = May 15
25 Taur. = May 16
26 Taur. = May 17
27 Taur. = May 18
28 Taur. = May 19
29 Taur. = May 20

GEMINI

0 Gem. = May 21
1 Gem. = May 22
2 Gem. = May 23
3 Gem. = May 24
4 Gem. = May 25
5 Gem. = May 26
6 Gem. = May 27
7 Gem. = May 28
8 Gem. = May 29
9 Gem. = May 30
10 Gem. = May 31
11 Gem. = Jun 2
12 Gem. = Jun 3
13 Gem. = Jun 4
14 Gem. = Jun 5
15 Gem. = Jun 6
16 Gem. = Jun 7
17 Gem. = Jun 8
18 Gem. = Jun 9
19 Gem. = Jun 10
20 Gem. = Jun 11
21 Gem. = Jun 12
22 Gem. = Jun 13
23 Gem. = Jun 14
24 Gem. = Jun 15
25 Gem. = Jun 16
26 Gem. = Jun 17
27 Gem. = Jun 18
28 Gem. = Jun 19
29 Gem. = Jun 20

CANCER

0 Canc. = Jun 22
1 Canc. = Jun 23
2 Canc. = Jun 24
3 Canc. = Jun 25
4 Canc. = Jun 26
5 Canc. = Jun 27
6 Canc. = Jun 28
7 Canc. = Jun 29
8 Canc. = Jun 30
9 Canc. = Jul 1
10 Canc. = Jul 2
11 Canc. = Jul 3
12 Canc. = Jul 4
13 Canc. = Jul 5
14 Canc. = Jul 6
15 Canc. = Jul 7
16 Canc. = Jul 8
17 Canc. = Jul 9
18 Canc. = Jul 11
19 Canc. = Jul 12
20 Canc. = Jul 13
21 Canc. = Jul 14
22 Canc. = Jul 15
23 Canc. = Jul 16
24 Canc. = Jul 17
25 Canc. = Jul 18
26 Canc. = Jul 19
27 Canc. = Jul 20
28 Canc. = Jul 21
29 Canc. = Jul 22

LEO

0 Leo = Jul 23
1 Leo = Jul 24
2 Leo = Jul 25
3 Leo = Jul 26
4 Leo = Jul 27
5 Leo = Jul 28
6 Leo = Jul 29
7 Leo = Jul 30
8 Leo = Aug 1
9 Leo = Aug 2
10 Leo = Aug 3
11 Leo = Aug 4
12 Leo = Aug 5
13 Leo = Aug 6
14 Leo = Aug 7
15 Leo = Aug 8
16 Leo = Aug 9
17 Leo = Aug 10
18 Leo = Aug 11
19 Leo = Aug 12
20 Leo = Aug 13
21 Leo = Aug 14
22 Leo = Aug 15
23 Leo = Aug 16
24 Leo = Aug 17
25 Leo = Aug 18
26 Leo = Aug 19
27 Leo = Aug 20
28 Leo = Aug 21
29 Leo = Aug 22

VIRGO

0 Virgo = Aug 23
1 Virgo = Aug 24
2 Virgo = Aug 25
3 Virgo = Aug 26
4 Virgo = Aug 27
5 Virgo = Aug 28
6 Virgo = Aug 29
7 Virgo = Aug 30
8 Virgo = Aug 31
9 Virgo = Sep 2
10 Virgo = Sep 3
11 Virgo = Sep 4
12 Virgo = Sep 5
13 Virgo = Sep 6
14 Virgo = Sep 7
15 Virgo = Sep 8
16 Virgo = Sep 9
17 Virgo = Sep 10
18 Virgo = Sep 11
19 Virgo = Sep 12
20 Virgo = Sep 13
21 Virgo = Sep 14
22 Virgo = Sep 15
23 Virgo = Sep 16
24 Virgo = Sep 17
25 Virgo = Sep 18
26 Virgo = Sep 19
27 Virgo = Sep 20
28 Virgo = Sep 21
29 Virgo = Sep 22

LIBRA

0 Libra = Sep 23
1 Libra = Sep 24
2 Libra = Sep 25
3 Libra = Sep 26
4 Libra = Sep 27
5 Libra = Sep 28
6 Libra = Sep 29
7 Libra = Sep 30
8 Libra = Oct 2
9 Libra = Oct 3
10 Libra = Oct 4

11 Libra = Oct 5
12 Libra = Oct 6
13 Libra = Oct 7
14 Libra = Oct 8
15 Libra = Oct 9
16 Libra = Oct 10
17 Libra = Oct 11
18 Libra = Oct 12
19 Libra = Oct 13
20 Libra = Oct 14
21 Libra = Oct 15
22 Libra = Oct 16
23 Libra = Oct 17
24 Libra = Oct 18
25 Libra = Oct 19
26 Libra = Oct 20
27 Libra = Oct 21
28 Libra = Oct 22
29 Libra = Oct 23

SCORPIO

0 Scor. = Oct 24
1 Scor. = Oct 25
2 Scor. = Oct 26
3 Scor. = Oct 27
4 Scor. = Oct 28
5 Scor. = Oct 29
6 Scor. = Oct 30
7 Scor. = Oct 31
8 Scor. = Nov 1
9 Scor. = Nov 2
10 Scor. = Nov 3
11 Scor. = Nov 4
12 Scor. = Nov 5
13 Scor. = Nov 6
14 Scor. = Nov 7
15 Scor. = Nov 8
16 Scor. = Nov 9
17 Scor. = Nov 10
18 Scor. = Nov 11
19 Scor. = Nov 12
20 Scor. = Nov 13
21 Scor. = Nov 14

22 Scor. = Nov 15
23 Scor. = Nov 16
24 Scor. = Nov 17
25 Scor. = Nov 18
26 Scor. = Nov 19
27 Scor. = Nov 20
28 Scor. = Nov 21
29 Scor. = Nov 22

SAGITTARIUS

0 Sag. = Nov 23
1 Sag. = Nov 24
2 Sag. = Nov 25
3 Sag. = Nov 26
4 Sag. = Nov 27
5 Sag. = Nov 28
6 Sag. = Nov 29
7 Sag. = Nov 30
8 Sag. = Nov 30
9 Sag. = Dec 1
10 Sag. = Dec 2

11 Sag. = Dec 3
12 Sag. = Dec 4
13 Sag. = Dec 5
14 Sag. = Dec 6
15 Sag. = Dec 7
16 Sag. = Dec 8
17 Sag. = Dec 9
18 Sag. = Dec 10
19 Sag. = Dec 11
20 Sag. = Dec 12
21 Sag. = Dec 13
22 Sag. = Dec 14
23 Sag. = Dec 15
24 Sag. = Dec 16
25 Sag. = Dec 17
26 Sag. = Dec 18
27 Sag. = Dec 19
28 Sag. = Dec 20
29 Sag. = Dec 21

CAPRICORN

0 Capr. = Dec 22
1 Capr. = Dec 23
2 Capr. = Dec 24
3 Capr. = Dec 25
4 Capr. = Dec 26
5 Capr. = Dec 27
6 Capr. = Dec 28
7 Capr. = Dec 29
8 Capr. = Dec 30
9 Capr. = Dec 31
10 Capr. = Jan 1
11 Capr. = Jan 2
12 Capr. = Jan 3
13 Capr. = Jan 4
14 Capr. = Jan 5
15 Capr. = Jan 6
16 Capr. = Jan 7
17 Capr. = Jan 8
18 Capr. = Jan 9
19 Capr. = Jan 10
20 Capr. = Jan 11
21 Capr. = Jan 12

22 Capr. = Jan 13
23 Capr. = Jan 14
24 Capr. = Jan 15
25 Capr. = Jan 16
26 Capr. = Jan 17
27 Capr. = Jan 18
28 Capr. = Jan 18
29 Capr. = Jan 19

AQUARIUS

0 Aqua. = Jan 20
1 Aqua. = Jan 21
2 Aqua. = Jan 22
3 Aqua. = Jan 23
4 Aqua. = Jan 24
5 Aqua. = Jan 25
6 Aqua. = Jan 26
7 Aqua. = Jan 27
8 Aqua. = Jan 28
9 Aqua. = Jan 29

10 Aqua. = Jan 30
11 Aqua. = Jan 31
12 Aqua. = Feb 1
13 Aqua. = Feb 2
14 Aqua. = Feb 3
15 Aqua. = Feb 4
16 Aqua. = Feb 5
17 Aqua. = Feb 6
18 Aqua. = Feb 7
19 Aqua. = Feb 8
20 Aqua. = Feb 9
21 Aqua. = Feb 10
22 Aqua. = Feb 11
23 Aqua. = Feb 12
24 Aqua. = Feb 13
25 Aqua. = Feb 14
26 Aqua. = Feb 15
27 Aqua. = Feb 16
28 Aqua. = Feb 17
29 Aqua. = Feb 18

PISCES

0 Pisc. = Feb 19
1 Pisc. = Feb 20
2 Pisc. = Feb 21
3 Pisc. = Feb 22
4 Pisc. = Feb 23
5 Pisc. = Feb 24
6 Pisc. = Feb 25
7 Pisc. = Feb 26
8 Pisc. = Feb 27
9 Pisc. = Feb 28
10 Pisc. = Mar 1
11 Pisc. = Mar 2
12 Pisc. = Mar 3
13 Pisc. = Mar 4
14 Pisc. = Mar 5
15 Pisc. = Mar 6
16 Pisc. = Mar 7
17 Pisc. = Mar 8
18 Pisc. = Mar 9
19 Pisc. = Mar 10
20 Pisc. = Mar 11
21 Pisc. = Mar 12

22 Pisc. = Mar 13
23 Pisc. = Mar 14
24 Pisc. = Mar 15
25 Pisc. = Mar 16
26 Pisc. = Mar 17
27 Pisc. = Mar 18
28 Pisc. = Mar 19
29 Pisc. = Mar 20

It should be noted that in using Astrological Power Periods to bring our dreams into reality, it is favorable to utilize all the resources available. Using the yearly Grandaddy Power Period, AND the Spring Equinox Treasure Map, AND the monthly New Moon, for writing down wishes is the best bet. These are magical time periods in which we can personally access a special boost of power from the Universe to assist us in making our lives easier. We don't have to pick and choose, we can use *all* the power at our disposal!

Maximizing Results

Moving Beyond Personal Limitations

Once you have written down your wishes during a New Moon Power Period, your job is complete . . . it's up to the angels and the synchronicity of life itself to make them come true. Some wishes take longer to manifest than others, depending on the amount of inner resistance you have built up from past experiences. Have no fear. Simply continue to use Power Days to plant the seeds, and the Universe will unfold your life in ways that enable your wishes to materialize.

If you have faithfully entered a wish for several months and it has not borne fruit, it may be an indication that it's time to take an honest look at yourself in that area. Usually when a wish doesn't manifest right away, it is a sign that what you have wished for involves a deeper purification of your character before it can come true. Ultimately, the only thing prohibiting us from having the things in our life that we desire is our own inner resistance (generally subconscious—see chapter on karma, page 135) or our not really believing that it's possible to have what we want. Your dreams are *meant* to come true, which is why you want them in the first place, but it may take time to grow beyond current personal limitations to the point where a particular wish *can* happen.

For example, if you want a happy romance and have been listing "I want to easily attract, recognize, and begin a happy romantic relationship with the right mate for me" for several months without results, you might try making a more basic wish having to do with your own readiness, such as: "I want all inner resistance to having a happy romance totally lifted from me"; "I want lots of healthy, happy charisma in my relationships with men (women)"; or "I want to easily find myself participating in situations where I meet a potential romantic partner." Further, you might make some wishes to improve your basic attitude: "I want right ideas to occur to me, helping me to see romance from a positive, confident perspective," or "I want to easily find myself genuinely *liking* the women (men) I meet."

In the end, you will find that having the wish come true is not the only benefit. The growth and inner strength gained along the path to manifesting the wish may prove to be the deepest and most gratifying result. And you can apply the power and confidence you have gained in the process to manifest other wishes!

DO believe in and pursue your dreams! Trust your ability to go through the tests of character that open the way to experiencing your own inner happiness!

Taking Responsibility

One of the most powerful ways we can grow personally on our path to manifesting our wishes is to learn to take responsibility for our own lives. When making wishes, we may encounter the idea that we can't have what we want because someone else is standing in our way; and this engenders feelings of powerlessness and thoughts of "giving up." Whenever we blame another for our circumstance or inner state of being, we are giving them our power. This leads to frustration, anger, and resentment—unpleasant feelings for us to experience and not conducive to reaching our goals. It is only when we take full responsibility for being exactly where we are in our lives that we have the power to change our circumstances.

For example, if I say: "I can't park my car because that red car is in my spot!," I am stuck waiting and fuming until someone comes out and moves the red car. On the other hand if I say: "That red car is in my parking spot. Hmmm . . . there must be a higher reason for this . . . maybe I'm supposed to meet someone who will be in a different part of the parking lot. . . . Well, where else can I park?"—suddenly, my options and my horizons are open, and my energy is no longer blocked. When we blame others, we drastically limit our perception of how to create the success we want. When we choose to not blame either ourselves or others and open our vision, the next step we can take to create practical success becomes apparent. Our focus shifts from being contracted and fixed on the problem and expands to see the wider picture, including ways we can bypass the obstruction to get what we want.

Another self-sabotaging block for some of us is thinking that if we achieve our heart's desire, those who have wronged us in the past may no longer feel guilty for what they have done to us (i.e., if we are happy now, then what they did to us must not have been so bad). So we subconsciously limit ourselves from success in order to make someone else feel badly for their behavior toward us, even though it's clear that we can only benefit by releasing these old wounds. After all, it's only ourselves we are hurting by holding on to past resentments.

If you find you have trouble letting them go, use one or two of your Power Day wishes until you find these resentments lifted from you completely. For example: "I want all negative memories totally lifted from me"; "I want all feelings of resentment toward ———— totally lifted from me"; "I want the negative bond between myself and

————— totally severed"; "I want the energy of forgiveness to enter into the relationship between me and————, totally freeing me from bondage to————"; "I want to be totally free of seeing myself through————'s eyes"; "I want————'s expectations of me totally removed from my consciousness"; "I want all hopeful expectations that ————— will change their behavior toward me, totally lifted from me."

The Power of Intention

In the process of remaining single-minded and removing all the obstructions between ourselves and the dreams of our heart, what we want will become manifest in our lives. The effort of focusing to decide what it is we want and the act of writing our wishes down on paper requires effort and commitment. If we postpone taking this action, that is also a decision—the decision to stay where we are. It's up to us. Nothing in our lives changes until we *decide* what we want and state our intention for it to happen, as we do when we write it down on a New Moon Power Day!

You are in charge of your life. By consciously *taking* charge during a Power Period, you will change from being a "victim" to being the creator of your own happiness. For maximum results, I would suggest focusing primarily on one area of your life until things begin to shift for you in the right direction. There is a lot of power in making one thing FIRST VALUE until it happens. For example, if getting a job is your chief concern, then the idea would be to make several wishes around getting a job each Power Period, approaching your goal from different angles until you actually have the job you want.

To find the right job, there may be several wishes appropriate to moving you forward: "I want to easily attract, recognize, and begin working in the right job for me"; "I want right ideas to occur to me, causing me to be in the right place to apply for and get the job that will make me happy"; "I want all inner resistance to getting the right job for me totally lifted from me"; "I want to easily find myself embracing the next right, happy job for me"; "I want any negative attitudes around working totally lifted from me"; "I want lots of enthusiasm around working, which will easily attract the right job to me!"

Once you find yourself in the right job, then you can look at the next thing you want: perhaps it's increasing your number of friends. If so, make THAT your FIRST VALUE until you again see progress.

If there is an area in life in which you feel a lot of resistance, it may take wishes coming in like laser beams from several different directions to remove the obstructions and make a clear path for the wish to be fulfilled. And other times we may repeat a wish worded almost exactly the same way if it is particularly crucial to us at the moment. For example, at one point in my life a tendency to procrastination became such a problem that on my wish list that month I wrote only four wishes, and three of them involved procrastination repeated and worded in three very similar ways: "I want all tendencies to procrastination *totally* lifted from me!"; "I want the habit of procrastination totally removed from me"; "I want all procrastination *totally lifted and removed* from me!" Fortunately, the results took hold within a few hours!

If you prefer a less intense approach, you may want to make wishes each month around several areas that will steadily progress in the direction of manifesting your dreams.

DO believe in yourself. Keep repeating wishes on your list until they begin coming true.
DO make more than one wish around an area that is especially difficult, or important to you.

Cooperation

As soon as a wish is made on a New Moon Power Day, personal tastes begin to change, attitudes shift, and you will find yourself viewing life differently and responding in different ways. Some of your wishes will begin to manifest almost immediately. However, if your wish is calling for a radical life change, give it a little time and keep repeating the wish every Power Day.

Willpower is not required; simply cooperate with the new you and accept the new attitudes that you find are beginning to emerge. For example, if you have been making wishes about weight loss, suddenly you may find yourself less hungry. Cooperate with that. Or perhaps you're out in public and suddenly you're not afraid to initiate in a situation where you used to feel fear—go ahead and initiate! This is the power of wishing . . . you start to feel differently and you naturally begin responding to life in a way that makes your wishes come true! All you have to do is to partner with this new energy.

When you make a wish during a Power Period, all the "stuff" in your subconscious mind will arise—the voices in your head that are contrary to having what you want in your life. And it's good when this negativity reveals itself so it can pass through your mind and you can dump it out! This "garbage" needs to be recognized and released, leaving the fertile ground of your subconscious free to receive the seeds of your wishes and dreams. When fears, self-doubt, or anxiety emerge, say to those thoughts: "Thank you for sharing!" and release them. Don't hold on to them, ponder them, or take them seriously. Simply allow them to pass through you and release them. Focus on your dreams, not your fears, and you will find them manifesting in amazing ways!

DO move with the new energy that emerges.
DO NOT let yourself stay stuck in old, habitual responses!

Wording

The WORDING of your wishes is very important—not the grammar used, but the "feeling" engendered by the way each wish is worded. Also, since your wishes *will* come true, it's important not to be careless about what you wish for! I recall during one especially potent Power Day, I made a wish involving a relationship. It was a really long, precise wish, and from a logical point of view, it sounded great! However, something in it didn't "feel" right, so I put a question mark by it. At the end of the day I reread my wishes, and something about that wish still didn't "feel right," so I took my pen and crossed it out. I have no idea what would have happened if that wish had come true, but it wouldn't have made me happy, and something within me knew it. It is very important to trust yourself. If a wish doesn't feel right, cross it out. You can always reword it and add it to next month's wish list if it feels right at that time.

In the "sample wishes" I often begin with the phrase: "I want to easily find myself. . . ." This is because I prefer change to happen easily, rather than in a stressful way. Using the word "easily" brings ease to the way the change occurs. "I want to find myself" implies that somehow the desired situation is just magically "happening," and takes the tendency to exert personal will out of the equation. When I am concerned that a wish may be too potent, or leave the way open for drastic, unpleasant change, I may add the phrase "in a healthy, happy way." For example, I would be hesitant to write down the wish: "I want to be rich" (who knows how it would come about—perhaps a tragedy . . .) and would rather make the request: "I want to be rich in a happy way."

Ultimately, the wording of our wishes is a personal decision. Only you know what wording feels right to you. You may not feel empowered by the phrase "I want to easily find myself . . ." and prefer a more direct wording such as: "I want to. . . ." Check your inner knowing and use the wording that leaves you fully open to receiving the abundance of your wish coming true.

DO trust your inner knowing when writing down wishes. Make sure the way the wish is worded leaves you feeling harmonious and empowered!

Another consideration about how to word wishes is that we can only be ready for some wishes to happen in stages. For example, a person may have the idea that eventually he or she would like to marry, but to write down the wish: "I want to attract and marry the right person for me" may evoke resistance and fear at the beginning. In that case, it would be better to begin with a wish you are comfortable with at the present time. For example, "I want to begin a happy friendship with a positive romantic partner" may be as far as you are ready to go and still feel internally comfortable. Or, you may only feel comfortable going as far as: "I want to be willing to begin a happy romantic relationship with the right person for me." Don't rush yourself or try to force your life in a direction where you are not really ready to go. You can always add the next stage of the wish in the future, when you feel comfortable with it.

DO NOT write down wishes that you don't feel completely comfortable with, even if they make sense logically.

Even if two or more wishes seem related, it is important not to combine them. When wishes are combined, my experience has shown that neither one will come true. I don't know why this is—possibly the wishes in some way negate each other, or take energy from one another. For example, in the wish "I want the habits of smoking and drinking alcohol totally lifted from me," neither area is likely to shift. However, worded as two separate wishes—"I want the habit of smoking totally lifted from me," and "I want the habit of drinking alcohol totally lifted from me"—each wish gains power of its own.

DO keep wishes separate from one another; otherwise they won't come true.

Rules of the Road

✧ *DO write down your wish list within eight hours following the exact time of the New Moon, whenever possible.*

✧ *DO write your wishes down by hand each month.*

✧ *DO NOT write more than ten wishes on any one Power Day.*

✧ *DO write more than one wish on each Power Day.*

✧ *DO date and keep your wish lists.*

✧ *DO trust yourself in writing down those wishes that truly make you feel harmonious on the exact day of the New Moon.*

✧ *DO trust your own process. The Universe wants you to be happy. If a wish doesn't come true immediately, keep repeating it, or watch to see what unexpected benefit comes in its place.*

✧ *DO NOT make wishes for other people. It won't work.*

✧ *DO make wishes shifting YOUR approach to other people whom you want to influence.*

✧ *DO combine the visual power of a Treasure Map during the New Moon in Aries each year.*

✧ *DO experiment with making wishes during your Grandaddy Power Period. It REALLY works at a super potent level!*

✧ *DO include a wish on your Grandaddy list to release any intense anxiety that might arise during the following month.*

✧ DO believe in and pursue your dreams! Trust your ability to go through the tests of character that open the way to experiencing your own inner happiness!

✧ DO believe in yourself. Keep repeating wishes on your list until they begin coming true.

✧ DO make more than one wish around an area that is especially important or difficult for you.

✧ DO move with the new energy as it emerges.

✧ DO NOT let yourself stay stuck in old, habitual responses!

✧ DO trust your inner knowing when writing down wishes. Does the way the wish is worded leave you feeling harmonious?

✧ DO NOT write down wishes that you don't feel completely comfortable with, even if they make sense logically.

✧ DO keep wishes separate from one another, otherwise they won't come true.

Tables of the New Moon, Through 2050

Wishes can be made up to forty-eight hours after the exact time of the New Moon; however, the most potent time is in the <u>first eight hours</u>.

EST

2001

JAN 24	Aquarius	08:08 AM
FEB 23	Pisces	03:21 AM
MAR 24	Aries	08:21 PM
APR 23	Taurus	10:27 AM
MAY 22	Gemini	09:47 PM
JUN 21	Cancer	06:58 AM
JUL 20	Cancer	02:45 PM
AUG 18	Leo	09:56 PM
SEP 17	Virgo	05:27 AM
OCT 16	Libra	02:24 PM
NOV 15	Scorpio	01:41 AM
DEC 14	Sagittarius	03:48 PM

2002

JAN 13	Capricorn	08:29 AM
FEB 12	Aquarius	02:42 AM
MAR 13	Pisces	09:03 PM
APR 12	Aries	02:21 PM
MAY 12	Taurus	05:46 AM
JUN 10	Gemini	06:48 PM
JUL 10	Cancer	05:26 AM
AUG 08	Leo	02:16 PM
SEP 06	Virgo	10:11 PM
OCT 06	Libra	06:18 AM
NOV 04	Scorpio	03:35 PM
DEC 04	Sagittarius	02:35 AM

2003

JAN 02	Capricorn	03:24 PM
FEB 01	Aquarius	05:49 AM
MAR 02	Pisces	09:35 PM
APR 01	Aries	02:20 PM
MAY 01	Taurus	07:15 AM ✓
MAY 30	Gemini	11:20 PM ✓
JUN 29	Cancer	01:40 PM
JUL 29	Leo	01:53 AM —
AUG 27	Virgo	12:26 PM
SEP 25	Libra	10:10 PM
OCT 25	Scorpio	07:51 AM
NOV 23	Sagittarius	05:59 PM
DEC 23	Capricorn	04:44 AM

2004

JAN 21	Aquarius	04:06 PM
FEB 20	Pisces	04:19 AM

MAR 20	Aries	05:42 PM
APR 19	Aries	08:22 AM
MAY 18	Taurus	11:53 PM
JUN 17	Gemini	03:27 PM
JUL 17	Cancer	06:24 AM
AUG 15	Leo	08:25 PM
SEP 14	Virgo	09:29 AM
OCT 13	Libra	09:48 PM
NOV 12	Scorpio	09:28 AM
DEC 11	Sagittarius	08:30 PM

2005

JAN 10	Capricorn	07:03 AM
FEB 08	Aquarius	05:29 PM
MAR 10	Pisces	04:12 AM
APR 08	Aries	03:33 PM
MAY 08	Taurus	03:46 AM
JUN 06	Gemini	04:56 PM
JUL 06	Cancer	07:03 AM
AUG 04	Leo	10:05 PM
SEP 03	Virgo	01:46 PM
OCT 03	Libra	05:29 AM
NOV 01	Scorpio	08:25 PM
DEC 01	Sagittarius	10:01 AM
DEC 30	Capricorn	10:13 PM

2006

JAN 29	Aquarius	09:15 AM
FEB 27	Pisces	07:31 PM
MAR 29	Aries	05:16 AM
APR 27	Taurus	02:45 PM
MAY 27	Gemini	12:26 AM
JUN 25	Cancer	11:06 AM
JUL 24	Leo	11:32 PM
AUG 23	Virgo	02:10 PM
SEP 22	Virgo	06:45 AM
OCT 22	Libra	12:15 AM
NOV 20	Scorpio	05:19 PM
DEC 20	Sagittarius	09:01 AM

2007

JAN 18	Capricorn	11:02 PM
FEB 17	Aquarius	11:15 AM
MAR 18	Pisces	09:43 PM
APR 17	Aries	06:37 AM
MAY 16	Taurus	02:29 PM
JUN 14	Gemini	10:14 PM
JUL 14	Cancer	07:04 AM
AUG 12	Leo	06:03 PM
SEP 11	Virgo	07:45 AM
OCT 11	Libra	12:01 AM
NOV 09	Scorpio	06:04 PM
DEC 09	Sagittarius	12:41 PM

2008

JAN 08	Capricorn	06:37 AM
FEB 06	Aquarius	10:45 PM
MAR 07	Pisces	12:15 PM
APR 05	Aries	10:56 PM
MAY 05	Taurus	07:19 AM
JUN 03	Gemini	02:24 PM
JUL 02	Cancer	09:20 PM
AUG 01	Leo	05:13 AM
AUG 30	Virgo	02:58 PM
SEP 29	Libra	03:13 AM
OCT 28	Scorpio	06:14 PM
NOV 27	Sagittarius	11:55 AM
DEC 27	Capricorn	07:23 AM

2009

JAN 26	Aquarius	02:56 AM
FEB 24	Pisces	08:35 PM
MAR 26	Aries	11:07 AM
APR 24	Taurus	10:24 PM
MAY 24	Gemini	07:12 AM
JUN 22	Cancer	02:36 PM
JUL 21	Cancer	09:36 PM
AUG 20	Leo	05:02 AM
SEP 18	Virgo	01:44 PM

OCT 18	Libra	12:34 AM		JUN 19	Gemini	10:02 AM
NOV 16	Scorpio	02:15 PM		JUL 18	Cancer	11:25 PM
DEC 16	Sagittarius	07:02 AM		AUG 17	Leo	10:56 AM
				SEP 15	Virgo	09:11 PM
				OCT 15	Libra	07:03 AM
				NOV 13	Scorpio	05:09 PM
				DEC 13	Sagittarius	03:42 AM

2010

JAN 15	Capricorn	02:12 AM
FEB 13	Aquarius	09:53 PM
MAR 15	Pisces	04:02 PM
APR 14	Aries	07:29 AM
MAY 13	Taurus	08:06 PM
JUN 12	Gemini	06:16 AM
JUL 11	Cancer	02:41 PM
AUG 09	Leo	10:09 PM
SEP 08	Virgo	05:31 AM
OCT 07	Libra	01:45 PM
NOV 05	Scorpio	11:52 PM
DEC 05	Sagittarius	12:37 PM

2013

JAN 11	Capricorn	02:44 PM
FEB 10	Aquarius	02:21 AM
MAR 11	Pisces	02:52 PM
APR 10	Aries	04:36 AM
MAY 09	Taurus	07:29 PM
JUN 08	Gemini	10:58 AM
JUL 08	Cancer	02:15 AM
AUG 06	Leo	04:51 PM
SEP 05	Virgo	06:38 AM
OCT 04	Libra	07:35 PM
NOV 03	Scorpio	07:50 AM
DEC 02	Sagittarius	07:23 PM

2011

JAN 04	Capricorn	04:03 AM
FEB 02	Aquarius	09:31 PM
MAR 04	Pisces	03:47 PM
APR 03	Aries	09:33 AM
MAY 03	Taurus	01:51 AM
JUN 01	Gemini	04:03 PM
JUL 01	Cancer	03:55 AM
JUL 30	Leo	01:40 PM
AUG 28	Virgo	10:04 PM
SEP 27	Libra	06:10 AM
OCT 26	Scorpio	02:57 PM
NOV 25	Sagittarius	01:10 AM
DEC 24	Capricorn	01:07 PM

2014

JAN 01	Capricorn	06:15 AM
JAN 30	Aquarius	04:39 PM
MAR 01	Pisces	03:00 AM
MAR 30	Aries	01:46 PM
APR 29	Taurus	01:15 AM
MAY 28	Gemini	01:40 PM
JUN 27	Cancer	03:10 AM
JUL 26	Leo	05:43 PM
AUG 25	Virgo	09:13 AM
SEP 24	Libra	01:15 AM
OCT 23	Scorpio	04:58 PM
NOV 22	Sagittarius	07:33 AM
DEC 21	Capricorn	08:36 PM

2012

JAN 23	Aquarius	02:41 AM
FEB 21	Pisces	05:35 PM
MAR 22	Aries	09:38 AM
APR 21	Taurus	02:20 AM
MAY 20	Gemini	06:48 PM

2015

JAN 20	Aquarius	08:15 AM
FEB 18	Pisces	06:48 PM
MAR 20	Pisces	04:37 AM
APR 18	Aries	01:58 PM
MAY 17	Taurus	11:15 PM
JUN 16	Gemini	09:06 AM
JUL 15	Cancer	08:25 PM
AUG 14	Leo	09:55 AM
SEP 13	Virgo	01:42 AM
OCT 12	Libra	07:06 PM
NOV 11	Scorpio	12:49 PM
DEC 11	Sagittarius	05:30 AM

2016

JAN 09	Capricorn	08:31 PM
FEB 08	Aquarius	09:40 AM
MAR 08	Pisces	08:56 PM
APR 07	Aries	06:24 AM
MAY 06	Taurus	02:30 PM
JUN 04	Gemini	10:01 PM
JUL 04	Cancer	06:02 AM
AUG 02	Leo	03:45 PM
SEP 01	Virgo	04:04 AM
SEP 30	Libra	07:13 PM
OCT 30	Scorpio	12:39 PM
NOV 29	Sagittarius	07:19 AM
DEC 29	Capricorn	01:55 AM

2017

JAN 27	Aquarius	07:08 PM
FEB 26	Pisces	09:59 AM
MAR 27	Aries	09:59 PM
APR 26	Taurus	07:17 AM
MAY 25	Gemini	02:45 PM
JUN 23	Cancer	09:32 PM
JUL 23	Leo	04:47 AM
AUG 21	Leo	01:31 PM
SEP 20	Virgo	12:30 AM
OCT 19	Libra	02:13 PM
NOV 18	Scorpio	06:43 AM
DEC 18	Sagittarius	01:30 AM

2018

JAN 16	Capricorn	09:18 PM
FEB 15	Aquarius	04:07 PM
MAR 17	Pisces	08:12 AM
APR 15	Aries	08:58 PM
MAY 15	Taurus	06:49 AM
JUN 13	Gemini	02:44 PM
JUL 12	Cancer	09:48 PM
AUG 11	Leo	04:59 AM
SEP 09	Virgo	01:02 PM
OCT 08	Libra	10:47 PM
NOV 07	Scorpio	11:03 AM
DEC 07	Sagittarius	02:22 AM

2019

JAN 05	Capricorn	08:29 PM
FEB 04	Aquarius	04:04 PM
MAR 06	Pisces	11:05 AM
APR 05	Aries	03:51 AM
MAY 04	Taurus	05:46 PM
JUN 03	Gemini	05:03 AM
JUL 02	Cancer	02:18 PM
JUL 31	Leo	10:12 PM
AUG 30	Virgo	05:38 AM
SEP 28	Libra	01:28 PM
OCT 27	Scorpio	10:39 PM
NOV 26	Sagittarius	10:06 AM
DEC 26	Capricorn	12:14 AM

2020

JAN 24	Aquarius	04:43 PM
FEB 23	Pisces	10:32 AM
MAR 24	Aries	04:29 AM
APR 22	Taurus	09:27 PM
MAY 22	Gemini	12:39 PM

JUN 21	Cancer	01:42 AM
JUL 20	Cancer	12:34 PM
AUG 18	Leo	09:42 PM
SEP 17	Virgo	06:00 AM
OCT 16	Libra	02:32 PM
NOV 15	Scorpio	12:08 AM
DEC 14	Sagittarius	11:17 AM

2021

JAN 13	Capricorn	12:01 AM
FEB 11	Aquarius	02:07 PM
MAR 13	Pisces	05:22 AM
APR 11	Aries	09:31 PM
MAY 11	Taurus	02:01 PM
JUN 10	Gemini	05:54 AM
JUL 09	Cancer	08:17 PM
AUG 08	Leo	08:51 AM
SEP 06	Virgo	07:53 PM
OCT 06	Libra	06:06 AM
NOV 04	Scorpio	04:15 PM
DEC 04	Sagittarius	02:44 AM

2022

JAN 02	Capricorn	01:35 PM
FEB 01	Aquarius	12:47 AM
MAR 02	Pisces	12:36 PM
APR 01	Aries	01:26 AM
APR 30	Taurus	03:28 PM
MAY 30	Gemini	06:31 AM
JUN 28	Cancer	09:54 PM
JUL 28	Leo	12:56 PM
AUG 27	Virgo	03:17 AM
SEP 25	Libra	04:56 PM
OCT 25	Scorpio	05:50 AM
NOV 23	Sagittarius	05:58 PM
DEC 23	Capricorn	05:18 AM

2023

JAN 21	Aquarius	03:55 PM
FEB 20	Pisces	02:07 AM
MAR 21	Aries	12:24 PM
APR 19	Aries	11:14 PM
MAY 19	Taurus	10:54 AM
JUN 17	Gemini	11:37 PM
JUL 17	Cancer	01:33 PM
AUG 16	Leo	04:39 AM
SEP 14	Virgo	08:40 PM
OCT 14	Libra	12:56 PM
NOV 13	Scorpio	04:29 AM
DEC 12	Sagittarius	06:33 PM

2024

JAN 11	Capricorn	06:58 AM
FEB 09	Aquarius	06:00 PM
MAR 10	Pisces	04:02 AM
APR 08	Aries	01:22 PM
MAY 07	Taurus	10:23 PM
JUN 06	Gemini	07:39 AM
JUL 05	Cancer	05:58 PM
AUG 04	Leo	06:13 AM
SEP 02	Virgo	08:57 PM
OCT 02	Libra	01:50 PM
NOV 01	Scorpio	07:48 AM
DEC 01	Sagittarius	01:23 AM
DEC 30	Capricorn	05:28 PM

2025

JAN 29	Aquarius	07:36 AM
FEB 27	Pisces	07:46 PM
MAR 29	Aries	05:59 AM
APR 27	Taurus	02:32 PM
MAY 26	Gemini	10:03 PM
JUN 25	Cancer	05:33 AM
JUL 24	Leo	02.12 PM
AUG 23	Virgo	01:07 AM
SEP 21	Virgo	02:55 PM

OCT 21	Libra	07:27 AM
NOV 20	Scorpio	01:48 AM
DEC 19	Sagittarius	08:44 PM

2026

JAN 18	Capricorn	02:53 PM
FEB 17	Aquarius	07:02 AM
MAR 18	Pisces	08:24 PM
APR 17	Aries	06:53 AM
MAY 16	Taurus	03:03 PM
JUN 14	Gemini	09:55 PM
JUL 14	Cancer	04:44 AM
AUG 12	Leo	12:38 PM
SEP 10	Virgo	10:28 PM
OCT 10	Libra	10:50 AM
NOV 09	Scorpio	02:03 AM
DEC 08	Sagittarius	07:53 PM

2027

JAN 07	Capricorn	03:25 PM
FEB 06	Aquarius	10:57 AM
MAR 08	Pisces	04:31 AM
APR 06	Aries	06:52 PM
MAY 06	Taurus	05:59 AM
JUN 04	Gemini	02:42 PM
JUL 03	Cancer	10:03 PM
AUG 02	Leo	05:06 AM
AUG 31	Virgo	12:42 PM
SEP 29	Libra	09:37 PM
OCT 29	Scorpio	08:37 AM
NOV 27	Sagittarius	10:25 PM
DEC 27	Capricorn	03:13 PM

2028

JAN 26	Aquarius	10:13 AM
FEB 25	Pisces	05:38 AM
MAR 25	Aries	11:33 PM
APR 24	Taurus	02:48 PM
MAY 24	Gemini	03:17 AM

JUN 22	Cancer	01:29 PM
JUL 21	Cancer	10:03 PM
AUG 20	Leo	05:45 AM
SEP 18	Virgo	01:24 PM
OCT 17	Libra	09:58 PM
NOV 16	Scorpio	08:19 AM
DEC 15	Sagittarius	09:07 PM

2029

JAN 14	Capricorn	12:25 PM
FEB 13	Aquarius	05:33 AM
MAR 14	Pisces	11:20 PM
APR 13	Aries	04:41 PM
MAY 13	Taurus	08:44 AM
JUN 11	Gemini	10:52 PM
JUL 11	Cancer	10:52 AM
AUG 09	Leo	08:57 PM
SEP 08	Virgo	05:46 AM
OCT 07	Libra	02:15 PM
NOV 05	Scorpio	11:25 PM
DEC 05	Sagittarius	09:53 AM

2030

JAN 03	Capricorn	09:50 PM
FEB 02	Aquarius	11:08 AM
MAR 04	Pisces	01:36 AM
APR 02	Aries	05:04 PM
MAY 02	Taurus	09:12 AM
JUN 01	Gemini	01:22 AM
JUN 30	Cancer	04:36 PM
JUL 30	Leo	06:12 AM
AUG 28	Virgo	06:08 PM
SEP 27	Libra	04:56 AM
OCT 26	Scorpio	03:18 PM
NOV 25	Sagittarius	01:47 AM
DEC 24	Capricorn	12:33 PM

2031

JAN 22	Aquarius	11:32 PM
FEB 21	Pisces	10:50 AM
MAR 22	Aries	10:50 PM
APR 21	Taurus	11:59 AM
MAY 21	Gemini	02:18 AM
JUN 19	Gemini	05:25 PM
JUL 19	Cancer	08:42 AM
AUG 17	Leo	11:34 PM
SEP 16	Virgo	01:47 PM
OCT 16	Libra	03:22 AM
NOV 14	Scorpio	04:11 PM
DEC 14	Sagittarius	04:07 AM

2032

JAN 12	Capricorn	03:07 PM
FEB 11	Aquarius	01:26 AM
MAR 11	Pisces	11:26 AM
APR 09	Aries	09:40 PM
MAY 09	Taurus	08:37 AM
JUN 07	Gemini	08:33 PM
JUL 07	Cancer	09:42 AM
AUG 06	Leo	12:12 AM
SEP 04	Virgo	03:58 PM
OCT 04	Libra	08:27 AM
NOV 03	Scorpio	12:46 AM
DEC 02	Sagittarius	03:54 PM

2033

JAN 01	Capricorn	05:18 AM
JAN 30	Aquarius	05:00 PM
MAR 01	Pisces	03:25 AM
MAR 30	Aries	12:53 PM
APR 28	Taurus	09:47 PM
MAY 28	Gemini	06:37 AM
JUN 26	Cancer	04:08 PM
JUL 26	Leo	03:14 AM
AUG 24	Virgo	04:40 PM
SEP 23	Libra	08:41 AM
OCT 23	Scorpio	02:30 AM
NOV 21	Sagittarius	08:40 PM
DEC 21	Capricorn	01:48 PM

2034

JAN 20	Aquarius	05:03 AM
FEB 18	Pisces	06:11 PM
MAR 20	Pisces	05:16 AM
APR 18	Aries	02:28 PM
MAY 17	Taurus	10:14 PM
JUN 16	Gemini	05:27 AM
JUL 15	Cancer	01:16 PM
AUG 13	Leo	10:54 PM
SEP 12	Virgo	11:15 AM
OCT 12	Libra	02:33 AM
NOV 10	Scorpio	08:18 PM
DEC 10	Sagittarius	03:15 PM

2035

JAN 09	Capricorn	10:04 AM
FEB 08	Aquarius	03:24 AM
MAR 09	Pisces	06:11 PM
APR 08	Aries	05:59 AM
MAY 07	Taurus	03:05 PM
JUN 05	Gemini	10:22 PM
JUL 05	Cancer	05:00 AM
AUG 03	Leo	12:12 PM
SEP 01	Virgo	09:01 PM
OCT 01	Libra	08:08 AM
OCT 30	Scorpio	09:59 PM
NOV 29	Sagittarius	02:39 PM
DEC 29	Capricorn	09:32 AM

2036

JAN 28	Aquarius	05:18 AM
FEB 27	Pisces	12:00 AM
MAR 27	Aries	03:58 PM
APR 26	Taurus	04:34 AM
MAY 25	Gemini	02:18 PM

JUN 23	Cancer	10:11 PM
JUL 23	Leo	05:18 AM
AUG 21	Leo	12:36 PM
SEP 19	Virgo	08:52 PM
OCT 19	Libra	06:52 AM
NOV 17	Scorpio	07:16 PM
DEC 17	Sagittarius	10:35 AM

2037

JAN 16	Capricorn	04:36 AM
FEB 14	Aquarius	11:56 PM
MAR 16	Pisces	06:37 PM
APR 15	Aries	11:09 AM
MAY 15	Taurus	12:56 AM
JUN 13	Gemini	12:11 PM
JUL 12	Cancer	09:33 PM
AUG 11	Leo	05:43 AM
SEP 09	Virgo	01:26 PM
OCT 08	Libra	09:35 PM
NOV 07	Scorpio	07:04 AM
DEC 06	Sagittarius	06:40 PM

2038

JAN 05	Capricorn	08:42 AM
FEB 04	Aquarius	12:53 AM
MAR 05	Pisces	06:17 PM
APR 04	Aries	11:44 AM
MAY 04	Taurus	04:20 AM
JUN 02	Gemini	07:26 PM
JUL 02	Cancer	08:34 AM
JUL 31	Leo	07:41 PM
AUG 30	Virgo	05:14 AM
SEP 28	Libra	01:59 PM
OCT 27	Scorpio	10:54 PM
NOV 26	Sagittarius	08:48 AM
DEC 25	Capricorn	08:04 PM

2039

JAN 24	Aquarius	08:38 AM
FEB 22	Pisces	10:18 PM
MAR 24	Aries	01:01 PM
APR 23	Taurus	04:36 AM
MAY 22	Gemini	08:39 PM
JUN 21	Cancer	12:22 PM
JUL 21	Cancer	02:56 AM
AUG 19	Leo	03:51 PM
SEP 18	Virgo	03:23 AM
OCT 17	Libra	02:10 PM
NOV 16	Scorpio	12:47 AM
DEC 15	Sagittarius	11:33 AM

2040

JAN 13	Capricorn	10:26 PM
FEB 12	Aquarius	09:26 AM
MAR 12	Pisces	08:47 PM
APR 11	Aries	09:01 AM
MAY 10	Taurus	10:29 PM
JUN 09	Gemini	01:04 PM
JUL 09	Cancer	04:15 AM
AUG 07	Leo	07:28 PM
SEP 06	Virgo	10:15 AM
OCT 06	Libra	12:26 AM
NOV 04	Scorpio	01:57 PM
DEC 04	Sagittarius	02:35 AM

2041

JAN 02	Capricorn	02:09 PM
FEB 01	Aquarius	12:44 AM
MAR 31	Aries	08:31 PM
MAR 02	Pisces	10:41 AM
APR 30	Taurus	06:47 AM
MAY 29	Gemini	05:57 PM
JUN 28	Cancer	06:18 AM
JUL 27	Leo	08:03 PM
AUG 26	Virgo	11:17 AM
SEP 25	Libra	03:43 AM

OCT 24	Scorpio	08:32 PM
NOV 23	Sagittarius	12:37 PM
DEC 23	Capricorn	03:08 AM

2042

JAN 21	Aquarius	03:43 PM
FEB 20	Pisces	02:40 AM
MAR 21	Aries	12:24 PM
APR 19	Taurus	09:21 PM
MAY 19	Taurus	05:56 AM
JUN 17	Gemini	02:49 PM
JUL 17	Cancer	12:53 AM
AUG 15	Leo	01:03 PM
SEP 14	Virgo	03:51 AM
OCT 13	Libra	09:04 PM
NOV 12	Scorpio	03:30 PM
DEC 12	Sagittarius	09:31 AM

2043

JAN 11	Capricorn	01:54 AM
FEB 09	Aquarius	04:09 PM
MAR 11	Pisces	04:11 AM
APR 09	Aries	02:08 PM
MAY 08	Taurus	10:23 PM
JUN 07	Gemini	05:37 AM
JUL 06	Cancer	12:52 PM
AUG 04	Leo	09:24 PM
SEP 03	Virgo	08:19 AM
OCT 02	Libra	10:13 PM
NOV 01	Scorpio	02:58 PM
DEC 01	Sagittarius	09:38 AM
DEC 31	Capricorn	04:49 AM

2044

JAN 29	Aquarius	11:05 PM
FEB 28	Pisces	03:14 PM
MAR 29	Aries	04:28 AM
APR 27	Taurus	02:43 PM
MAY 26	Gemini	10:41 PM

JUN 25	Cancer	05:26 AM
JUL 24	Leo	12:12 PM
AUG 22	Virgo	08:06 PM
SEP 21	Virgo	06:05 AM
OCT 20	Libra	06:38 PM
NOV 19	Scorpio	09:58 AM
DEC 19	Sagittarius	03:54 AM

2045

JAN 17	Capricorn	11:27 PM
FEB 16	Aquarius	06:52 PM
MAR 18	Pisces	12:16 PM
APR 17	Aries	02:28 AM
MAY 16	Taurus	01:28 PM
JUN 14	Gemini	10:06 PM
JUL 14	Cancer	05:30 AM
AUG 12	Leo	12:41 PM
SEP 10	Virgo	08:28 PM
OCT 10	Libra	05:38 AM
NOV 08	Scorpio	04:51 PM
DEC 08	Sagittarius	06:43 AM

2046

JAN 06	Capricorn	11:24 PM
FEB 05	Aquarius	06:11 PM
MAR 07	Pisces	01:17 PM
APR 06	Aries	06:53 AM
MAY 05	Taurus	09:57 PM
JUN 04	Gemini	10:24 AM
JUL 03	Cancer	08:40 PM
AUG 02	Leo	05:26 AM
AUG 31	Virgo	01:27 PM
SEP 29	Libra	09:27 PM
OCT 29	Scorpio	06:18 AM
NOV 27	Sagittarius	04:51 PM
DEC 27	Capricorn	05:41 AM

2047

JAN 25	Aquarius	08:45 PM
FEB 24	Pisces	01:27 PM
MAR 26	Aries	06:46 AM
APR 24	Taurus	11:41 PM
MAY 24	Gemini	03:28 PM
JUN 23	Cancer	05:37 AM
JUL 22	Leo	05:51 PM
AUG 21	Leo	04:17 AM
SEP 19	Virgo	01:32 PM
OCT 18	Libra	10:29 PM
NOV 17	Scorpio	08:00 AM
DEC 16	Sagittarius	06:39 PM

2048

JAN 15	Capricorn	06:34 AM
FEB 13	Aquarius	07:33 PM
MAR 14	Pisces	09:28 AM
APR 13	Aries	12:21 AM
MAY 12	Taurus	03:59 PM
JUN 11	Gemini	07:51 AM
JUL 10	Cancer	11:05 PM
AUG 09	Leo	01:01 PM
SEP 08	Virgo	01:26 AM
OCT 07	Libra	12:46 PM
NOV 05	Scorpio	11:40 PM
DEC 05	Sagittarius	10:32 AM

2049

JAN 03	Capricorn	09:25 PM
FEB 02	Aquarius	08:17 AM
MAR 03	Pisces	07:14 PM
APR 02	Aries	06:41 AM
MAY 01	Taurus	07:12 PM
MAY 31	Gemini	09:02 AM
JUN 29	Cancer	11:52 PM
JUL 29	Leo	03:08 PM
AUG 28	Virgo	06:20 AM
SEP 26	Libra	09:07 PM

OCT 26	Scorpio	11:16 AM
NOV 25	Sagittarius	12:36 AM
DEC 24	Capricorn	12:53 PM

2050

JAN 22	Aquarius	11:58 PM
FEB 21	Pisces	10:04 AM
MAR 22	Aries	07:42 PM
APR 21	Taurus	05:28 AM
MAY 20	Gemini	03:52 PM
JUN 19	Gemini	03:23 AM
JUL 18	Cancer	04:19 PM
AUG 17	Leo	06:49 AM
SEP 15	Virgo	10:50 PM
OCT 15	Libra	03:50 PM
NOV 14	Scorpio	08:43 AM
DEC 14	Sagittarius	12:19 AM

Table courtesy of the Astrology Center of America

Part II

What to Wish for
When the New Moon
Is in Each Sign

Basic Information:

✧ The New Moon occurs once approximately every twenty-nine and a half days, when the orbiting Moon aligns with the Sun in each of the twelve signs of the zodiac. The dates of each monthly New Moon are listed in the table on page 35.

In this New Moon section, the word "rules" is used. This is a traditional astrological term meaning "holds dominion over" or "influences." For example, the sign of Gemini rules communication. To determine a person's style and issues regarding communication, an astrologer would notice how factors related to the sign of Gemini interact in the birth chart.

At the end of the section about each sign, some health areas ruled by that sign are mentioned. It is to be noted that there is NO direct correlation between your Sun sign and health challenges related to each New Moon. For example, if your Sun sign is Libra, it does not mean you have a kidney weakness (the kidneys are ruled by Libra). Health challenges are shown by much more complex astrological compilations: the sign and ruler of the 6th House, the planets in the

6th House, the ruler of the ascendant—and difficult aspects between those rulers—are some of the factors taken into account in foreseeing what health related areas may need special attention.

This section discusses the unique issues stimulated when the New Moon is in each sign of the zodiac. Wishes that are in harmony with the energy currently activated in the atmosphere are especially potent. For example, Taurus rules money, and wishes around money are most powerful when the New Moon is in the sign of Taurus. So I suggest that you include at least one or two wishes connected with the special energies of each New Moon on your monthly wish list. Sample wishes are given for each sign. You may choose to put these wishes on your list only one time, or some of them may become regulars. Keep in mind, for best results, a maximum of ten wishes TOTAL is recommended on each New Moon day.

When considering which attributes of each New Moon to include on your wish list, select those qualities you FEEL that you want to work with or develop *at the time*. For example, when the New Moon is in the sign of Gemini, one year you may feel attracted to making the wish: "I want to be open to listening and learning from the various people I speak with." Another year, as the direction of your personal growth and desires change, you may choose the wish: "I want to easily find myself open to speaking and sharing messages and information with the various people I meet." Both wishes would reflect the particular energy of the New Moon in Gemini.

When making wishes, trust yourself and tune in to where your energy resonates. The idea is to be in touch with what you would really like to have happen and what feels appropriate to you as you absorb the energy of the current New Moon. For best results, use your intuition—what you feel *drawn* to wish for, not what you logically *think* you "should" wish for.

WHAT TO WISH FOR
WHEN THE NEW MOON IS IN

ARIES

New beginnings

Self-focus

Innocence/
authenticity

Self-discovery

Independence

Courage

Disengaging
self-absorption

*For more wishes in areas of life ruled by Aries,
see Ongoing Wishes and North Node in Aries.*

ARIES RULES NEW BEGINNINGS, INCLUDING:

Blazing new trails
Initiating
High energy
Taking action
Innovative approaches

Sample Wishes to Stimulate High Energy, Initiative:

℮ "I want to easily find myself initiating action in regard to————";
"I want lots of high energy and vitality!"; "I want to easily find myself
pursuing those activities that increase my energy"; "I want a successful
new beginning in the area of————"; "I want all fears around my as-
sertively blazing new beginnings with ———— easily lifted from me";
"I want all fears of being 'the first' totally lifted from me"; "I want to
easily find myself initiating in ways that create mutual trust and support in my relationship with————"; "I want to initiate a happy new
beginning in my relationship with————."

ARIES RULES THE SELF, INCLUDING:

The physical body
Survival issues
Instincts
Assertiveness

Sample Wishes to Strengthen the Self:

"I want the habit of losing the boundary of my own identity totally
lifted from me"; "I want the practice of abandoning myself easily lifted
from me"; "I want to easily find inner radiance and joy manifesting in

my face and physical appearance"; "I want to easily find myself trust-ing my instincts"; "I want to be consciously aware of myself, and ac-cepting of myself, as walking the earth as a beautiful (handsome) ———— (woman/man)"; "I want to easily find myself taking *myself* into account in all situations"; "I want to easily find myself making choices that are in the best interests of my own survival"; "I want to easily find myself embracing and loving myself"; "I want to easily find myself consistently asserting myself in healthy ways."

ARIES RULES INNOCENCE, INCLUDING:

Honesty
Authenticity
Impulsiveness
Straightforwardness

Sample Wishes to Encourage Authenticity:

"I want to easily find myself *acting* on my constructive inner im-pulse"; "I want to easily find myself behaving in ways that allow ———— to see who I am and to respect me"; "I want to easily find my-self honestly revealing my thoughts and feelings"; "I want total confi-dence in simply being myself"; "I want to easily find myself saying the right words to others that are a reflection of my true self"; "I want to easily find myself being authentic with others: letting them know what I am experiencing inwardly in a kind, nonblaming way"; "I want to easily find myself being more honest about who I am in my relation-ship with ————"; "I want to easily find myself being more straight-forward in all my relationships."

ARIES RULES SELF-DISCOVERY, INCLUDING:

Exploration
Taking risks
Eagerness
Competition

Sample Wishes to Further Self-Discovery:

"I want to easily find myself taking those risks that lead to personal growth and positive renewal!"; "I want to easily find myself filled with eagerness for exploring each new day!"; "I want to view any 'setbacks' as an opportunity for creative self-discovery"; "I want to easily find myself filled with the joy of self-discovery in every area of my life"; "I want all aversion to exploring new paths totally lifted from me"; "I want to easily find myself competing and winning in a healthy, nonabrasive way"; "I want to connect with others in ways that awaken my own sense of self-discovery."

ARIES RULES INDEPENDENCE, INCLUDING:

Self-direction
Self-reliance
Autonomy
Self-sufficiency

Sample Wishes to Bolster Independence:

"I want to easily find myself accepting the leadership of my own life"; "I want to easily find myself being kind and generous with myself"; "I want to experience independence in my relationship with ————"; "I want to easily find myself going in independent directions that are healthy and constructive for me"; "I want to easily find myself cultivating the habit of self-reliance"; "I want to easily find myself making decisions that are in my own best interests"; "I want to easily find myself *trusting* myself"; "I want to easily find myself following my own constructive instincts in making decisions."

ARIES RULES OUR "WARRIOR NATURE," INCLUDING:

Courage
Leadership
Strength
Vigilance
Boldness

Sample Wishes to Evoke Courage:

"I want the *courage* to be myself"; "I want lots of vital, healthy energy and courage in every area of my life"; "I want to easily find myself confidently taking the lead in the matter of ———"; "I want to be filled with courage and awareness in actively pursuing my own aims"; "I want to be filled with strength and boldness in my approach to ———"; "I want to remain consistently vigilant in the matter of ——— (keeping my weight at 130 pounds/remaining aware of my children/not procrastinating on work projects, etc.)."

ARIES ALSO RULES SELF-ABSORPTION, INCLUDING:

Lack of awareness of others
Selfishness
Vanity
Impulsive action that alienates others
Anger
Impatience

Sample Wishes to Disengage Self-Absorption:

"I want the tendency to isolating selfishness totally lifted from me"; "I want to stop taking impulsive actions that are against my own best interests"; "I want the habits of vanity and judgment totally lifted from me"; "I want all nonconstructive anger easily lifted from me"; "I want any survival instincts that are socially counterproductive easily lifted from me"; "I want all impatience easily lifted from me"; "I want all self-defeating lack of awareness of others totally lifted from me."

IN MATTERS OF RESTORING HEALTH, ARIES RULES:

Acne
Eyes
Head, face, scalp, and brain
Headaches and dizziness

Sample Wishes to Maximize Good Health in Areas of the Body Specifically Ruled by Aries:

"I want a total healing to occur in the area of my ———— (above body area ruled by Aries)"; "I want to easily attract, recognize, and begin working with the right healers for me that restore my ————

(body area ruled by Aries) to perfect health"; "I want to attract right information that leads to a total healing of my tendency to ——————— (body distress associated with Aries)"; "I want to easily find myself taking action that leads to my successfully restoring my ——————— (body area ruled by Aries) to perfect health and beauty."

WHAT TO WISH FOR
WHEN THE NEW MOON IS IN

TAURUS

Money

Sensual pleasure

Contentment

Perseverance

Patience

Self-worth

Releasing
stubbornness

For more wishes in areas of life ruled by Taurus,
see Ongoing Wishes and North Node in Taurus.

TAURUS RULES ACCUMULATION, INCLUDING:

Money
Material comforts
Ownership
Possessions

Sample Wishes to Appropriately Increase Money and Possessions:
"I want to easily find myself creating financial independence in a happy way"; "I want lots of money in a happy way!"; "I want all self-sabotaging anxieties around money totally lifted from me"; "I want to attract and purchase the right ——— (possession) for me at a price I can afford"; "I want to easily find myself taking steps that lead to owning my own ——— (home/car, etc.)"; "I want clear thinking regarding money, leading to my handling my resources in ways that are in my overall best interests"; "I want to easily find myself living in comfortable surroundings."

TAURUS RULES THE PHYSICAL SENSES, INCLUDING:

Sensuality
Heightened tactile enjoyment
Massage
Physical comfort
Aromas
Tastes

Sample Wishes to Increase Sensual Experience and Pleasure:
"I want to easily find myself enjoying the sensual side of life in a happy, healthy way"; "I want to find myself successfully initiating an

enjoyable experience of massage with my mate at least ———— times each month"; "I want to discover and begin using body oils that enhance both my and my mate's enjoyment of our bodies"; "I want to begin purchasing clothing that feels sensual and comfortable on my body"; "I want to easily find myself taking the time to cook, savor, and appreciate my meals"; "I want to find myself enjoying and appreciating the tastes, smells, and textures of the foods I eat"; "I want to easily attract, recognize, and begin working with the right massage therapist for me"; "In my sexual relationship with ————, I want to fully experience joyous sensual pleasure."

TAURUS RULES ENJOYMENT OF LIFE ON EARTH, INCLUDING:

Appreciation
Gratitude
Simple physical pleasures
Rapport with nature
Satisfaction
Contentment

Sample Wishes to Enhance Enjoyment of Life:

"I want to enjoy and appreciate my life"; "I want to count my blessings and feel thankful for the good things that are in my life"; "I want to easily find myself consciously enjoying the simple pleasures of everyday life"; "I want to easily find myself gardening a minimum of ———— days a week"; "I want to easily find myself consciously and consistently appreciating the abundance of life and Mother Nature"; "I want to experience a feeling of contentment with my life"; "I want to easily find myself experiencing a sense of satisfaction with the good things that are in my life."

TAURUS RULES BUILDING, INCLUDING:

Solid foundations
Persistence
Progressing step by step
Thoroughness
Perseverance

Sample Wishes to Aid in Building Successful Results:
    "I want to easily find myself filled with persistence—continually pressing on until my goal of ———— is reached"; "I want to easily find myself taking the time to build solid foundations that I can depend on in every area of my life"; "I want to easily find myself slowing down and doing each task with thoroughness"; "I want the consistency to steadily progress, step by step, until I accomplish my goal of ————"; "I want the habit of trying to rush results easily lifted from me."

TAURUS RULES RELIABILITY, INCLUDING:

Patience
Dependability
Trustworthiness
Steadfastness

Sample Wishes to Encourage Reliability:
    "I want to easily find myself *keeping my word,* and being a person that others can rely on"; "I want the quality of loving patience and steady progress to enter every area of my life"; "I want to easily find myself patiently, step by step, accomplishing my goal of ————"; "I want to determine my current "first value" and then steadfastly stay

focused on it until it is reached"; "I want to easily find myself relying on my own efforts for success"; "I want to easily find myself saying the right words that inspire others to be more reliable and loyal toward me"; "I want the quality of dependability to enter into my relationships; for me to manifest consistently dependable behavior and to inspire dependability in others."

TAURUS RULES SELF-WORTH, INCLUDING:

Awareness of personal needs
Setting appropriate boundaries
Strong values
Determination
Self-acceptance

Sample Wishes to Increase Self-Worth:

"I want lots of strength and determination, leading to my maintaining ——— (a decision, a stance, etc.)"; "I want to define what's important to me, and easily find myself living according to those values"; "I want to easily find myself communicating my needs to others in a way that encourages them to support me"; "I want to easily find myself stating my needs without an attachment to results"; "I want to easily find myself establishing boundaries that make my life stronger"; "I want to consciously and consistently experience feelings of self-worth in every area of my life"; "I want the tendency to undervalue myself easily lifted from me"; "I want to easily find myself being true to my own timing and comfort zones."

TAURUS ALSO RULES INFLEXIBILITY, INCLUDING:

Stubbornness
Attachment
Resistance to change
Possessiveness
Holding dogmatic opinions
Stagnation

Sample Wishes to Aid in Releasing Inflexibility:
"I want all self-defeating stubbornness easily lifted from me"; "I want all possessiveness totally lifted from me"; "I want to easily find myself expressing my views in ways that do not shut others out of the conversation"; "I want the habit of lazy stagnation totally lifted from me"; "I want all attachment to excessive accumulation totally lifted from me"; "I want all nonconstructive resistance to change easily lifted from me"; "I want to easily find myself *embracing* constructive change."

IN MATTERS OF RESTORING HEALTH, TAURUS RULES:

Coughs
Throat, chin, and neck
Thyroid gland
Voice and vocal cords

Sample Wishes to Maximize Good Health in Areas of the Body Specifically Ruled by Taurus:
 ✸ "I want a total healing to occur in the area of my ———— (above body area ruled by Taurus)"; "I want to easily attract, recognize, and begin working with the right healers for me that restore my ————

(body area ruled by Taurus) to perfect health"; "I want to attract right information that leads to a total healing of my tendency to —————— (body distress associated with Taurus)"; "I want to easily find myself taking action that leads to my successfully restoring my —————— (body area ruled by Taurus) to perfect health and beauty."

WHAT TO WISH FOR
WHEN THE NEW MOON IS IN

GEMINI

Motion/activity

Learning

Communication skills

Logic/cleverness

Social ease

Positive daily
interactions

Calming mental
anxiety

*For more wishes in areas of life ruled by Gemini,
see Ongoing Wishes and North Node in Gemini.*

GEMINI RULES MOTION, INCLUDING:

Automobiles (and mechanics)
Short trips
Transportation
Restless energy
Excitability

Sample Wishes to Facilitate Appropriate Motion:
  "I want to attract, recognize, and purchase the right car for me at a price I can easily afford"; "I want to easily find myself taking positive steps that result in my selling my car at a price I am happy with"; "I want to easily attract the right auto mechanic for me who restores my car to perfect running condition at a fair price"; "I want to easily find myself driving safely without stress"; "I want all self-limiting anxiety around driving easily lifted from me"; "I want to easily find myself taking short vacations at least ———— times each year"; "I want the fear of flying totally lifted from me"; "I want to easily find myself taking day trips to explore new places at least ———— time(s) each month"; "I want all ———— (restlessness/nervous anxiety/excitability) totally lifted from me."

GEMINI RULES LEARNING, INCLUDING:

Factual information
Formal education
Print media
The Internet
Curiosity

Sample Wishes to Enhance Learning:

"I want to find myself navigating the Internet with ease"; "I want to easily attract, recognize, and purchase the right ———— (subject) book for me that empowers me to further my goal of ————!"; "I want to easily find myself successfully completing my schoolwork in a straightforward, nonstressful way"; "I want to easily find myself going back to school, taking a minimum of ———— classes each semester/quarter"; "I want total clarity showing me what educational environment is going to be the best for ————"; "I want to easily attract those sources of information that will give me the answer to ————"; "I want healthy curiosity prompting me to get the information I need to resolve the issue of ————."

GEMINI RULES COMMUNICATION, INCLUDING:

Writing
Speaking
Effective listening and teaching
Mental rapport
Understanding different opinions

Sample Wishes to Promote Effective Communication:

"I want to easily find myself asking the right questions that lead to my understanding how other people think"; "I want to easily find myself writing in my journal a minimum of ———— days a week, a minimum of ———— minutes each time"; "I want to easily find myself writing a letter to ———— that successfully ———— (intended goal)"; "I want to easily find myself taking a class in public speaking that results in my having self-confidence in this area"; "I want to easily find myself communicating with ——————— in ways that restore the love in our relationship"; "I want to more effectively listen and learn from others, and communicate in a way that allows them to hear me"; "I want to easily find myself understanding other people's points of view, and feeling the pleasure of a deep mental rapport."

GEMINI RULES LOGIC, INCLUDING:

Awareness of options
Cleverness
Short-term results /
Handyman skills
Ingenuity
Variety

Sample Wishes to Enhance Logic:

"I want clear logic to enter my relationship with ———————"; "I want to easily find myself accepting other people's ideas as true for them"; "I want to consciously enjoy the variety in life, rather than only looking for what is familiar"; "I want to easily find myself creating positive short-term results in the moment"; "I want to clearly see my options for constructive change in my relationship with ———————"; "I want the cleverness to navigate life in a way that is in my best overall interests"; "I want to easily find myself focusing on what is positive in my relationship with ———————, rather than on what is "missing""; "I want all resistance to being handy around the house easily lifted from me"; "I want to easily find myself filled with ingenuity, understanding how mechanical things work and being able to fix them."

GEMINI RULES SOCIAL SKILLS, INCLUDING:

Tact
Acceptance
Quick thinking
Enjoying the moment
Wittiness
Having a sociable nature

Sample Wishes to Enhance Social Skills:
   "I want all fear of socializing with others easily lifted from me"; "I want to easily find myself consistently using tact, courtesy, and wit in all my relationships"; "I want to easily find myself totally comfortable in having light, interesting conversations with others"; "I want to easily find myself communicating in a way that others can understand and accept"; "I want to easily find myself accepting other people's points of view as true for them, without feeling I have to agree or disagree with them"; "I want to easily find myself 'thinking on my feet' and giving accurate and intelligent responses"; "I want to easily find myself having a more positive, lighthearted approach to life."

GEMINI RULES RELATIONSHIPS BASED ON PROXIMITY, INCLUDING:

Brothers
Sisters
Neighbors
Schoolmates
Roommates

Sample Wishes to Encourage Positive Communication in Social Relationships:

"I want easy, constructive communication to occur in my relationship with ————"; "I want to easily find myself constructively communicating in ways that ———— (my brother/roommate, etc.) can clearly hear and accept"; "I want more alertness and better judgment in dealing with ———— (sister/neighbor/roommate, etc.)"; "I want to easily find myself saying the right words to ———— that result in more harmony and cooperation in our relationship"; "I want to easily find myself interacting with ———— (sister/neighbor/roommate) in a way that creates ———— (loyalty/mutual support/mutual helpfulness, etc.)"; "I want to easily find myself going out and meeting new people socially at least ———— times each month."

GEMINI ALSO RULES OVERACTIVE MENTAL PROCESSES, INCLUDING:

Excessive questioning
Trickery with words
Superficiality
Nervousness
Indecision

Sample Wishes to Calm Mental Anxiety:

"I want all self-defeating tendencies to superficiality totally lifted from me"; "I want the tendency to deceive others or myself with words totally lifted from me"; "I want the habit of 'second-guessing' totally lifted from me"; "I want mental overactivity easily lifted from me"; "I want the habit of constantly changing my mind totally lifted from me"; "I want the mental habits leading to insomnia easily lifted from me"; "When I feel emotionally anxious, I want to easily find myself taking three deep breaths to relax."

IN MATTERS OF RESTORING HEALTH, GEMINI RULES:

Hands, wrists, arms, and shoulders
Hay fever
Lungs, breathing
Nervous system

Sample Wishes to Maximize Good Health in Areas of the Body Specifically Ruled by Gemini:

"I want a total healing to occur in the area of my ————— (above body area ruled by Gemini)"; "I want to easily attract, recognize, and begin working with the right healers for me that restore my ————— (body area ruled by Gemini) to perfect health"; "I want to attract right information that leads to a total healing of my tendency to ————— (body distress associated with Gemini)"; "I want to easily find myself taking action that leads to my successfully restoring my ————— (body area ruled by Gemini) to perfect health and beauty."

CANCER

Home/family

Safety

Growing

Intimacy/caring skills

Feelings/moods

Nurturing

Releasing
insecurity

For more wishes in areas of life ruled by Cancer,
see Ongoing Wishes and North Node in Cancer.

CANCER RULES FOUNDATIONS, INCLUDING:

Your internal frame of reference
Home
Family
Gut instincts

Sample Wishes to Strengthen Your Personal Foundation:
   "I want to easily attract, recognize, and purchase the right happy home for me"; "I want to attract, work with, and list with the right real estate broker who sells my home easily at a price I am happy with"; "I want to easily find myself initiating the refinancing of my home at the right time with an institution that gives me a fabulous deal!"; "I want to easily attract, recognize, and find myself living in the right happy ———— (room/apartment/condo) for me at a price I can easily afford"; "I want to easily find myself filling the atmosphere of my home with music, sweet scents, and other accents that brighten the atmosphere"; "I want to find myself spending more happy time with my family"; "Internally, I want to experience a feeling of increased security and joy"; "I want to easily find myself listening to, and honoring, my gut instincts."

CANCER RULES SAFETY, INCLUDING:

Security
Feelings of belonging
Protection
Tenacity
Financial security

Sample Wishes to Increase Feelings of Safety:

"I want to easily find myself handling my finances in ways that create a stable base I can count on"; "I want to feel an overriding sense of security in every area of my life"; "I want to easily find myself interacting with ———— in a way that gives me a sense of happy belonging"; "I want to easily find myself not giving up on ————"; "I want to easily find myself protecting myself in wholesome ways."

CANCER RULES PROCESSES, INCLUDING:

Training and practicing
Early childhood conditioning
Growth
Nurturing new beginnings

Sample Wishes to Encourage Positive Growth:

"I want to become aware of my early childhood conditioning in a way that frees me from unwholesome patterns"; "I want to easily find myself joyously learning and growing from all the significant events that happen in my life"; "I want to consciously and consistently practice positive new approaches in my relationships"; "I want to easily find myself aware of putting positive, caring energy into the beginning stages of my new relationship with ————"; "I want to easily find myself successfully training myself to ————"; "I want to easily find myself embracing the process of my own expansion and personal growth"; "In the matter of ————, I want to easily find myself more concerned with the integrity of the process and less concerned with results."

CANCER RULES EMOTIONAL CLOSENESS, INCLUDING:

Caring
Empathy
Vulnerability
Intimacy

Sample Wishes to Increase Emotional Closeness:
    "I want to easily find myself experiencing a reciprocal feeling of caring in my relationships with others"; "I want to easily find myself asking for help in a way that is empowering for myself and others"; "I want all fears around intimacy totally lifted from me"; "I want to easily find myself cocreating intimacy in a way that is healthy for me"; "I want to experience empathy and constructive emotional closeness with others"; "I want to easily find myself empathetically understanding others in a way that results in mutual caring and support"; "I want to easily find myself being vulnerable in a way that evokes positive acceptance and support from others."

CANCER RULES FEELINGS, INCLUDING:

Changing moods
Awareness of our own feelings
Sensitivity to others' feelings
Tenderness
Awareness of needs

Sample Wishes to Enhance Feeling Experiences:
    "I want to consciously, consistently find myself communicating my feelings in responsible, appropriate ways"; "I want all moodiness easily

lifted from me"; "I want all nonconstructive, overemotional responses easily lifted from me"; "I want the tendency to be ruled by my moods easily lifted from me"; "I want to easily find myself consciously aware of how I am feeling in various life situations"; "I want to easily find myself consciously aware of the feelings of others"; "I want to easily find myself experiencing the tenderness of deeply caring about someone else."

CANCER RULES NURTURING, INCLUDING:

Being supportive / accepting support
Food
Mother
Close family relations
Taking care of others
Being taken care of by another

Sample Wishes to Promote Positive Nurturing:
❧ "I want all self-destructive habits around food easily lifted from me"; "I want to experience the satisfaction of mutual emotional nourishment in all my relationships"; "I want to feel emotionally nourished from things that are healthy for me"; "I want to easily find myself sharing quality time with my mother, enjoying visits or recreational activities"; "I want to easily find myself saying the right words to my mother that create an experience of mutual understanding, respect, support, and love"; "I want to easily find myself maintaining my own identity while in the company of my family"; "I want to easily find myself avoiding the tendency to take care of others at my own expense"; "I want to easily find myself taking care of ———— in a way that is also healthy for me."

CANCER ALSO RULES EXCESSIVE SELF-PROTECTION, INCLUDING:

Clinginess
Feelings of insecurity
Possessiveness
Overly cautious behaviors
Fears of rejection
A lack of definite goals

Sample Wishes to Release Self-Defeating Insecurity:
   "I want the habit of clinginess totally lifted from me"; "I want the urge to possess others replaced by awareness of a deep sense of security within myself"; "Regarding taking responsibility for ————, I want all overprotective tendencies easily lifted from me"; "When caution interferes with my success, I want hesitation easily lifted from me"; "I want all insecurity totally lifted from me"; "I want to easily find myself *free* of being emotionally caught up in ————'s games"; "I want the fear of rejection totally lifted from me"; "I want to easily find myself defining goals that empower me to rise above current limitations."

IN MATTERS OF RESTORING HEALTH, CANCER RULES:

Breasts and chest cavity
Pancreas
Stomach, stomach gas, and ulcers
Tumors

Sample Wishes to Maximize Good Health in Areas of the Body Specifically Ruled by Cancer:

"I want a total healing to occur in the area of my ———— (above body area ruled by Cancer)"; "I want to easily attract, recognize, and begin working with the right healers for me that restore my ———— (body area ruled by Cancer) to perfect health"; "I want to attract right information that leads to a total healing of my tendency to ———— (body distress associated with Cancer)"; "I want to easily find myself taking action that leads to my successfully restoring my ———— (body area ruled by Cancer) to perfect health and beauty."

What to Wish for
When the New Moon Is in

LEO

> Love and romance
>
> Creativity
>
> Generosity
>
> Celebration &
> play/fun
>
> Dignity
>
> Determination
>
> Tempering
> arrogance

For more wishes in areas of life ruled by Leo,
see Ongoing Wishes and North Node in Leo.

LEO RULES PERSONAL HEART CONNECTIONS, INCLUDING:

Romance
Children
Dating
Intense love encounters
Giving and seeking approval

Sample Wishes to Encourage Personal Love:

"I want to attract and experience a healthy, happy romantic relationship"; "In romance, I want to easily find myself being honest with the other person about who I am and what I want, so that I become involved with a person who really resonates with my true inner spirit"; "I want to easily find myself giving verbal approval to others"; "I want to easily find myself seeing life afresh, with the eyes of a child"; "I want to successfully create a feeling of romance and play in my relationship with ———"; "I want to easily find myself spending more time enjoying my children"; "I want to easily find myself interacting with my children in a way that creates mutual understanding, respect, cooperation, and love"; "I want to easily find myself reentering the dating scene in a way that is successful and pleasurable for me."

LEO RULES CREATIVITY, INCLUDING:

Enthusiasm
Creative projects
Artistic expression
Total subjective involvement
Self-actualization
Passion

Sample Wishes to Stimulate Creative Involvement:

"I want to easily find myself beginning each day with a feeling of enthusiasm"; "I want to be filled with creative, new ideas relative to ————"; "I want to easily find myself expressing my creativity for its own sake, without an eye to the results"; "I want to easily find myself choosing projects that cause my creativity to flow freely and that bring me joy"; "I want to easily find myself allowing my natural enthusiasm to shine forth"; "I want to easily find myself actively following the path that is dictated by my own sense of inner joy and happiness"; "I want the tendency to sabotage the successful fulfillment of my heart's desires easily lifted from me"; "I want to easily find myself involved in activities that evoke my passion and vital interest."

LEO RULES GIVING LOVE, INCLUDING:

Loyalty
Generosity
Bringing joy
Encouragement
Kindness

Sample Wishes to Encourage Giving Love:

"I want to express myself in ways that result in others knowing that I love them"; "I want to easily find myself honoring the individual personalities of the people around me"; "I want to easily find myself actively giving love, approval, and support to the people who are important to me"; "I want to easily find myself interacting with others in a way that demonstrates loyalty and support"; "I want to easily find myself giving others the benefit of the doubt"; "I want to easily find myself encouraging others to be the best that they can be"; "I want to easily find myself being generous with those around me"; "I want to easily find myself adding to the energy of fun and laughter when I am with others."

LEO RULES PLEASURE AND CELEBRATION, INCLUDING:

Fun
Play
Games
Parties
Vacations
Recreational sports
Taking risks for excitement

Sample Wishes to Increase Pleasure in Life:

"I want to easily find myself doing at least one thing that brings me pleasure each day"; "I want to easily find myself open to experiencing the pleasure available in my daily life"; "I want my relationship with ———— to be filled with fun, playfulness, and lighthearted enjoyment"; "I want to easily find myself consciously taking time to play and enjoy life"; "I want to be filled with right ideas about exactly the right, happy vacation for me to take this year!"; "I want to easily find myself actively participating in the sport/activity of ———— a minimum of ———— times each (week/month)"; "I want to easily find myself taking those risks that bring more joy and vitality into my life"; "I want the habit of shutting down and not experiencing the joy of life easily lifted from me"; "I want to easily find myself initiating activities that are fun for all concerned, including me!"; "When attending parties, I want to find myself filled with self-confidence and easy, genuine interest in those around me."

LEO RULES DIGNITY, INCLUDING:

Recognition
Being center stage
Self-confidence
Powerful individual expression
Radiance
Benevolence

Sample Wishes to Enhance Dignity:

"I want to easily find myself happily participating in the right the-
ater group for me"; "I want to easily find myself putting others on center stage in a way that creates positive mutual energy!"; "I want to
easily find myself enjoying being center of the stage in a healthy, happy
way"; "I want an aura of happy dignity to permeate my being"; "I want
true self-confidence to enter into every area of my life"; "I want to easily allow the radiance of my inner being to shine openly"; "I want to
have a feeling of benevolence and goodwill toward ————"; "I want
to easily find myself taking the right actions ———— (at work/with
family/with friends, etc.) that cause me to be recognized in a positive
way."

Career?

LEO RULES DETERMINATION, INCLUDING:

Leadership
Concentrated focus
Follow through
Strength of purpose
Resoluteness
Stamina

Sample Wishes to Strengthen Determination:

"I want to be filled with the determination that easily carries my plans through to completion"; "I want to easily find myself consciously and consistently connecting with my own inner determination, so that I willingly and happily ———— (exercise) on a regular basis"; "I want the habit of wavering or being distracted from my purpose totally lifted from me"; "I want plenty of stamina leading to my completing the process of ————"; "I want all resistance to completing things totally lifted from me"; "I want to easily find myself assuming leadership in ———— (all areas of my life)"; "I want to experience an increase in my ability to focus in a concentrated way"; "I want to easily find myself focused on completing one thing at a time, and completing it."

LEO ALSO RULES ARROGANCE, INCLUDING:

Pride
Being overly dramatic
Self-centeredness
Extravagance
Bossiness

Sample Wishes to Curtail Overconfidence:

"I want self-defeating extravagance totally lifted from me"; "I want any feeling of arrogance easily lifted from me"; "I want the habit of feeling either superior or inferior totally lifted from me"; "I want all self-isolating pride totally lifted from me"; "I want the habit of using unpleasant drama to get my way easily lifted from me"; "I want all nonconstructive self-centeredness totally lifted from me"; "I want the habit of bossing people around totally lifted from me."

IN MATTERS OF RESTORING HEALTH, LEO RULES:

Back and spine
Exhaustion, heat exhaustion
Heart
Inflammations

Sample Wishes to Maximize Good Health in Areas of the Body Specifically Ruled by Leo:

"I want a total healing to occur in the area of my ———— (above body area ruled by Leo)"; "I want to easily attract, recognize, and begin working with the right healers for me that restore my ———— (body area ruled by Leo) to perfect health"; "I want to attract right information that leads to a total healing of my tendency to ———— (body distress associated with Leo)"; "I want to easily find myself taking action that leads to my successfully restoring my ———— (body area ruled by Leo) to perfect health and beauty."

WHAT TO WISH FOR
WHEN THE NEW MOON IS IN

VIRGO

Physical
health/diet/exercise

Work/job

Efficient organizing

Clear discrimination

Helpfulness

Order

Relaxing
perfectionism

*For more wishes in areas of life ruled by Virgo,
see Ongoing Wishes and North Node in Virgo.*

VIRGO RULES PHYSICAL HEALTH, INCLUDING:

Diet
Exercise
Establishing good health habits
Weight control
Healing
Healers (nurses, doctors, chiropractors, etc.)

Sample Wishes to Enhance Physical Health:

"I want to easily find myself attracted to and consuming only those foods that are low fat, low calorie, and healthy for my body"; "I want to easily find myself doing ———— (aerobic/yoga/weight lifting/etc.) exercises for a minimum of ———— hours a day, ———— days a week"; "I want the addiction to ———— (sugar, cigarettes, alcohol, coffee, etc.) totally lifted from me"; "I want to easily establish my weight at ———— pounds in a healthy way that is beautifying for my body"; "I want to easily find myself establishing routines that lead to vibrant health"; "I want all feelings of inadequacy relative to health totally lifted from me"; "I want to easily attract, recognize, and begin working with those healers who can successfully help me restore my body to perfect health"; "I want to easily attract, recognize, and begin taking those herbs, vitamins, minerals, that help me restore my body and mind to perfect health and vitality."

VIRGO RULES WORK, INCLUDING:

Jobs
Work projects
Tasks and errands
Co-workers
Structured routines

Sample Wishes to Prompt Positive Participation:

"I want to easily attract, recognize, and begin working at the right job for me"; "I want to easily find myself completing work projects with a minimum of stress and a maximum of efficiency"; "I want to be filled with healthy self-confidence in every area of my job"; "I want to easily find myself adopting an attitude that allows me to enjoy my work"; "I want to easily find myself creating a routine that gives me plenty of time for work, play, time with my family, and —————"; "I want all resistance to hard work easily lifted from me"; "I want to easily find myself replacing daydreaming with productive action"; "I want all tendencies to postpone doing tasks and errands totally lifted from me"; "I want to easily find myself saying the right words to my co-workers that lead to mutual respect, support, cooperation, and —————."

VIRGO RULES CREATIVE ORGANIZATION, INCLUDING:

Orderly environments
Handling details
Efficiency and planning
Paperwork
Punctuality

Sample Wishes to Begin Creating Efficient Systems and Order:

"I want to easily find myself creating neatness and order in my home"; "I want to easily find myself paying my bills on the ————— day of each month"; "I want to easily find myself organizing my paperwork—completing all filing and throwing away whatever I no longer need"; "I want the habit of being late easily lifted from me"; "I want to easily find myself restoring my environment to order on a daily basis"; "I want all resistance to 'cleaning up the mess' easily lifted from me"; "I want clear planning that will empower me to successfully reach my goal of ————."

VIRGO RULES DISCRIMINATION, INCLUDING:

Analysis
Critical thinking
Focus
Discernment

Sample Wishes to Promote Accurate Discrimination:
"I want to easily find myself analyzing the problem of ———— in a way that produces productive, happy results"; "I want all confusion and overanalyzing of my situation with ———— easily lifted from me"; "I want to easily find myself accurately discerning what is important to me and what is not"; "I want to easily find myself effectively responding to external crisis without inner tension"; "I want to easily find myself focusing on, and appreciating, the opportunities that are being offered to me"; "I want to easily find myself consistently focusing on the here-and-now moment, using it to make my dreams come true."

VIRGO RULES SERVICE, INCLUDING:

Willingness to adapt
Practical helpfulness
Purity of intent
Conscientiousness

Sample Wishes to Increase Awareness of Pure Intent:
   "I want to consciously feel satisfaction from being of service to others in my work"; "I want to easily find myself *adjusting* to the ———— situation in a way that is in my best overall interest"; "I want to easily find myself adapting to those changes that are to my advantage"; "I want to easily find myself responding to disorder and confusion with an approach of practical helpfulness"; "I want to easily find myself doing my part to bring order and calm to my environment"; "I want to easily find myself being conscientious—aware of not interfering with the activities of others"; "I want to consciously be aware of the purity of my intention to benefit others."

VIRGO RULES SYNTHESIS, INCLUDING:

Desire for perfection
Processing
Bringing order out of chaos
The ability to see how the pieces fit

Sample Wishes to Activate the Ability for Synthesis:
   "I want to easily find myself aware of—and accepting of—good fortune when it comes to me"; "I want to easily find myself focusing on what is RIGHT with my life, rather than what is "wrong"; "I want

to easily find myself 'taking hold'—seeing and following practical action in the issue of ———"; "I want to easily find myself processing my relationship with ——— in a way that leads to a total healing for me"; "I want to clearly see the situation with ——— in a way that shows me how to bring order out of the chaos"; "I want accurate clarity in seeing 'how the pieces fit' in the situation of ———"; "I want to easily find myself focusing on the positive results I want to create in the situation of ———."

VIRGO ALSO RULES EXCESSIVE PERFECTIONISM, INCLUDING:

Worry
Criticism
Blame and judgment
Workaholic tendencies

Sample Wishes to Curb Perfectionism:

"I want all self-defeating tendencies to perfectionism easily lifted from me"; "I want the habit of obsessive worrying totally lifted from me"; "I want to stand free of critical judgments of myself and others"; "I want the compulsion to 'fix others' totally lifted from me"; "I want my mind's habit of using negative, critical language easily lifted from me"; "I want the habit of compulsively blaming others totally lifted from me"; "I want the compulsion to be 'right' easily lifted from me"; "I want the habit of working at the expense of living a balanced, happy life easily lifted from me."

IN MATTERS OF RESTORING HEALTH, VIRGO RULES:

Bowels and intestines
Constipation and diarrhea
Digestion and assimilation
Solar plexus

Sample Wishes to Maximize Good Health in Areas of the Body Specifically Ruled by Virgo:

"I want a total healing to occur in the area of my ———— (above body area ruled by Virgo)"; "I want to easily attract, recognize, and begin working with the right healers for me that restore my ———— (body area ruled by Virgo) to perfect health"; "I want to attract right information that leads to a total healing of my tendency to ———— (body distress associated with Virgo)"; "I want to easily find myself taking action that leads to my successfully restoring my ———— (body area ruled by Virgo) to perfect health and beauty."

WHAT TO WISH FOR
WHEN THE NEW MOON IS IN

LIBRA

Marriage

Negotiation skills

Harmony

Teamwork

Sociability/
diplomacy

Refinement

Healing
codependency

*For more wishes in areas of life ruled by Libra,
see Ongoing Wishes and North Node in Libra.*

LIBRA RULES MARRIAGE, INCLUDING:

Partnerships
Agreements
Sharing
Interdependence

Sample Wishes to Inspire Happiness in Marriage:
"I want to easily attract and begin a happy, monogamous, committed relationship with a man (woman) with whom I experience mutual ———— (support, respect, appreciation, love, passion, etc.)"; "I want to be filled with right ideas showing me the best possible relationship between ———— and myself"; "I want the exchange of love, support, and sharing to reenter my marriage"; "I want to attract and recognize the right marriage partner for me and begin a happy, healthy relationship with that person"; "I want to easily see and successfully follow the pathway to creating a happy marriage"; "I want to easily find myself saying the right words to ———— (my partner) that encourage him/her to be more loving toward me"; "I want to easily find myself filled with accurate discrimination in terms of relationships, leading to my committing to those opportunities that are in my overall best interests."

LIBRA RULES FAIRNESS, INCLUDING:

Balance
Equality
Appreciation of opposite viewpoints
Negotiation
Counseling

Sample Wishes to Promote Fairness:

"I want all thoughts of not being equal with others easily lifted from me"; "I want to easily find myself putting myself in the other person's shoes in order to perceive them accurately"; "I want to easily find myself open to understanding points of view opposite to my own"; "I want all upsetting preoccupation with fairness easily lifted from me"; "I want to effectively negotiate my situation with ———— in a way that creates a win-win situation"; "I want to easily find myself saying the right words to ———— that result in our going to counseling together"; "I want to feel internally balanced and peaceful"; "I want to easily attract, recognize, and begin working with the right counselor for me who is a healing and empowering influence in my life."

LIBRA RULES HARMONY, INCLUDING:

Peace

Beauty

Art

Decorations

Sample Wishes to Enhance Harmony:

❧"I want to easily find myself adding those decorating touches to my environment that create a feeling of peace, happiness, and serenity"; "I want to begin consciously experiencing peace and harmony in my life"; "I want to easily relax into the graciousness of my own beauty as a ———— (woman/man)"; "I want to easily find myself *being* myself in a way that is harmonious for others and happy for me"; "I want to easily attract and begin working with the right feng shui specialist for me who makes those shifts in my home environment that result in my attracting into my life those things that I want"; "I want to easily find myself decorating my home in a way that totally pleases me."

LIBRA RULES TEAMWORK, INCLUDING:

Giving and receiving support
Collaboration
Supportive relationships
Cooperation
Team identity

Sample Wishes to Encourage Teamwork:

"I want to consciously be aware that we are 'all in this together' and easily lend my support to others"; "I want to easily find myself supporting ———— in a way that also works for me"; "I want to easily find myself cooperating with others in a healthy, happy way"; "I want all resistance to being a team player totally lifted from me"; "I want to easily find myself creating a strong sense of mutual support in my relationship with ————"; "I want to easily find myself collaborating with ———— in a way that results in a win-win situation."

LIBRA RULES SOCIABILITY, INCLUDING:

Being companionable
Tact
Getting along with other people
One-on-one interactions

Diplomacy
Affinity for others

Sample Wishes to Enhance Sociability:

"I want to easily find myself feeling affinity for others and wanting to interact with them"; "I want to speak to others tactfully, resulting in them wanting to cooperate with me"; "I want to easily find myself employing diplomacy as a regular habit"; "I want to easily find myself relating with others in a tactful, courteous, and cooperative manner"; "I want to be aware of feeling agreeable and at ease in social situations"; "I want to be filled with total, accurate clarity in seeing how to make my relationships more satisfying."

LIBRA RULES REFINEMENT, INCLUDING:

Luxury
Elegance
Pampering
Good taste
Grace

Sample Wishes to Develop Refinement:

"I want to be fully receptive to and appreciative of being pampered by others"; "I want to easily find myself filled with the energy of grace and elegance as I move through my daily life"; "I want to naturally find myself attracted to purchasing items that are in good taste at a price I can easily afford"; "I want to easily find myself fully appreciating the luxury that is in my life"; "I want to easily find myself graciously accepting gifts from others in a happy, healthy way"; "I want to consciously and consistently be aware of the grace that is present in every moment"; "I want to easily find myself dressing in a style that others perceive to be elegant."

LIBRA ALSO RULES LOSS OF SELF-IDENTITY, INCLUDING:

Codependency
Appeasing behaviors
Indecision
Aimless debate

Sample Wishes to Strengthen Self-Identity:
   "I want the compulsion to like—and be liked by—everybody totally lifted from me"; "I want the compulsion to gain 'peace at any price' easily lifted from me"; "I want the habit of comparing myself to others totally lifted from me"; "I want all paralyzing indecision lifted from me"; "I want the habit of always taking an opposing point of view easily lifted from me"; "I want the notion that I must always be a 'nice person' totally lifted from me"; "I want to no longer need to experience inner accord with ———— in order to have peace of mind."

IN MATTERS OF RESTORING HEALTH, LIBRA RULES:

Adrenal glands
Buttocks
Diabetes (sugar imbalance)
Kidneys

Sample Wishes to Maximize Good Health in Areas of the Body Specifically Ruled by Libra:

"I want a total healing to occur in the area of my ———— (above body area ruled by Libra)"; "I want to easily attract, recognize, and begin working with the right healers for me that restore my ———— (body area ruled by Libra) to perfect health"; "I want to attract right information that leads to a total healing of my tendency to ———— (body distress associated with Libra)"; "I want to easily find myself taking action that leads to my successfully restoring my ———— (body area ruled by Libra) to perfect health and beauty."

WHAT TO WISH FOR
WHEN THE NEW MOON IS IN
SCORPIO

Empowerment

Change

Crisis skills

Self-mastery

Sex/soul mates

Financial
partnerships

Avoiding power
struggles

*For more wishes in areas of life ruled by Scorpio,
see Ongoing Wishes and North Node in Scorpio.*

SCORPIO RULES POWER, INCLUDING:

Secrets
Awareness of others' needs and motives
Politics
Psychology
Charisma

Sample Wishes to Enhance Personal Power:

"I want to easily find myself keeping secrets"; "I want a heightened awareness in seeing the real needs of my significant other"; "I want to easily find myself working with the politics at my job in a way that is beneficial to me and others"; "I want right ideas to occur to me relative to mutual empowerment in my relationships"; "I want to easily find myself using my power constructively"; "I want lots of healthy, happy charisma in my relationships"; "I want to easily attract, recognize, and begin working with the right person who facilitates a psychological healing for me."

SCORPIO RULES TRANSCENDENCE, INCLUDING:

Transformation
Eliminating old "baggage"
Change
Restoration
Forgiveness

Sample Wishes to Encourage Change:

"I want a positive transformation to occur in the area of ————";
"I want to easily find myself *releasing* old 'baggage' from ———— (my

childhood/all previous relationships)"; "I want to confidently find myself embracing change in the area of ————"; "I want to easily find myself restoring my relationship with ———— to one of mutual support, understanding, and respect"; "I want to easily find myself forgiving ———— in a way that is empowering for me"; "I want to easily find myself gaining power by ceasing to blame others for my circumstance"; "I want positive change to enter into my relationship with ————."

SCORPIO RULES CRISIS, INCLUDING:

Taking risks to gain power
Compulsions
Obsessions
Intense interactions
Living on the edge

Sample Wishes to Reduce Stress in Crisis:

"I want to easily find myself responding to crisis with clear, competent thinking and action"; "I want the habit of constantly creating stress and crisis in my life totally lifted from me"; "I want the habit of entering disastrous situations totally lifted from me"; "I want to easily find myself taking those constructive risks that lead to a new sense of empowerment"; "I want to easily find myself expressing my intensity in ways that are not threatening to others"; "I want to easily find myself noticing the intensity of others without taking it personally"; "I want my ———— (obsession/compulsion) with ———— totally lifted from me"; "I want to easily find myself experiencing mutual empowerment with others in a way that is healthy and happy for me."

SCORPIO RULES SELF-MASTERY, INCLUDING:

Good versus evil
Strength
Self-discipline
Commitment
Depth of character

Sample Wishes to Foster Self-Mastery:

"I want to easily find myself choosing good over evil: the high road of integrity that is best for me in every area of my life"; "I want to easily find myself filled with strength and making changes in my life that are in my overall best interests"; "I want to easily manifest self-discipline in the area of ————"; "I want to easily manifest self-mastery over ———— (smoking/drinking/excessive eating/etc.)"; "I want to easily find myself accepting my own emotional depth"; "I want to easily find myself fully committed to success in ————"; "I want the fear of commitment easily lifted from me."

SCORPIO RULES BONDING, INCLUDING:

Sex
Absorption
Soul mates
Deep emotional connections
Mutual validation

Sample Wishes to Cultivate Positive Bonding:

"I want to participate in making the sexuality in my relationship with ———— more passionate, facilitating a stronger bond between us"; "I want to easily find myself valuing those people in my life who are important to me and giving them my full support"; "I want the tendency to be absorbed in the force fields of others easily lifted from me"; "I want to attract, recognize, and experience a happy soul-mate relationship"; "I want to easily find myself saying the right words to ———— that create a situation of mutual empowerment and support"; "I want clarity and wisdom showing me the proper course to take in creating a happy soul-mate relationship"; "I want to easily find myself getting along with ————, growing in our love and bonding every day in a way that is also positive for us as individuals"; "I want to easily find myself saying the right words to ———— that create an atmosphere resulting in a deep emotional connection."

SCORPIO RULES FINANCIAL PARTNERSHIPS, INCLUDING:

Loans

Taxes

Debts

Grants

Wills and inheritances

Contracts and business

Sample Wishes to Successfully Manage Financial Partnerships:

"I want to easily find myself applying for and receiving a loan that is in my overall best interests"; "In my financial negotiations with ————, I want to easily find myself feeling full self-confidence in a positive way"; "I want all tendencies to postpone completing my tax return for ———— easily lifted from me"; "I want to easily find myself taking those actions that directly result in my becoming debt free in a happy way"; "I want to easily find myself using my full power and strength to get rid of my credit-card debt in a happy way"; "In the inheritance from ————, I want to easily find myself saying the right words to those involved that allow the situation to be resolved with fairness and goodwill for all concerned"; "I want to easily find myself completing my personal will"; "I want right ideas to occur to me regarding how to approach ———— in getting them to pay me back the money they owe me."

SCORPIO ALSO RULES THE MISUSE OF POWER, INCLUDING:

Revenge
Jealousy
Harsh judgments
Destructive urges
Power struggles
Abandonment
Suspicion
Guilt

Sample Wishes to Help Release Any Tendency to Misuse Power:
"I want all tendencies to get involved in power struggles easily lifted from me"; "I want the fear of abandonment totally lifted from me"; "I want all guilt regarding ———— easily and totally lifted from me"; "I want all desires for revenge against ———— totally lifted from me"; "I want all jealousy totally lifted from me"; "I want to easily find myself consciously suspending judgment of self and others"; "I want all destructive urges *totally* lifted from me"; "I want to easily find myself using my power *constructively* in all situations."

IN MATTERS OF RESTORING HEALTH, SCORPIO RULES:

Rectum, colon, bladder, and organs of elimination
PMS and menstruation
Sexual diseases
Sexual organs, male and female

Sample Wishes to Maximize Good Health in Areas of the Body Specifically Ruled by Scorpio:

"I want a total healing to occur in the area of my ——— (above body area ruled by Scorpio)"; "I want to easily attract, recognize, and begin working with the right healers for me that restore my ——— (body area ruled by Scorpio) to perfect health"; "I want to attract right information that leads to a total healing of my tendency to ——— (body distress associated with Scorpio)"; "I want to easily find myself taking action that leads to my successfully restoring my ——— (body area ruled by Scorpio) to perfect health and beauty"; "I want all PMS totally lifted from me."

SAGITTARIUS

Quest for Truth

Peace of mind

Travel/freedom/
adventure

Legal issues

Faith/optimism

Finding solutions

Overcoming excess

*For more wishes in areas of life ruled by Sagittarius,
see Ongoing Wishes and North Node in Sagittarius.*

SAGITTARIUS RULES THE QUEST FOR TRUTH, INCLUDING:

Religion
Prayer and higher guidance
Places of worship
Frankness and honesty
Direct communication

Sample Wishes to Promote a Personal Connection with Truth:

"I want to regularly find myself enlisting the help of a Higher Power in directing my life"; "I want a totally clear connection and communication with my positive Spiritual Guides"; "I want clear guidance showing me how to pray in a way that connects me directly to —————— (God/Higher Power/my Angels)"; "I want to easily find myself regularly attending a place of worship or meditation class a minimum of —————— times each week/month"; "I want all fears surrounding my being honest with others easily lifted from me"; "I want to easily find myself filled with courage in standing for, and enacting, my beliefs"; "I want to easily find myself —————— (praying/meditating/reading spiritual books) a minimum of —————— days a week, a minimum of —————— minutes each time."

SAGITTARIUS RULES THE NATURAL WORLD, INCLUDING:

Connections to nature
Intuition
Peace of mind

Sample Wishes to Promote Connections with the Natural World:

"I want to easily find myself listening with respect to my intuitive voices, and trusting my Guides to lead me in the right direction"; "I want to experience the joy of spiritual fullness"; "I want to easily find myself taking action on what my intuitive knowing tells me is the correct path for me"; "I want my intuitive sense to become stronger and more accurate"; "I want to easily find myself appreciating the beauty of nature"; "I want to easily find myself consistently experiencing peace of mind."

SAGITTARIUS RULES FREEDOM, INCLUDING:

Spontaneity
Adventure
Positive expectations
Exploration
Foreign travel

Sample Wishes to Inspire Freedom:

"I want to easily find myself taking a trip to ———— at a price I can afford"; "I want to easily find myself taking trips and traveling on a regular basis"; "I want to experience the freedom and enjoyment of living my life"; "I want to have more positive adventures in life"; "I want to easily find myself viewing life as a happy adventure"; "I want to easily find myself enjoying the benefits available in spontaneous interactions with others"; "In the situation regarding ————, I want to be filled with optimism and a positive solution"; "I want to easily find myself successfully exploring ————."

SAGITTARIUS RULES THE LAW, INCLUDING:

Attorneys
Lawsuits
Ethics
Morality
Conscience
Court proceedings

Sample Wishes to Encourage a Positive Relationship with the Law:

"I want to easily find myself obeying my conscience, leading to peace of mind"; "I want to easily find myself acting with integrity on the prompting of my inner being"; "I want to easily find myself consistently choosing the ethical path in the matter of —————"; "I want clear discrimination in choosing the right attorney who will handle my ————— case in a positive way at a price I can easily afford"; "I want clarity in the court proceedings with —————, allowing me to actively create a positive outcome"; "I want total clarity in my lawsuit with —————, resulting in my making those decisions that are in my overall best interests."

SAGITTARIUS RULES OPTIMISM, INCLUDING:

Faith
Friendliness
Good luck
Generous spirit
Gallantry

Sample Wishes to Evoke Optimism:

"I want to easily find myself behaving in a gallant manner with those who need my help"; "I want easy, friendly relationships with people"; "I want to easily find myself filled with confidence in the positive outcome of events"; "I want to solidly know within myself that there is a positive way out of any situation"; "I want all blocks to experiencing the joy of generosity easily lifted from me"; "I want to easily find myself having faith that a positive Higher Power is involved in every aspect of my life"; "I want to easily find myself receptive to good luck entering into every area of my life."

SAGITTARIUS RULES HIGHER EDUCATION, INCLUDING:

Mentors
Colleges and universities
Philosophy
Seeking answers
Finding solutions

Sample Wishes to Enhance Higher Education:

"I want to successfully enroll in the right college for me"; "I want to easily find myself seeing my life from a more philosophical point of view"; "I want to easily attract, recognize, and begin reading those spiritual texts that advance me on my spiritual path in a positive way"; "I want clear discrimination in choosing the spiritual teacher/teaching that will uplift my soul and help free my spirit"; "I want to easily attract, recognize, and begin working with the right mentor for me who will help me learn ———"; "I want to easily find myself actively seeking answers to my dilemma of ———"; "I want to find the solution to ——— in a clear, straightforward way."

SAGITTARIUS ALSO RULES CARELESSNESS, INCLUDING:

Shortcuts
Self-righteousness
Making assumptions
Excesses
Extravagance
Blunt communication
Pollyanna approaches

Sample Wishes to Eliminate Self-Defeating Carelessness:

"I want the habit of being blunt easily lifted from me"; "I want the habit of taking foolhardy risks in the area of ———— totally lifted from me"; "I want the tendency to take shortcuts that result in making mistakes easily lifted from me"; "I want all self-sabotaging carelessness in the area of ———— (money/joy/spouse, etc.) easily lifted from me"; "I want all self-righteousness totally lifted from me"; "I want the tendency to 'assume'—without checking out the facts—easily lifted from me"; "I want the tendency to excess and overdoing things totally lifted from me"; "I want the habit of Pollyanna approaches that undermine my life totally lifted from me."

IN MATTERS OF RESTORING HEALTH, SAGITTARIUS RULES:

Hips
Liver
Sciatica
Thighs, upper legs

Sample Wishes to Maximize Good Health in Areas of the Body Specifically Ruled by Sagittarius:

"I want a total healing to occur in the area of my ———— (above body area ruled by Sagittarius)"; "I want to easily attract, recognize, and begin working with the right healers for me that restore my ———— (body area ruled by Sagittarius) to perfect health"; "I want to attract right information that leads to a total healing of my tendency to ———— (body distress associated with Sagittarius)"; "I want to easily find myself taking action that leads to my successfully restoring my ———— (body area ruled by Sagittarius) to perfect health and beauty."

WHAT TO WISH FOR
WHEN THE NEW MOON IS IN
CAPRICORN

Future security

Handling
responsibility

Reaching goals

Success/recognition

Management skills

Authority figures

Releasing controlling
tendencies

*For more wishes in areas of life ruled by Capricorn,
see Ongoing Wishes and North Node in Capricorn.*

CAPRICORN RULES FUTURE NEEDS, INCLUDING:

Time
Making sensible decisions
Maturity
Retirement
Old age

Sample Wishes to Promote Preparing for the Future:
    "I want to easily find myself responding to the aging process in a way that is in my best interests"; "I want all fears of growing old totally lifted from me"; "I want clear thinking leading me to make those decisions that result in my having the best time of my life during my retirement!"; "I want to easily find myself approaching the situation of ———— in a mature, sensible way that is in my best interests"; "I want to easily find myself making decisions that provide a secure financial base for my golden years"; "I want to easily find myself handling my money in a way that allows me to retire at age ————"; "I want to easily find myself consciously using time to my best advantage."

CAPRICORN RULES RESPONSIBILITY, INCLUDING:

Self-discipline
Adult behavior
Keeping commitments
Competency
Public image

Sample Wishes to Encourage Responsible Behavior Leading to Success:
    "I want to easily find myself approaching my relationship with

——— from an adult position"; "I want to easily find myself behaving in ways that create a better public image"; "I want to easily find myself accepting responsibility for my situation with ——— in a way that empowers me to change it to my advantage"; "I want to easily find myself demonstrating my competency in ———"; "I want all fears of incompetency totally lifted from me"; "I want to easily find myself willing to commit to those things that are in my best interests"; "I want to easily find myself keeping my commitments"; "I want to easily find myself embracing the habit of self-discipline"; "I want to be filled with confidence and self-discipline, successfully reaching my goal of ———."

CAPRICORN RULES GOALS, INCLUDING:

Ambition
Defining goals
Using opportunities
Professions
Hard work

Sample Wishes to Assist in Reaching Goals:
"I want to easily find myself filled with the energy of ambition!"; "I want to clearly see which goals, when attained, will make me happy"; "I want total clarity in setting appropriate goals that lead to success in the areas I desire"; "I want to easily find myself using existing opportunities to reach my goal of ———"; "I want to easily find myself recognizing and utilizing opportunities when they arise"; "I want clarity in seeing how to most successfully proceed in order to realize my ambitions in my career"; "I want to easily attract, recognize, and find myself successfully pursuing the right career for me!";

"I want to easily find myself welcoming the hard work that leads to success."

CAPRICORN RULES SUCCESS, INCLUDING:

Accomplishments
Recognition
Social status
Achieving goals

Sample Wishes to Help Achieve Success:
"I want all anxiety around success totally lifted from me"; "I want to easily find myself filled with right ideas leading to success in the area of ————"; "I want to find myself believing that I can pull myself up by the bootstraps and succeed in life!"; "I want to achieve my goal of ———— with ease and a sense of authority"; "I want to experience positive recognition in my profession"; "I want right ideas to occur to me, leading to a successful promotion at work"; "I want to easily find myself steadily accomplishing my goal of ————"; "I want to easily find myself taking those actions that lead to an enhanced social status."

CAPRICORN RULES MANAGEMENT, INCLUDING:

Following protocol
Delegating responsibility
Being in charge
Respect

Sample Wishes to Enhance Management Skills:

"I want to easily find myself managing my life in a way that allows plenty of time for work, play, and family"; "I want to easily find myself successfully taking charge in every area of my life"; "I want all fears surrounding taking charge totally lifted from me"; "I want to easily find myself behaving in a way that naturally puts me in charge of —————"; "I want to easily attract right knowledge concerning successful management techniques"; "I want to easily find myself being in charge in a way that does not discount others"; "I want to accurately discern the talents of those around me and delegate those tasks that they are capable of doing and want to do"; "In the meeting about —————, I want to easily find myself focusing on the common goal, rather than the personalities involved"; "I want to easily find myself experiencing healthy self-respect and respect for others in all situations."

Capricorn Rules Authority, Including:

Fathers
Bosses and other authority figures
Tradition
Reputation

Sample Wishes to Promote Successful Interactions with Authority:

"I want to easily find myself following traditional routes leading to success"; "I want to easily find myself taking a more formal, respectful approach in the matter of —————"; "I want to easily find myself listening to the authority of my own inner being"; "I want to easily find myself behaving in ways that enhance my reputation"; "I want clear vision in seeing how I can best heal my relationship with my father"; "I want to easily find myself interacting with my father in a constructive way that maintains my own self-identity"; "I want to clearly see how I can support my boss in a mutually beneficial way"; "I want all fears around interacting with my boss totally lifted from me"; "I want to easily find myself successfully interacting with authority figures in a healthy way that does not make me feel diminished."

CAPRICORN ALSO RULES EXCESSIVE CONTROL, INCLUDING:

Lack of joy
Sternness
Fear of new approaches
Pessimism
Inflexibility
Self-justification

Sample Wishes to Release Controlling Tendencies:
   "I want the compulsive need to take personal credit easily lifted from me"; "I want all self-sabotaging tendencies to control others totally lifted from me"; "I want the habit of justifying myself to others totally lifted from me"; "I want all sternness easily lifted from me"; "I want to easily find myself seeing life in a way that brings me joy"; "I want all limiting, inflexible approaches totally lifted from me"; "I want to experience pessimism being mitigated by an awareness of the potential for positive outcomes"; "I want to welcome the possibility that a new approach will make my goals easier to reach"; "I want the habit of usurping others' responsibility easily lifted from me."

In Matters of Restoring Health, Capricorn Rules:

Bones and joints
Arthritis and rheumatism
Gall bladders and gallstones
Knees
Skin, psoriasis and itching

Sample Wishes to Maximize Good Health in Areas of the Body Specifically Ruled by Capricorn:

"I want a total healing to occur in the area of my ———— (above body area ruled by Capricorn)"; "I want to easily attract, recognize, and begin working with the right healers for me that restore my ———— (body area ruled by Capricorn) to perfect health"; "I want to attract right information that leads to a total healing of my tendency to ———— (body distress associated with Capricorn)"; "I want to easily find myself taking action that leads to my successfully restoring my ———— (body area ruled by Capricorn) to perfect health and beauty."

WHAT TO WISH FOR
WHEN THE NEW MOON IS IN
AQUARIUS

Inventive solutions

Seeing the future

Humanitarian
attitudes

Revelations

Humor

Friends

Avoiding excessive
detachment

*For more wishes in areas of life ruled by Aquarius,
see Ongoing Wishes and North Node in Aquarius.*

AQUARIUS RULES INVENTIONS, INCLUDING:

Innovative ideas
Brilliance
Eccentricity
Understanding how things work

Sample Wishes to Stimulate Inventive Energy:
"I want a brilliant, inventive solution to occur to me regarding the situation of ———"; "I want to be totally open to seeing life from a nonconventional point of view"; "I want to easily see a new and successful approach to the problem of ———"; "I want to give myself and others plenty of room to be eccentric and unique as individuals"; "I want all fears of being unique totally lifted from me"; "I want inspiring new ideas to occur to me regarding my dream of ———"; "I want to understand how ——— works in a way that summons an innovative solution."

AQUARIUS RULES THE FUTURE, INCLUDING:

New trends and unconventional approaches
High technology
Long-range goals
Following your heart's desire

Sample Wishes to Successfully Navigate the Future:
"I want to be aware of the beginning of new trends, and cooperate with them in a way that is in my best interests"; "I want to easily find myself filled with the courage to revolutionize my life!"; "I want to easily find myself courageously and successfully following my dream of ———"; "I want confidence in continuing to apply changes

in technology to my personal life"; "I want to easily find myself taking the first step toward making my dream of ———— come true"; "I want clarity in seeing those long-range goals that will give meaning to my life."

AQUARIUS RULES HUMANITARIANISM, INCLUDING:

Seeking outcomes that are good for everyone involved
Identification with humankind
Interest in others
Operating from a larger worldview

Sample Wishes to Stimulate Humanitarianism:
   "I want to easily find myself supporting outcomes that are good for others, as well as myself"; "I want to easily find myself seeing myself as part of a community"; "I want total clarity regarding the best ways I can participate with others to create successful win-win outcomes"; "I want to feel a sense of comfortable equality with others"; "I want to easily find myself actively involved in furthering the cause of ———— at least ———— hours each ———— (week/month)"; "I want to easily find myself genuinely interested in others"; "I want to easily find myself responding to others with warmth and friendliness"; "I want to become consciously aware of the larger picture of what is happening in the area of ————."

AQUARIUS RULES REVELATIONS, INCLUDING:

Excitement
Unexpected results
Surprises

Revitalizing experiences
Freedom

Sample Wishes to Attract Exciting Experiences:
"I want to greet unexpected events as positive opportunities for growth"; "I want all fears that lead to my refusing new revitalizing experiences totally lifted from me"; "I want a new revelation to show me the right path for me in the matter of ———"; "When sudden change occurs, I want to see the hidden opportunity that will allow me to benefit"; "I want to easily find myself making those changes that create a greater feeling of freedom in my relationship with ———"; "I want to find myself embracing the possibility of happy surprises in my daily life"; "I want to easily find myself open to attracting exciting, revitalizing experiences."

AQUARIUS RULES THE BIG PICTURE, INCLUDING:

Objectivity
Seeking knowledge
Tools of divination (Astrology, Numerology, Tarot, I Ching, etc.)
Humor
Manifesting dreams

Sample Wishes to Aid in Accessing "the Big Picture":
"I want to see life in a way that sparks my sense of humor"; "I want to be aware of—and act on—good timing"; "I want to be more objective in my perceptions regarding ———"; "I want to easily gain the knowledge that will empower me to manifest my dream of ———"; "I want to easily attract and enroll in the right ———

(Tarot, I Ching, Astrology, etc.) class for me that will open me to the knowledge I seek"; "I want to easily find myself realigning my thinking in cooperation with my destiny"; "I want right insights that lead to my dream of ———— coming true"; "I want to easily find myself ceasing to take things personally."

AQUARIUS RULES FRIENDSHIP, INCLUDING:

Friends
Groups
Networking
Open, friendly approaches
Forthrightness
Giving and receiving platonic love

Sample Wishes to Promote Friendship:

"I want to easily find myself making choices that are in my highest interests in promoting healthy friendships"; "I want to reestablish support and friendship in my relationship with ————"; "I want to easily find myself being honest about where I stand in my friendships, even if the other person feels differently"; "I want to easily find myself graciously accepting help, love, and support from others"; "I want to be filled with happy, healthy self-confidence in welcoming new people into my life"; "I want to attract and begin lots of happy, healthy new friendships"; "I want to easily find myself feeling comfortable and self-confident in group situations, relating to others with helpfulness"; "I want to easily find myself networking with my peers, successfully cooperating for the fulfillment of commonly held goals"; "I want my instinctive response to others to be one of friendliness, encouragement, and support."

Aquarius Also Rules Excessive Detachment, Including:

Cold aloofness
Fear of involvement
Erratic or shocking behavior
Inflexible opinions

Sample Wishes to Help Break the Bondage of Self-Defeating Detachment:

"I want self-sabotaging tendencies to withdrawal easily lifted from me"; "I want all self-defeating fears of involvement and intimacy easily lifted from me"; "I want the habit of isolating aloofness totally lifted from me"; "I want all destructive rebellion totally lifted from me"; "I want the habit of hurtfully shocking others totally lifted from me"; "I want all stubborn attachment to my own perceptions totally lifted from me"; "I want to easily find myself open to considering alternative points of view."

In Matters of Restoring Health, Aquarius Rules:

Ankles and calves
Circulation
Cramps and spasms
Varicose veins

Sample Wishes to Maximize Good Health in Areas of the Body Specifically Ruled by Aquarius:

"I want a total healing to occur in the area of my ———— (above body area ruled by Aquarius)"; "I want to easily attract, recognize, and begin working with the right healers for me that restore my ————

(body area ruled by Aquarius) to perfect health"; "I want to attract right information that leads to a total healing of my tendency to ———— (body distress associated with Aquarius)"; "I want to easily find myself taking action that leads to my successfully restoring my ———— (body area ruled by Aquarius) to perfect health and beauty."

WHAT TO WISH FOR
WHEN THE NEW MOON IS IN

PISCES

Imagination

Inner happiness

Psychic sensitivity

Trust/mystic
awareness

Spiritual healing

Compassion

Releasing
helplessness

*For more wishes in areas of life ruled by Pisces,
see Ongoing Wishes and North Node in Pisces.*

PISCES RULES ILLUSIVE STATES, INCLUDING:

Confusion
Sleep
Fantasy
Imagination
Chaos

Sample Wishes to Enhance Positive Illusive States:
"I want to easily find myself dealing with times of confusion in a constructive way that leads to growth"; "I want to easily find my mind and body deeply relaxing at night, for a minimum of ——— hours deep and restful sleep"; "I want the habit of insomnia easily lifted from me"; "I want the tendency to escape through sleeping too much totally lifted from me"; "I want to easily find myself replacing fantasy with constructive action to bring about the things that I want in my life"; "I want to easily find myself embracing chaos in a way that leads to peace of mind and serenity"; "I want my imagination activated, leading to new and positive views about life."

PISCES RULES JOYFUL STATES, INCLUDING:

Internal happiness
Bliss
Ecstasy
Universal love

Sample Wishes to Encourage Joyful States:
"I want to consciously and consistently experience the joy of my inner being"; "I want to feel spiritually fulfilled and happy"; "I want all

resistance to experiencing bliss easily lifted from me"; "I want to easily find myself embracing the ecstacy of pleasure"; "I want to consciously and consistently experience the loving bliss within me"; I want to experience the peace of universal love."

PISCES RULES PSYCHIC SENSITIVITY, INCLUDING:

Emotional sensitivity
Gentleness
Awareness of subtle energies
Mystical states
Harmlessness

Sample Wishes to Support Psychic Sensitivity:
   "I want to easily find myself staying in my own kind, loving nature"; "I want to easily find myself being more sensitive to others"; "I want the clear mind of the mystic in viewing my life and circumstances"; "I want to easily find myself attuned to the positive spiritual forces around me"; "I want the quality of gentleness to become a stronger part of my character"; "I want to easily find myself consciously living my life in a way that is harmless toward others"; "I want all debilitating sensitivity easily lifted from me."

PISCES RULES RELIANCE ON A HIGHER POWER, INCLUDING:

Surrender
Trust

Spiritual awareness
Channeling of spiritual power

Sample Wishes to Increase Connection with a Higher Power:
  "I want to easily surrender all worries and anxieties into the healing hands of a Higher Power"; "In my daily life, I want to consciously and consistently remember that "Source is doing it all"; "I want to easily find myself trusting a Higher Power to successfully guide my life"; "I want to easily find myself trusting that everything that occurs in my life is working towards my higher good"; "I want to easily find myself wordlessly channeling healing, spiritual power as I walk through my daily life"; "I want to easily attract, recognize, and begin working with the right spiritual teacher for me"; "I want to attract, recognize, and begin spending time with those who are on a spiritual path that is similar to my own."

PISCES RULES SPIRITUAL HEALING, INCLUDING:

Meditation and yoga
Desire for inner peace
Angelic assistance
Quiet time
Spiritual purification

Sample Wishes to Promote Spiritual Healing:
  "I want to easily find myself focused on the inner peace of my own nature"; "I want to easily find myself meditating at least ———— days a week, a minimum of ———— minutes each time"; "I want to easily attract, recognize, and begin attending the right yoga class for me at

least ——— day(s) a week"; "When I am creating ———
(art/music/writing, etc.) I want to find myself fully receptive to the
support and influence of the Angels"; "I want to easily find myself creating regular quiet time for myself a minimum of ——— days a
week, a minimum of ——— minutes each time"; "I want to experience the healing power of love"; "I want to easily find myself surrendering to a Higher Power and experiencing a total healing
in ———."

PISCES RULES UNCONDITIONAL LOVE, INCLUDING:

Forgiveness
Understanding
Nonjudgmental thinking
Tolerance
Acceptance
Compassion
Acknowledging oneness

Sample Wishes to Promote Unconditional Love:
   "I want to experience total forgiveness in the situation
with ———"; "I want to feel love and compassion for ———"; "I
want to easily find myself responding to ruckus with tolerance and understanding"; "I want to easily find myself remembering that everyone
is doing the very best they can, with the information and tools they
have"; "I want wisdom leading to loving people unconditionally"; "I
want to easily find myself understanding why others are where they
are, without judgment"; "I want to easily find myself responding with
compassion to those who are in need"; "I want to easily find myself
lovingly accepting ——— without trying to 'fix' her/him."

PISCES ALSO RULES VICTIM MENTALITY, INCLUDING:

Defeatist attitudes
Procrastination
Panic attacks
Deception
Addictions
Disappointments

Sample Wishes to Release Helplessness:
    "I want all tendencies to self-deception or deceiving others easily lifted from me"; "I want all thoughts of suicide totally lifted from me"; "I want to easily find myself free of the addiction to ————— (drugs/alcohol/smoking/watching television, etc.)"; "I want to easily surrender my addiction to————— and find it replaced by natural spiritual contentment within myself"; "I want all feelings of helplessness easily lifted from me"; "I want to easily find myself saying no when it is in my overall best interests to do so"; "I want the habit of passive behavior easily lifted from me"; "I want the habit of playing the victim role easily lifted from me"; "I want the habit of procrastination totally lifted from me"; "I want all psychic disturbance totally lifted from me"; "I want feelings of panic to dissolve into the conscious recognition that I am protected and cared for by a Higher Power"; "I want all anxiety totally lifted from me"; "I want all feelings of disappointment replaced by the recognition that everything is working toward my highest good."

IN MATTERS OF RESTORING HEALTH, PISCES RULES:

Colds
Feet, bunions and corns

Lymphatic system
Poisoning and toxicity

Sample Wishes to Maximize Good Health in Areas of the Body Specifically Ruled by Pisces:

"I want a total healing to occur in the area of my ———— (above body area ruled by Pisces)"; "I want to easily attract, recognize, and begin working with the right healers for me that restore my ———— (body area ruled by Pisces) to perfect health"; "I want to attract right information that leads to a total healing of my tendency to ———— (body distress associated with Pisces)"; "I want to easily find myself taking action that leads to my successfully restoring my ———— (body area ruled by Pisces) to perfect health and beauty."

Part III

Releasing Past Karma Through the Power of Wishing

In addition to using New Moon Power Days to attract what you want, you can also use them to rid yourself of unconscious habits and behaviors that have been working against you. These strong patterns, which often keep us from attaining the desires of our heart, can be seen as past-life (or karmic) "residue." They are habitual responses that worked to our advantage in past lives and/or early childhood, but are detrimental in our current adult life. These patterns block our happiness at every turn, yet we will continue to enact them until we realize what's going on and break their hold on our behavior.

In order to reveal these unconscious influences, it is helpful to look at them in the larger context of karma. I use the term "karma" to describe the process of balancing out what we have experienced in past lives. For example, if part of our character has been overdeveloped from too many incarnations focused on the home environment, in this lifetime we may need to consciously prompt ourselves to get out of the home and into the work world in order to regain a sense of inner balance.

Each of us has an aspect of our character that has been underdeveloped. Astrologically, this neglected part is specifically shown by the position of the North and South Nodes of the Moon in the birth chart. The Nodes of the Moon are not planetary bodies; they are points formed by the Moon's orbit around the Earth as it intersects with the Earth's orbit around the Sun. Consequently, they take into account the relationship between the Sun, Moon, and the Earth at the time of birth. This chapter includes a table that will assist you in locating the position of your North Node, as well as specific wishes that will be useful for your nodal sign. As you read about your North Node (which includes the lessons shown by the South Node), you will find a description of the imbalances that have been subtly undermining your life and the qualities that must be developed for inner equilibrium to occur and your dreams to manifest. For example, if your North Node is in the sign of Taurus, you may have an unconscious resentment of having to deal with money, which can manifest in chronic financial problems in this lifetime. (If you would like to learn more about any of the nodal groups, they are described in depth in my book *Astrology for the Soul,* Bantam, 1997.)

Of course, we do not intentionally take actions that cause us to lose what we value, but this karmic imbalance in the personality structure results in a lopsided approach to life that does not create success. It's like a leg that has atrophied through lack of use—it's difficult to make forward progress. By identifying the area of neglect and consciously stimulating it in a positive way (as in exercising the leg to rebuild the muscles), that part of ourselves becomes stronger and comes into balance with the rest of our personality. Yet RESISTANCE to implementing necessary new behaviors can be so strong that we continue to enact these karmic tendencies, even though this creates loss and discomfort in our lives. To get what we want in the outer world, and experience the resulting satisfaction and personal growth, these inner blockages to success must be released. From extensive work with myself and my clients, I've found that surrendering these tendencies for removal during an Astrological Power Period—either on New Moon Power Days or during the Grandaddy Power Period—can often initiate the easiest of healings.

It is the purpose of this chapter to describe the karmic, or undeveloped, parts of our character and then to offer wishes specifically tailored to dislodge our habitual negative reactions and awaken a healthy equilibrium in the personality structure. As that part of our character that needs to be emphasized is stimulated through the power of wishing, a strong inner balance is attained that serves as a foundation from which we can begin to produce the results we want in the outer world in a positive, happy way. What needs to change is not your dreams, but rather the approach you have been using to attain them.

THE LOCATION OF YOUR NORTH NODE

*Locate the span that includes your birth date in the chart below.
Your North Node position is listed to the right of these dates.*

May 10, 1899–Jan. 21, 1901 . . . . Sagittarius	Apr. 24, 1924–Oct. 26, 1925 . . . Leo	Jan. 27, 1949–July 26, 1950 . . . Aries
Jan. 22, 1901–July 21, 1902 . . . . Scorpio	Oct. 27, 1925–Apr. 16, 1927. . . . Cancer	July 27, 1950–Mar. 28, 1952. . . Pisces
July 22, 1902–Jan. 15, 1904 . . . . Libra	Apr. 17, 1927–Dec. 28, 1928 . . . Gemini	Mar. 29, 1952–Oct. 9, 1953. . . . Aquarius
Jan. 16, 1904–Sept. 18, 1905 . . . Virgo	Dec. 29, 1928–July 7, 1930. . . . . Taurus	Oct. 10, 1953–Apr. 2, 1955 . . . . Capricorn
Sept. 19, 1905–Mar. 30, 1907 . . . Leo	July 8, 1930–Dec. 28, 1931. . . . . Aries	Apr. 3, 1955–Oct. 4, 1956 . . . . . Sagittarius
Mar. 31, 1907–Sept. 27, 1908. . . Cancer	Dec. 29, 1931–June 24, 1933 . . . Pisces	Oct. 5, 1956–June 16, 1958 . . . . Scorpio
Sept. 28, 1908–Mar. 23, 1910 . . Gemini	June 25, 1933–Mar. 8, 1935. . . . Aquarius	June 17, 1958–Dec. 15, 1959 . . . Libra
Mar. 24, 1910–Dec. 8, 1911 . . . . Taurus	Mar. 9, 1935–Sept. 14, 1936 . . . Capricorn	Dec. 16, 1959–June 10, 1961 . . . Virgo
Dec. 9, 1911–June 6, 1913 . . . . . Aries	Sept. 15, 1936–Mar. 3, 1938 . . . Sagittarius	June 11, 1961–Dec. 23, 1962 . . . Leo
June 7, 1913–Dec. 3, 1914 . . . . . Pisces	Mar. 4, 1938–Sept. 12, 1939 . . . Scorpio	Dec. 24, 1962–Aug. 25, 1964 . . . Cancer
Dec. 4, 1914–May 31, 1916. . . . . Aquarius	Sept. 13, 1939–May 24, 1941 . . . Libra	Aug. 26, 1964–Feb. 19, 1966 . . . Gemini
June 1, 1916–Feb. 13, 1918. . . . . Capricorn	May 25, 1941–Nov. 21, 1942 . . . Virgo	Feb. 20, 1966–Aug. 19, 1967 . . . Taurus
Feb. 14, 1918–Aug. 15, 1919. . . . Sagittarius	Nov. 22, 1942–May 11, 1944 . . . Leo	Aug. 20, 1967–Apr. 19, 1969 . . . Aries
Aug. 16, 1919–Feb. 7, 1921. . . . . Scorpio	May 12, 1944–Dec. 13, 1945 . . . Cancer	Apr. 20, 1969–Nov. 2, 1970 . . . . Pisces
Feb. 8, 1921–Aug. 23, 1922 . . . . Libra	Dec. 14, 1945–Aug. 2, 1947 . . . . Gemini	Nov. 3, 1970–Apr. 27, 1972 . . . . Aquarius
Aug. 24, 1922–Apr. 23, 1924 . . . Virgo	Aug. 3, 1947–Jan. 26, 1949 . . . . Taurus	Apr. 28, 1972–Oct. 27, 1973. . . . Capricorn

Oct. 28, 1973–July 10, 1975 . . . Sagittarius
July 11, 1975–Jan. 7, 1977 . . . . . . Scorpio
Jan. 8, 1977–July 5, 1978 . . . . Libra
July 6, 1978–Jan. 12, 1980 . . . . . Virgo
Jan. 13, 1980–Sept. 24, 1981 . . . Leo
Sept. 25, 1981–Mar. 16, 1983 . . . Cancer
Mar. 17, 1983–Sept. 11, 1984 . . . Gemini
Sept. 12, 1984–Apr. 6, 1986 . . . . Taurus
Apr. 7, 1986–Dec. 2, 1987 . . . . . Aries
Dec. 3, 1987–May 22, 1989 . . . . . Pisces
May 23, 1989–Nov. 18, 1990 . . . Aquarius
Nov. 19, 1990–Aug. 1, 1992 . . . Capricorn
Aug. 2, 1992–Feb. 1, 1994 . . . . Sagittarius
Feb. 2, 1994–July 31, 1995 . . . . Scorpio
Aug. 1, 1995–Jan. 25, 1997 . . . Libra
Jan. 26, 1997–Oct. 20, 1998 . . . Virgo
Oct. 21, 1998–Apr. 9, 2000 . . . Leo
Apr. 10, 2000–Oct. 12, 2001 . . . Cancer
Oct. 13, 2001–Apr. 13, 2003 . . . Gemini
Apr. 14, 2003–Dec. 25, 2004 . . . Taurus
Dec. 26, 2004–June 21, 2006 . . . Aries

June 22, 2006–Dec. 18, 2007 . . . Pisces
Dec. 19, 2007–Aug. 21, 2009 . . . Aquarius
Aug. 22, 2009–Mar. 3, 2011 . . . Capricorn
Mar. 4, 2011–Aug. 29, 2012 . . . Sagittarius
Aug. 30, 2012–Feb. 18, 2014 . . . Scorpio
Feb. 19, 2014–Nov. 11, 2015 . . . Libra
Nov. 12, 2015–May 9, 2017 . . . Virgo
May 10, 2017–Nov. 6, 2018 . . . Leo
Nov. 7, 2018–May 4, 2020 . . . Cancer
May 5, 2020–Jan. 18, 2022 . . . Gemini
Jan. 19, 2022–July 17, 2023 . . . Taurus
July 18, 2023–Jan. 11, 2025 . . . Aries
Jan. 12, 2025–July 26, 2026 . . . Pisces
July 27, 2026–Mar. 26, 2028 . . . Aquarius
Mar. 27, 2028–Sept. 23, 2029 . . . Capricorn
Sept. 24, 2029–Mar. 20, 2031 . . . Sagittarius
Mar. 21, 2031–Dec. 1, 2032 . . . Scorpio
Dec. 2, 2032–June 3, 2034 . . . Libra
June 4, 2034–Nov. 29, 2035 . . . Virgo
Nov. 30, 2035–May 29, 2037 . . . Leo
May 30, 2037–Feb. 9, 2039 . . . Cancer

Feb. 10, 2039–Aug. 10, 2040 . . . Gemini
Aug. 11, 2040–Feb. 3, 2042 . . . Taurus
Feb. 4, 2042–Aug. 18, 2043 . . . Aries
Aug. 19, 2043–Apr. 18, 2045 . . . Pisces
Apr. 19, 2045–Oct. 18, 2046 . . . Aquarius
Oct. 19, 2046–Apr. 11, 2048 . . . Capricorn
Apr. 12, 2048–Dec. 14, 2049 . . . Sagittarius
Dec. 15, 2049–June 28, 2051 . . . Scorpio

Table courtesy of The Astrology Center of America

ARIES
North Node People
and North Node in the 1st House

ARIES NORTH NODE PEOPLE ARE LEARNING TO
OVERCOME CODEPENDENT TENDENCIES

Due to many lifetimes spent pouring their energy into strengthening their partner, these folks have lost touch with the strength of their independent identity. They think that supporting their partner is the key to their own survival because, subconsciously, they remember this process having worked for them before. However, in this lifetime when they depend on another for their survival, they will always end up being disappointed.

Sample Wishes to Strengthen Independence:
   "I want to easily find myself accepting responsibility for my own survival"; "I want all unhealthy codependent tendencies totally lifted from me"; "I want all resentment of other people being unfair with me totally lifted from me"; "I want to consciously and consistently honor my needs for independence"; "I want to easily find myself staying centered in my own identity"; "I want the thought that I need others for my survival totally lifted from me"; "I want to easily find myself de-

pending on others in a healthy way that does not lead to disappoint-ment"; "I want to easily find myself establishing my own material in-dependence."

ARIES NORTH NODE PEOPLE ARE DISCOVERING THEIR OWN UNIQUE IDENTITY AND LEADERSHIP POTENTIAL

In past lives, adapting to others was so important that in this life, Aries North Node people tend to form their identity to either coop-erate with—or totally resist—being the way that others see them. They are discovering their own true identity by simply being them-selves, without trying to see themselves through others' eyes. They will find that by being true to themselves and revealing themselves, they will automatically assume a healthy leadership role with others.

Sample Wishes to Encourage the Process of Self-Discovery:
"I want the habit of comparing myself to others totally lifted from me"; "I want to easily find myself honestly expressing what is true for *me* in my life"; "I want the habit of seeing myself through others' eyes easily lifted from me"; "I want to be so centered within myself that I am not distracted by others' perceptions of me"; "I want to con-sciously and consistently view life as a process of self-discovery"; "I want to consciously, consistently, be aware of my personal identity from inside of myself"; "I want all self-limiting images of 'who I should be' totally lifted from me"; "I want to easily find myself fol-lowing my own impulses for self-leadership."

ARIES NORTH NODE PEOPLE ARE OVERCOMING INDECISIVENESS AND LEARNING TO ACT ON THEIR IMPULSES

Aries North Node people are so accustomed to seeing both sides of an issue impartially that they unconsciously perceive any two situations as equal—and then have a hard time deciding what they want to do! They are learning to trust their impulses, which are true reflections of their own inner identity. In following their instincts they will naturally make the right decision.

Sample Wishes to Overcome Indecisiveness:
"I want to easily find myself ACTING on my impulses!"; "I want all guilt surrounding fulfilling my needs easily lifted from me"; "I want to easily find myself trusting my instincts"; "I want all self-defeating preoccupation with 'justice' totally lifted from me"; "I want to consciously and consistently take action on my own inner impulses"; "In making decisions, I want to easily find myself trusting and following my initial impulses."

ARIES NORTH NODE PEOPLE ARE LEARNING ASSERTIVENESS

These folks are experts at negotiating. However, in the process of ensuring fairness for everyone else they often leave themselves out of the equation, and then wonder why others never support THEIR desires! To counteract this tendency, Aries North Node people are learning to openly communicate what they want FIRST, and THEN ask the other person's preference so that a fair compromise can be achieved.

Sample Wishes to Promote Healthy Assertiveness:
"I want courage to fill every area of my life, empowering me to

speak my truth directly, in a loving way"; "I want to easily find myself saying the right words that allow others to really hear me"; "I want to easily find myself stating what I want *first,* and then listening to the desires of others"; "I want all fear of asserting myself totally lifted from me"; "I want to easily find myself initiating plans that are positive for me"; "I want to easily find myself asserting what I want and need in a self-revealing way that results in others cooperating with me"; "I want the notion that I have to always be 'a nice person' totally lifted from me; "I want to easily find myself handling my relationship with ———— in a way that is in my overall best interests."

ARIES NORTH NODE PEOPLE ARE LEARNING TO COPE WITH DISRUPTION IN THEIR RELATIONSHIPS BY FOCUSING ON THEIR OWN SERENITY

Through many past lives as a "team player," these folks developed a tremendous sensitivity to others in order to effectively help and support their partner. Now they are overly sensitive, and when those around them are upset they lose their own sense of balance and peace. They are learning to release their attachment to restoring harmony in others and focus on maintaining their own serenity.

Sample Wishes to Maintain Inner Peace in the Midst of External Disruption:

"I want to easily find myself experiencing the peace and love of my own energetic field when I am with others"; "I want the habit of merging with the personalities and force fields of others totally lifted from me"; "I want to easily find myself consciously and consistently centered within my own body and energy field"; "I want the habit of leaving my own serenity in order to restore harmony for others easily lifted from me"; "When external disruptions occur, I want to easily find myself resting in the harmonious love in my own nature"; "I want the idea that I am responsible for the harmony of others totally lifted from me."

ARIES NORTH NODE PEOPLE ARE STRENGTHENING SELF-LOVE AND AWARENESS OF THEIR OWN BEAUTY

Aries North Node people have had so many past incarnations recognizing the magnificence in others and pouring their love and support into their partner that they have forgotten to notice their own specialness and beauty. They lack confidence in just being themselves because they aren't aware of the loveliness of their own nature. Now they need to spend time consciously loving and supporting themselves and appreciating their radiance.

Sample Wishes to Strengthen Self-Love:
"I want to easily find myself appreciating the depth of love in my own nature"; "I want to easily find myself fully accepting and loving myself"; "I want to easily find myself consciously cooperating with the process of my metamorphosis, which will allow me to reflect more of my natural beauty"; "I want to easily find myself being my own best partner"; "I want to consciously and consistently be aware of loving myself and acting in my own best interests"; "I want to easily find myself feeling complete and confident in just being myself."

TAURUS
North Node People
and North Node in the 2nd House

TAURUS NORTH NODE PEOPLE ARE DEVELOPING AWARENESS OF THEIR OWN NEEDS AND BUILDING A SENSE OF SELF-WORTH

Due to many past incarnations when they put the wants of their powerful partner first, these folks have a subconscious habit of discounting their own needs. This pattern of denial leads to deep feelings of unworthiness. During this lifetime, a primary focus for Taurus North Node people is to develop a healthy sense of their own self-worth.

Sample Wishes to Promote Feelings of Self-Worth:
"I want to easily find myself consciously aware of what I NEED in various situations as they arise"; "I want all feelings of guilt around stating my needs to others totally lifted from me"; "I want the habit of invalidating my own needs totally lifted from me"; "I want to easily find myself communicating my needs as they arise"; "In choosing my direction, I want to easily find myself putting my own needs first"; "I want to easily find myself making choices that are in alignment with raising my self-worth."

TAURUS NORTH NODE PEOPLE ARE OVERCOMING THEIR DEPENDENCE ON VALIDATION FROM OTHERS

In past lives, the confirmation of those they were supporting was a barometer of whether or not these folks were "on track." Through many incarnations, this dependence on the validation of others in order to feel good about themselves has become debilitating. They may compromise their values and/or needs in order to gain others' approval, which erodes their sense of self-esteem.

Sample Wishes to Help Overcome Dependence on Validation from Others:
"I want all feelings of needing validation from others totally lifted from me"; "I want the idea that I need the energy of others to survive easily lifted from me"; "I want to consistently and successfully rely on my own energy for survival"; "I want all feelings of bondage to others' values totally lifted from me"; "I want all unhealthy attachment to other people's opinions of me totally lifted from me"; "I want all tendencies to manipulating the views and values of others totally lifted from me"; "I want to easily find myself actively pursuing my own independent directions."

TAURUS NORTH NODE PEOPLE ARE LEARNING TO HANDLE MONEY AND DEVELOP GRATITUDE

In past incarnations, these folks were supported financially in exchange for expending most of their life energy in nurturing their powerful partner. So in this lifetime, they lack experience in handling money. They are learning that by taking responsibility for earning and managing their own money, they gain power over their lives. They are also learning to appreciate what they already have, rather than always wanting more.

Sample Wishes to Help Increase Financial Responsibility:

"I want all self-sabotaging thoughts and actions around money totally lifted from me"; "I want all feelings of inadequacy around money totally lifted from me"; "I want healthy self-confidence to enter all my dealings with money"; "I want the notion that 'I don't know what to do' with money totally lifted from me"; "In the issue of money, I want to be comfortable beyond fear"; "I want to easily find myself taking charge with money in a way that is in my overall best interests"; "I want to easily find myself consciously and consistently experiencing gratitude in every area of my life"; "I want to easily find myself restoring my credit record to be acceptable for future loan applications."

TAURUS NORTH NODE PEOPLE ARE LEARNING ABOUT BOUNDARIES AND STAYING IN THEIR COMFORT ZONE

To merge more fully with their sexual or financial partners in past lives, these folks diffused the edges of their own boundaries. Now they are faced with the challenge of redefining them. By learning to live within the perimeters of their own values—not stepping outside their natural boundaries to accommodate others—they will reconnect with the feeling of inner comfort they are seeking.

Sample Wishes to Develop Healthy Boundaries:

"I want to easily find myself creating healthy boundaries between myself and those with whom I am close"; "I want to easily find myself verbally acknowledging my feelings when something makes me

uncomfortable, which will allow healthy boundaries to be identified";
"I want to easily find myself supporting others without losing myself";
"I want to easily find myself consistently asking the question: 'Do I feel
comfortable with this situation?' and acting in accordance with what
makes me feel at ease"; "I want to easily find myself consciously aware
of not crossing my own boundaries when I relate with others"; "I want
the habit of pushing past the boundaries of others easily lifted from
me"; "I want total clarity in seeing how to maintain healthy boundaries
with others in a happy way."

TAURUS NORTH NODE PEOPLE ARE LEARNING TO DEFINE THEIR OWN VALUES AND TO PROCEED STEP-BY-STEP TO ACHIEVE THEIR GOALS

Due to past alliances with powerful, wealthy people, these folks
are used to traveling in the "fast lane" and experiencing instant results
from their combined efforts. However, in this lifetime when they push
for quick results they skip the steps that are necessary for lasting success. They are learning to rely on their own efforts and to proceed one
step at a time to attain goals that are in alignment with their own personal values and comfort zone.

Sample Wishes to Promote a Step-by-Step Approach to Achieving Goals:
"I want to easily find myself consciously aware of what MY values
are in various situations as they arise"; "I want to consciously be aware
of what makes ME feel good about myself, and pursue those directions that give me a solid sense of self-worth"; "I want the habit of
postponing my own needs until my partner is 'ready,' totally lifted
from me"; "I want the habit of pressing for instant results easily lifted
from me"; "I want to easily find myself relying on my *own efforts* for

success"; "I want to easily find myself approaching my goals with a step-by-step process that assures my needs will be met"; "I want to easily find myself respecting myself for the steady progress I am making."

TAURUS NORTH NODE PEOPLE ARE OVERCOMING AN UNHEALTHY CONCERN WITH OTHER PEOPLE'S BUSINESS AND THE TENDENCY TO BE JUDGMENTAL

Due to their position in society, in past lives these folks became attuned to the "social mores" of the day, and judged those who didn't uphold them. They are aware of the dark side of society and can be harshly judgmental of others, "reading in" ulterior motives where none may exist. In judging others, they leave themselves open to judgment, and by not focusing on their own needs, they rob themselves of the opportunity to build a worthwhile life for themselves. They are learning to shift their attention from concern with the business of others to focusing on taking care of their own needs.

Sample Wishes to Help Release the Tendency to Be Overly Concerned with Others' Business:

"I want to easily find myself focusing on my OWN LIFE, rather than the needs and desires of others"; "I want to easily find myself learning from my experiences without self-judgment"; "I want the habit of being preoccupied with the wants and needs of others totally lifted from me"; "I want to easily find myself forgiving ———— in a way that is empowering for me"; "I want to easily find myself staying out of other people's business"; "I want to easily find myself enjoying what I have, without desiring to experience something from another person's life"; "I want all tendencies to abuse power totally lifted from me."

TAURUS NORTH NODE PEOPLE ARE LEARNING HOW TO STOP ACTIVATING CRISIS IN THEIR LIVES

These folks are accustomed to situations of high intensity, and have become addicted to the excitement of "living on the edge." Consequently, in this life they may subconsciously attract situations and people that bring chaos and uncertainty into their lives in order to trigger the adrenaline released by having to deal with crisis. They are learning to take a rest from the intensity of past incarnations and to make choices that include comfort and stability.

Sample Wishes to Help Release the Tendency to Create Crisis and Stress:
"I want to easily find myself making choices that lead to the inner experiences of comfort, serenity, and peace"; "I want all tendencies to overspending totally lifted from me"; "I want to easily find myself becoming CONSCIOUS around money in a way that leads to increased security and financial ease"; "I want the habit of attracting crisis-prone people into my life easily lifted from me"; "I want the addiction to crisis totally lifted from me"; "I want to consciously and consistently choose the path of peace over the path of crisis."

GEMINI
North Node People
and North Node in the 3rd House

GEMINI NORTH NODE PEOPLE ARE LEARNING HOW TO COMMUNICATE WITHOUT RIGHTEOUSNESS

Due to past incarnations where their position was to be the absolute authority on "Truth," Gemini North Node people have a tendency to do more talking than listening. They carry the conviction that their thinking must be right, and close out other points of view. They are learning to have two-way conversations in which each person values the ideas of the other, instead of one-way monologues.

Sample Wishes to Enhance the Ability for True Communication:
   "I want all tendencies to self-righteousness totally lifted from me"; "I want all attachment to 'being right' totally lifted from me"; "I want the need for others to agree with my ideas totally lifted from me"; "I want to easily find myself sincerely listening to the ideas of others with the intention of really understanding how they see the world"; "I want to easily find myself allowing others to share their thoughts, without feeling I need to either agree or disagree with them"; "I want to easily find myself deeply listening to the ideas of

others and respecting their right to have their own point of view"; "I want to easily find myself communicating my ideas in a way that is nonthreatening to others."

GEMINI NORTH NODE PEOPLE ARE LEARNING SOCIABILITY AND TACT

These folks spent a lot of time in monasteries and religious environments in past incarnations without much practice interacting with others. In this life they tend to speak their mind directly and spontaneously, without first establishing a sense of rapport with the other person, and their brusque approach alienates people who would otherwise like them. They are learning to slow down their communication and take time to implement some social skills, including: tact, openness to other points of view, showing a genuine interest in others, and presenting their own ideas in a less emotionally charged way.

Sample Wishes to Develop Tact:
"I want to easily find myself successfully and joyously connecting with a variety of different people"; "I want to easily find myself sharing my thoughts without needing others to agree with me"; "I want to easily find myself using the right words to say what I want in a way that others can easily understand"; "I want to easily find myself deeply listening to others to enhance my ability to supply them with the information they are asking for"; "I want to easily find myself saying the right words that lead to others understanding my point of view in a way they can accept"; "I want to easily find myself communicating my ideas in a way that creates love and closeness with others."

GEMINI NORTH NODE PEOPLE ARE OVERCOMING THEIR ANXIETY ABOUT REALLY LISTENING TO OTHERS

With so many past incarnations dedicated to memorizing religious texts and dogma, Gemini North Node people carry an inner anxiety that they must always "be right" and be able to provide "the answer" for others. They may avoid asking questions that could lead to a deeper understanding of what the other person is saying, for fear they might not have "the answer." They are learning that in this lifetime, it's not their responsibility to have all the answers. Instead, their task is to be curious about people and draw them out, learn about different personalities, and experience the mental rapport of deeply understanding others.

Sample Wishes to Promote Comfort When Really Listening to Others:
"I want all fears of 'not knowing what to say' totally lifted from me"; "I want to easily find myself breathing deeply whenever I feel anxious or upset"; "I want the compulsion to provide answers totally lifted from me"; "If I feel awkward, I want to easily find myself changing the subject by asking the person a friendly question about their life"; "I want to easily find myself listening and learning from others, feeling the pleasure of a deep mental connection and an understanding of their point of view"; "I want to easily find myself asking the right questions that lead to my understanding others on a deeper level."

GEMINI NORTH NODE PEOPLE ARE LEARNING THE VALUE OF FACTS, LOGIC, AND OPTIONS

These folks have spent many past incarnations following their intuition and a moralistic code of ethics, seeking the "one final answer."

They have become so solution oriented that now they tend to jump to hasty conclusions without considering all the facts. This subconscious trait can lead to painful misjudgments, misunderstandings with people, and feelings of social isolation. In this lifetime when they don't understand a situation, they are learning to respond by seeking more information while keeping their mind open to the facts.

Sample Wishes to Promote Openness to Facts and Logic:
    "When I have trouble making a decision, I want to easily find myself *verbalizing* my dilemma to the other people involved"; "When I become panicky, I want clear logic to enter my mind, showing me the facts of the situation and the logical way to proceed"; "I want to easily find myself verbalizing my point of view as 'truth' for me at this time, recognizing that I can always change my mind"; "I want to easily find myself successfully applying clear logic in every area of my life"; "When I become suspicious, I want to easily find myself checking more deeply into the *facts* of the situation"; "I want to easily find myself taking time to gain the factual information I need to feel comfortable making a decision."

GEMINI NORTH NODE PEOPLE ARE DEVELOPING THE HABIT OF JOURNALING ON A DAILY BASIS

With past incarnations spent memorizing religious dogma, these folks have lost touch with the fluidity of their own thoughts. They are learning to give themselves permission to have different points of view, to be indecisive, and to reveal their various perceptions to others—even when they don't have a solution. The process of writing in a journal or diary clarifies their thinking, brings new insights to problems, and empowers them to see more options.

Sample Wishes to Prompt the Habit of Daily Journaling:

"I want to easily find myself consciously valuing the process of writing in my life"; "I want to easily find myself acting on my urge to write"; "I want the habit of minimizing the importance of my need to write totally lifted from me"; "I want to easily find myself writing in my journal a minimum of ———— days a week, a minimum of ———— minutes each time"; "I want to easily find myself communicating my changing thoughts about a situation without needing to have a solution"; "When I feel indecisive, I want to easily find myself communicating my two different thoughts about the matter to the person involved."

GEMINI NORTH NODE PEOPLE ARE CHALLENGED WITH ACCEPTING AND ENJOYING PEOPLE AS THEY ARE

In past incarnations, these folks were the spiritual reformers of others—missionaries, priests, moral guides, and zealots. Due to this "crusading spirit," they tend to put their cause above the wants and needs of others. Gemini North Node people have a difficult time accepting others without trying to reform them. This leads to frustration when people won't just put their personalities aside and dedicate themselves to the purpose at hand. In this lifetime their goal is to learn to accept, understand, and enjoy the special personalities of others, allowing for individual differences while working together toward a common goal.

Sample Wishes to Increase Acceptance and Enjoyment of Others Just as They Are:

"I want the compulsion to reform others totally lifted from me"; "I want to easily find myself accepting others' ideas and points of view as true for them"; "I want to release the urgency of trying to influence or guide the outcome of things"; "I want to easily find myself not trying to do God's job"; "I want to easily find myself valuing the personalities I'm involved with more than the end results we're striving for"; "I want all righteous anger totally lifted from me."

CANCER
North Node People
and North Node in the 4th House

CANCER NORTH NODE PEOPLE ARE LEARNING TO
RECOGNIZE AND VALUE PERSONAL FEELINGS

Cancer North Node people have had many incarnations where they suppressed their personal feelings in order to support a public goal. In this lifetime they can be so out of touch with their internal responses that they have a problem identifying their feelings. Now they are awakening to the importance of recognizing their own emotional responses. They are learning to take care of themselves and to make choices that lead to happiness, security, and emotional satisfaction.

Sample Wishes to Increase Awareness of Personal Feelings:
  "I want all tendencies to suppress my feelings totally lifted from me"; "I want to easily find myself being AWARE of—and accepting of—the fact that I have moods and feelings"; "I want to easily find myself accepting, and succeeding in, situations where I experience feelings of love, caring, closeness, and happiness"; "I want to easily find myself consciously aware of and identifying what MY feelings are as they arise in various situations"; "I want all fears of closeness and inti-

macy totally lifted from me"; "I want all fear of not knowing how to respond when others approach me with the energy of intimacy totally lifted from me."

CANCER NORTH NODE PEOPLE ARE CHALLENGED WITH LETTING GO OF THE NEED TO CONTROL

Because of their past life inexperience in dealing with feelings, Cancer North Node people tend to respond to emotions by trying to control the situation so that feelings are no longer evoked. In the process, they suppress others' emotional responses, as well as their own. Now they are learning to ACCEPT their own emotional reactions, and those of others. They are finding that once the feeling is verbally acknowledged, they experience a psychological release, and a plan for handling the situation emerges naturally.

Sample Wishes to Help Release Controlling Tendencies:
"I want the tendency of trying to control others' reactions totally lifted from me"; "I want the tendency to be standoffish and formal totally lifted from me"; "I want to easily find myself graciously accepting help from others and acknowledging the value of their support"; "I want to cease controlling others through my expectation that they change their behavior to meet my needs"; "I want to easily find myself allowing others to communicate how they feel, without thinking that I have to 'do something'; "I want to easily find myself responding to others' feelings by first acknowledging and empathizing with their mood"; "I want to easily find myself focusing on the *process* and letting go of trying to control outcomes."

CANCER NORTH NODE PEOPLE ARE
LEARNING TO BE VULNERABLE

Due to so many incarnations of being the strong person whom others looked up to, the instinctive response for these folks is to not show their vulnerability. They are learning to share their feelings when relating to others, to expose what they are experiencing and reveal their true nature. In this process, they validate the importance of their inner selves, making them stronger and capable of the intimacy they long for.

Sample Wishes to Encourage Sharing One's True Feelings:
"I want to be aware of my feelings and easily find myself sharing them with others in a responsible way"; "I want to easily find myself asking for the support I need"; "I want to easily find myself sharing power by revealing my true feelings and inviting others to do the same"; "When there is an opportunity for intimacy, I want the tendency to withdraw or 'change the subject' totally lifted from me"; "I want to easily find myself communicating my true feelings in my close relationships with others"; "In times of emotional trauma, I want to easily find myself revealing my feelings."

CANCER NORTH NODE PEOPLE ARE DEVELOPING THEIR
FEMININE, SUPPORTIVE NATURE

These folks were authority figures in past incarnations; most often they utilize the male/father side of their personality. In this lifetime they are developing their caring/mother nature. When their initial approach is to demonstrate personal concern for the other person—

showing interest in their families, how their lives are going, etc.—
people automatically respond with appreciation and warmth. In caring about others, they open the door to others wanting to be close and
support them.

Sample Wishes to Promote a Caring and Supportive Approach:

"I want to easily find myself embracing the fact that others have
feelings, fears, and insecurities that are very real for them"; "I want to
easily find myself empathetically aware of others' feelings, without
feeling that I have to feel the same way"; "I want to easily find myself
being interested in the personal lives of others, asking questions that
let them know I care about them"; "I want all fears around others
sharing their feelings with me totally lifted from me"; "I want to be
sensitive to others' verbalized needs"; "I want to easily find myself accepting and understanding how others feel, and to experience closeness with them as a result"; "I want to easily find myself aware of
caring about others in their moments of need."

CANCER NORTH NODE PEOPLE ARE LEARNING TO
BE GUIDED BY THEIR GUT INSTINCTS

Cancer North Node people have had goal-oriented and highly
successful past lives. To accomplish their ambitious goals, they developed the habit of not allowing their feelings to distract them. Their
challenge in this life is to acknowledge their internal responses and to
allow those feelings to guide them. They are learning to trust themselves—when they follow their gut instincts, the choices they make
are on track.

Sample Wishes to Heighten Awareness of Gut Instincts:

"I want to easily find myself aware of my gut instincts"; "I want to easily find myself consciously and consistently following my gut instincts in decision making"; "I want to easily find myself accepting my personal feelings, fears, and insecurities"; "I want to be aware of which people make ME feel good and loved, and consciously choose to spend time with people who care about me"; "I want all self-defeating ploys to gain respect totally lifted from me"; "I want the habit of saying one thing when I really need something else totally lifted from me."

CANCER NORTH NODE PEOPLE ARE LEARNING TO ALLOW PERSONAL SATISFACTION

These folks have had so many incarnations where they postponed personal fulfillment for the sake of a higher commitment that they habitually postpone experiencing satisfaction in this lifetime until they "first reach a loftier goal." Their personal life gets perpetually postponed! In the process their feelings can become starved and "shriveled," and they run the risk of turning cold inside. They are learning to yield and ENJOY present opportunities for fulfillment on a personal level.

Sample Wishes to Prompt Satisfaction with the Present:

"I want to easily find myself focusing on joy in the *process* of developing things with others"; "I want to easily and happily stay in the 'now' moment, handling my life responsibly without being overly concerned for the future"; "I want to easily find myself allowing others the freedom to care for me and fill my needs in their own way!";

"I want to easily find myself TOTALLY RECEPTIVE and welcoming when others express their feelings of closeness with me"; "I want the tendency to manage things in the best interests of others at the expense of my own personal needs totally lifted from me"; "I want to feel a sense of ease and comfort when others approach me with the energy of intimacy and closeness."

LEO
North Node People
and North Node in the 5th House

LEO NORTH NODE PEOPLE ARE STRENGTHENING
THEIR SELF-CONFIDENCE

Success breeds solid confidence. Because of past incarnations where their individuality was discounted for the sake of a larger ideal, these folks didn't develop a strong personal will. They easily allow themselves to be distracted from their aims, and tend to rely on the help of friends, who generally let them down at a crucial moment. Now they are learning the value of taking responsibility for themselves, keeping their commitments, and letting their accomplishments show them that they are on track. In this lifetime, it is the path of INDIVIDUAL EFFORT that brings them the success they need to increase their self-confidence.

Sample Wishes to Help Build Self-Confidence:
"I want to be filled with healthy self-confidence in every area of my life"; "I want all inhibiting fear totally lifted from me"; "I want to easily find myself staying 'on track' until my goal of ———— is reached"; "I want all self-doubt totally lifted from me"; "I want to

easily find myself giving to others in a way that results in feelings of happy, healthy self-confidence"; "I want to easily find myself taking those risks that result in feelings of empowerment."

LEO NORTH NODE PEOPLE ARE CHALLENGED WITH BUILDING A DISTINCT EGO

Due to many past incarnations of "going with the flow" or being immersed in a morality dictated by others (society, religion, family), these folks have lost contact with their personal ego. They subconsciously consider those around them to have "superior knowledge," and too easily buckle under others' wants and needs. They tend to go along without resistance in order to support the overall happiness of the group. In this lifetime, they are challenged with acknowledging that THEY are actually the ones who have access to the bigger picture of what is for the common good. They are learning to take a stronger stand and to view others as children, responding to outrageous behavior by letting them know where the limits are.

Sample Wishes to Strengthen Personal Ego:
"I want to easily find myself responding to the drama of others in a way that creates new, positive directions for everyone concerned"; "I want to easily find myself stating my wants in ways that others can hear and support"; "I want to easily find myself effectively speaking up to shift situations in more positive directions"; "I want all fears of being overly dramatic easily lifted from me"; "I want to consciously and consistently be aware of the child in others, leading me to respond to them in ways that are *mutually* empowering"; "I want to easily find myself taking a stronger stand in actively creating situations that are also happy for *me*."

LEO NORTH NODE PEOPLE ARE LEARNING TO BE
WHO THEY REALLY ARE

Past incarnations spent in group environments have caused these folks to develop tremendous sensitivity to the opinions of their peers. Now this manifests in unnecessary self-censorship; they carry the fear that by being themselves they may be judged by others. They have often sought to express their individuality by either going along with how others see them, or by rebelling against others' views by doing the opposite. Now they are learning to actualize their own unique individuality by following the path that makes them happy.

Sample Wishes to Promote True Self-Actualization:
"I want the fear of being ridiculed by others totally lifted from me"; "I want the negative influence of peer pressure *totally* lifted from me"; "I want to easily find myself recognizing and honoring my *own* specialness"; "I want the habit of self-censorship totally lifted from me"; "I want to be consciously aware of when I am having fun, and then KNOW that it is the correct path for me!"; "I want to easily find myself pursuing the things that make me happy."

LEO NORTH NODE PEOPLE ARE LEARNING
TO CREATE THEIR OWN DESTINY

With so many incarnations spent in public service to further humanitarian causes, these folks are accustomed to life automatically bringing them joyful relationships and experiences as a natural reward. But in this lifetime they are challenged with creating their own destiny—to visualize and find those people and experiences that make them happy, and then actively focus on giving them love and attention to help them thrive. They are learning to use their intelligence and personal power to shift outcomes and create positive results and happiness for themselves.

Sample Wishes to Activate Creative Power:
    "I want to be consciously and consistently aware of my power to create positive results in any situation"; "I want to be filled with the determination to carry through and create a happy life for myself"; "I want to consciously and consistently be in touch with my power of creative visualization"; "I want to easily find myself using the power of my will to create the results I want"; "I want to easily find myself making choices that increase my vitality and enjoyment of life!"; "I want to easily find myself actively creating my own happy destiny."

LEO NORTH NODE PEOPLE ARE LEARNING TO REPLACE DETACHMENT WITH CREATIVE INVOLVEMENT

These folks have had so many past incarnations as scientists, inventors, and observers that they are accustomed to viewing life from a detached perspective. By objectively watching others—and themselves—they miss experiencing the pleasure of direct creative involvement. They are learning to become more immersed with the people and situations in their lives. When they take center stage and actively participate in making a situation fun and vital for everyone involved, they find the pleasure, love, and joy they are seeking!

Sample Wishes to Support Direct Creative Involvement:
    "I want all self-limiting detachment totally lifted from me"; "I

want the habit of withdrawing from dramatic situations easily lifted from me"; "I want all habits of 'ivory tower' isolation easily lifted from me"; "When a crisis arises, I want to easily find myself becoming involved in creating positive solutions"; "I want to easily find myself willing to give positive attention to my personal relationships"; "I want to easily find myself willing to take more risks in exploring my creative and artistic talents"; "I want to easily find myself living a creative and fun life!"

LEO NORTH NODE PEOPLE ARE LEARNING TO TAKE RISKS AND FOLLOW THEIR HEARTS

In past lives, Leo North Node people were instrumental in helping the race to evolve. They had special access to higher knowledge and guidance so that they could create an inventive new approach to life. They are accustomed to waiting for insights about the "big picture" before taking action, but in this lifetime they are learning that all the knowledge they need is now centered within their own hearts. So when they follow their hearts—the paths that bring them personal joy and fun—the risks they take will in the end turn out to be in the best interests of everyone involved.

Sample Wishes to Prompt Taking Risks:
"I want to easily find myself TAKING ACTION in pursuing those ventures that evoke feelings of joy and happiness within me"; "I want to easily find myself less fearful of the future and more concerned with what makes me happy in the present moment"; "I want to easily find myself pursuing activities that are fun for me"; "I want to

easily find myself following my inner joy and taking actions that are in alignment with that happy feeling"; "I want all fears of following my own heart totally lifted from me"; "I want to easily find myself taking those risks that add vitality, joy, and creative self-expression to my life!"

VIRGO
North Node People
and North Node in the 6th House

VIRGO NORTH NODE PEOPLE ARE LEARNING TO RESPOND TO CHAOS WITH CONSTRUCTIVE PARTICIPATION

These folks have had many past incarnations of self-purification—lifetimes spent in solitude, in monasteries, or perhaps even in jail. Consequently, when faced with something upsetting, their first response is to withdraw and turn inward, hoping the problem will go away. However, in this lifetime the situation will not get resolved until they actively participate to restore order.

Sample Wishes to Encourage Active Participation:
    "Rather than withdrawing or running away, I want to easily find myself participating in relationships in a way that brings about positive results"; "I want to easily find myself actively focusing on creating positive results in my life"; "I want to easily find myself successfully turning chaos into order in my environment through actively taking part"; "I want all resistance to participation totally lifted from me"; "I want the habit of withdrawing easily lifted from me"; "When other people

get into their issues, I want to easily find myself actively taking part to help them see their situation more clearly."

VIRGO NORTH NODE PEOPLE ARE
LEARNING TO STICK TO THEIR OBJECTIVES

Due to many past lifetimes of worldly sacrifice, these folks tend to "give up" and surrender their goals all too easily. However, without a purpose to focus on, worries begin to consume them. The antidote is for them to decide on a tangible objective and make a plan for reaching it. Then focused, productive energy emerges and they regain their confidence.

Sample Wishes to Prompt Adherence to Goals and Objectives:
"I want tendencies toward giving up magically transformed into renewed focus on creating success and happiness"; "I want all self-sabotaging confusion totally lifted from me"; "When worries arise, I want to easily find myself responding by focusing on a practical plan to restore order"; "I want to easily find myself clearly defining my goals and objectives"; "I want the habit of 'giving up' totally lifted from me"; "I want to easily find myself *persevering* in creating the positive tangible results I want."

VIRGO NORTH NODE PEOPLE ARE LEARNING THE POWER
OF FOCUSING ON THE HERE AND NOW

When these folks spend too much time being mentally unfocused, their minds churn up anxieties that result in a loss of confidence. They are learning to not allow their imaginations to dominate their experience. When they feel anxious, if they focus on the here and now—noticing tangible details such as the color of someone's clothing or the feel of the breeze on their skin—their fears will dissolve.

Sample Wishes to Increase Focus on the Here and Now:
   "I want all panic attacks totally lifted from me"; "I want to easily find myself focusing my awareness on the here and now"; "I want to easily find myself so focused in the here and now that I automatically remember when I need to do things that are in my best interests"; "I want to consciously and consistently be connected in the *here and now,* viewing people and situations with full awareness in the *present moment*"; "When I feel anxious, I want to easily find myself noticing the details in my physical environment"; "I want to easily find myself not allowing my imagination to dominate my experience."

VIRGO NORTH NODE PEOPLE ARE DEVELOPING AWARENESS OF DETAILS AND LEARNING DISCRIMINATION

Due to tremendous personal suffering in past lives, Virgo North Node people have spent many incarnations developing an attitude of acceptance and understanding. Now they tend to be careless and not pay attention to the events in their daily lives that would "tip them off" to situations that could hurt them. They are learning to pay attention, to attend to details, and to be more discriminating in order to keep their lives on a positive track.

Sample Wishes to Promote Discrimination:
   "I want the tendency to help others indiscriminately totally lifted from me"; "I want accurate discrimination guiding me in putting my

attention and energy in directions where I can create positive results"; "I want the habit of absorbing other people's negativity totally lifted from me"; "When I feel anxious about a situation, I want to easily find myself analyzing the details—the facts and figures—to restore my serenity"; "I want to easily find myself consciously and consistently aware of the important details in the situations around me"; "I want the tendency to overlook details totally lifted from me."

VIRGO NORTH NODE PEOPLE ARE OVERCOMING THEIR TENDENCY TO BE VICTIMS

Virgo North Node people have spent so many past lifetimes in self-reflection that they have experienced significant purification and dissolution of their personal ego. In this lifetime, they are born with great compassion for others. Even when others "step over the line" and hurt them, they tend to respond with understanding rather than setting limits and saying no. In this way they inadvertently support negative behavior in others. They are learning that nobody wins when they allow themselves to be victimized.

Sample Wishes to Help Dissolve Victim Tendencies:
"I want to easily find myself remembering, 'This is *not* a victim lifetime!' "; "I want clear *discrimination* entering into all my relationships, leading to my accurately discerning when to be supportive and when to say no"; "I want clear boundaries, empowering me to not allow abusive situations in my life"; "I want the habit of playing the victim easily lifted from me"; "I want to easily find myself saying no and meaning it when it serves my best interests"; "I want to easily find myself saying no in a way that others hear and respect."

VIRGO NORTH NODE PEOPLE ARE
LEARNING TO MAINTAIN HEALTHY ROUTINES

Due to past incarnations spent in monasteries and other situations where their schedules were set by others, these folks are not accustomed to taking responsibility for maintaining healthy routines on their own. However, without a plan to follow they become obsessed with inner anxieties. They are learning to take responsibility for creating an orderly lifestyle that includes proper diet, regular exercise, and scheduled time for work and play.

Sample Wishes to Support a Healthy Routine:

"I want the tendency to be late for appointments totally lifted from me"; "I want to easily find myself setting and following healthy routines that add strength and confidence to my life"; "I want right ideas to show me the best routine I can follow to create physical, mental, and emotional strength and integration"; "I want my attitude toward taking charge of my life and establishing a routine to be optimistic and joyful"; "I want to easily find myself taking charge of my diet in a self-empowering way"; "I want to easily find myself taking charge of my exercise program in a self-empowering way"; "I want to easily find myself taking care of bills, errands, and other responsibilities in a timely manner."

LIBRA
North Node People
and North Node in the 7th House

LIBRA NORTH NODE PEOPLE ARE
LEARNING TO RELAX THEIR FOCUS ON PERSONAL SURVIVAL

In past lives, Libra North Node people have been warriors, trained to be ever aware of enemies and concerned only with their own survival. In this lifetime they subconsciously feel that others are a potential threat. This leads to a naive self-centeredness and behaviors that repel others, preventing these folks from having the relationships they want. To expand their experience of personal love, they must learn to focus on encouraging and supporting the other person. Then their experience of love expands and they find the peace they are seeking.

Sample Wishes to Help Relax a Focus on Survival:
    "I want preoccupation with my own survival totally lifted from me"; "I want all tendencies to negative self-absorption totally lifted from me"; "I want all nonconstructive selfishness totally lifted from me"; "I want all resistance to openhearted sharing with another easily lifted from me"; "I want to be aware of others giving to me in non-

competitive ways"; "I want to easily find myself experiencing the joy of supporting others without thought of personal gain."

LIBRA NORTH NODE PEOPLE ARE CHALLENGED WITH A TENDENCY TO PROJECT THEIR STANDARDS ONTO OTHERS

Libra North Node people have spent many past lives in military environments where everyone knew "the rules" and followed the same guidelines. In this life, they are shocked and disillusioned when the actions of others reflect that they are not playing by the same rules as these folks. Instead of projecting their identity and standards onto others, they are learning to objectively discover the true character and compatibility of others before becoming involved on a personal level.

Sample Wishes to Help in Accurately Discerning the Identity of Others:
"I want the tendency to project my standards onto others totally lifted from me"; "I want to easily find myself releasing the expectation that others should be playing by my rules"; "I want to easily find myself questioning the other person, objectively discovering their realities, before deciding to partner with them"; "I want to easily find myself correctly assessing others by *first* wholly putting myself in their place"; "I want to approach others assuming everyone I encounter has their own set of rules and find myself being interested in discovering what they are"; "I want to easily find myself open to seeing other people's true identities and appreciating their unique talents and temperaments."

LIBRA NORTH NODE PEOPLE ARE
LEARNING TACT AND DIPLOMACY

From their past life experiences, Libra North Node people are so overinvolved with themselves and their purpose that they tend to speak directly and forcefully. They state their position in a way that makes others feel excluded and uncomfortable. To stop alienating others and encourage cooperation, these folks are learning to use tact and diplomacy to probe the thinking of the other person before stating their opinion. In this way they can gain an understanding of the other person's views and modify their approach accordingly.

Sample Wishes to Help Develop Tact and Diplomacy:
    "I want the habit of giving orders to others totally lifted from me"; "I want to easily find myself making diplomacy more important than direct disclosure"; "Before correcting another, I want to easily find myself asking questions to discover the rationale behind their opinion or behavior"; "I want to easily find myself slowing down to allow time for input and cooperation with others, before rushing toward the goal"; "I want to easily find myself aware of using words in a way that supports others in maintaining their inner harmony."

LIBRA NORTH NODE PEOPLE ARE OVERCOMING
SELF-CONSCIOUSNESS BY LEARNING TO
FOCUS THEIR ATTENTION ON OTHERS

Although these folks feel very sure of their own ability for accomplishment, they lack confidence in social situations. Their excessive self-consciousness can make them feel awkward in their interactions with others; from many past incarnations as "loners" they are not accustomed to the social rituals of relating. When they stop focusing on themselves ("Will I say the right thing? Do I look all right?") and focus on how they can serve the other person, suddenly their self-consciousness disappears and they feel confident in the relationship. They are learning that they have to enter the other person's world to truly establish a connection.

Sample Wishes to Promote Confidence in Social Situations:
   "I want all inhibiting self-consciousness totally lifted from me"; "I want the distraction of 'watching myself' when interacting with others *totally* lifted from me"; "I want to easily find myself feeling self-confident and comfortable in social situations"; "I want to easily find myself consciously and consistently taking the time and energy to discover who other people are"; "I want to easily find myself relating with others in THEIR world, rather than solely from my own world"; "In social situations, I want to easily find myself focusing my attention on the other person and on what I can do to support them."

LIBRA NORTH NODE PEOPLE ARE
LEARNING TO BE SENSITIVE TO THE FEELINGS OF OTHERS

Due to so many past lifetimes focused on awareness of self, Libra North Node people have developed tremendous sensitivity to their own personal feelings. In this lifetime, their interactions often consist of trying to get the other person to go along with what they need so that they can feel harmonious. However, this process usually results in their feeling alone, without the sense of peace that comes from sharing mutual support. They are learning to turn their sensitivity outward to become aware of others' needs. And as they start using their awareness to help others regain balance, their own sense of serenity will automatically be restored.

Sample Wishes to Stimulate Sensitivity to Others:

"In relationships, I want to easily find myself as sensitive to others as I am to myself"; "I want to easily find myself *naturally* being more patient and loving with others"; "I want all tendencies to having a short temper easily lifted from me"; "I want to easily find myself supporting others in having what they need to survive"; "I want to easily find myself helping others to maintain their inner harmony"; "I want to easily find myself saying the right words to others that lead to positive, balanced interactions"; "I want to easily find myself taking the feedback of others to heart, allowing them to show me the road to true partnership."

LIBRA NORTH NODE PEOPLE ARE DISCOVERING THE STRENGTH OF TEAMWORK

These folks have had many incarnations of developing independence, self-reliance, and confidence as "the loner." They are self-starters and have an innate sense of discipline. Yet in this lifetime nothing happens for them without partnership. Whatever they approach, if they try to do it on their own their success will fall far short of what it would be if they had a partner. Teamwork is the key to their wildest dreams coming true, on both the personal and professional level.

Sample Wishes to Activate Teamwork:

"I want to easily find myself being a team player with others"; "I want all resistance to awareness of others easily lifted from me";

"I want to easily attract, recognize, and begin a supportive partnership with the right ——— (romantic partner/business partner/exercise partner, etc.) for me"; "I want to easily find myself regularly putting the interests of the other person first"; "I want to easily find myself constructively supporting others in a way they can appreciate"; "I want to easily find myself creating patterns of cooperation, healthy interdependence, and happy commitment in the right ——— (romantic/business) partnership for me."

SCORPIO
North Node People
and North Node in the 8th House

SCORPIO NORTH NODE PEOPLE ARE
CHALLENGED WITH RELEASING STUBBORNNESS

Because these folks were so totally reliant on themselves for survival in past incarnations, they feel an exaggerated importance around doing a job with absolute thoroughness, making sure they can create success with their own efforts. If someone suggests a plan that is contrary to their way of doing things, a reaction of stubborn rebelliousness immediately arises within them. This is counterproductive for Scorpio North Node people and for those around them. They are learning to bypass this stubbornness by taking time to investigate the reasoning behind the other person's plan.

Sample Wishes to Help Release the Habit of Stubbornness:
　　"I want all self-defeating stubbornness totally lifted from me"; "I want the reaction of instinctive rebelliousness totally lifted from me"; "When the feeling of stubbornness arises, I want to easily find myself *investigating* the reasons for the other person's suggestion"; "I want the response of automatically fighting with others easily lifted from me";

"I want to easily find myself investigating the *motives* of others before saying no"; "When in doubt, I want to easily find myself saying: 'I don't really have an answer for that right now. Let me think about it.'"

SCORPIO NORTH NODE PEOPLE ARE LEARNING TO CHOOSE VITALITY, EMPOWERMENT, AND PERSONAL TRANSFORMATION OVER COMFORT

In past lives, these folks held comfort as their highest value, and if they felt comfortable with an idea it indicated that they were "on track." However, too many lifetimes of opulence resulted in stagnation. To regain their vitality, their challenge is to relinquish the ideal of comfort and choose paths of greater empowerment and personal transformation. They are learning to opt for an exciting risk instead of maintaining the status quo.

Sample Wishes to Help Release the Attachment to Comfort:
"I want all self-defeating attachment to comfort totally lifted from me"; "I want all resistance to change totally lifted from me"; "I want all thoughts about money that are blocking my prosperity totally lifted from me"; "I want the habit of personally identifying with possessions totally lifted from me"; "I want the fear of being engulfed in the unknown totally lifted from me"; "I want to consciously embrace the excitement of positive change!"

SCORPIO NORTH NODE PEOPLE ARE LEARNING TO LET GO OF EVERYTHING THAT OPPRESSES THEM

These folks accumulated tremendous wealth and many belongings in past lives, which is why money is an issue for them in this lifetime. They equated their personal value with their possessions, and still carry the tendency to "accumulate," often keeping things far beyond the point of usefulness. But now they are finding that this attachment to possessions is very oppressive. They are learning to let go of EVERYTHING that weights them down: ideas, material possessions, habits, people from their past. By releasing what they have, they open themselves to new vitality.

Sample Wishes to Help Release Accumulation:
"I want all fears of 'not having enough' totally lifted from me"; "I want to easily find myself giving away material possessions I no longer use"; "I want the habit of looking back at what I have already released *totally* lifted from me"; "I want to easily find myself going through my ———— (wardrobe/storage shed/hall closet/kitchen, etc.) and donating everything to charity that I have not used in the past three years"; "I want the notion that 'I may need this in the future' totally lifted from me"; "I want to easily find myself letting go of everything that oppresses me."

SCORPIO NORTH NODE PEOPLE ARE LEARNING THE BENEFITS OF PARTNERSHIP

Due to a tremendous amount of self-sufficiency in past lives, these folks became attached to the idea of doing things "their way, the hard way." But in this lifetime, their greatest benefits come through using their energy and intelligence to support another person who has similar values. In fact, Scorpio North Node people now have the opportunity to experience soul mate relationships. They are learning to fully merge with another, and embrace the financial and emotional benefits of true partnership.

Sample Wishes to Promote Partnership:

"I want the compulsive feeling that I have to do everything by myself, 'my way—the hard way'—totally lifted from me"; "I want to easily find myself open to receiving the benefit of other people's energy"; "I want to easily find myself accepting gifts from others in a healthy, happy way"; "I want to easily find myself consciously *aware* of how valuable other people are"; "I want to easily find myself supporting others in a way that leads to mutual gain"; "I want to easily find myself seeing what others need and giving it to them in a happy way."

SCORPIO NORTH NODE PEOPLE ARE LEARNING TO DISCOVER THE VALUES AND NEEDS OF OTHERS

In past incarnations, Scorpio North Node people built a solid set of values to live by, and in this lifetime they tend to assume that those they are close to share those values. So if their partner betrays them in some way, it is even more hurtful because they didn't see it coming. They are learning to discover the *other person's* values and needs before allowing themselves to become deeply involved. By attuning themselves to what the other person wants and what is important to them, these folks will be able to make healthy decisions about whom to partner with.

Sample Wishes to Help Discover Others' Needs and Values:

"I want the habit of assuming others share my values easily lifted from me"; "I want to easily find myself actively INVESTIGATING the motives and desires of others—asking about what they want and why they approach certain situations in ways I do not understand"; "I want the notion that others don't want to be deeply understood totally lifted from me"; "I want to easily find myself genuinely interested in what motivates others, asking the appropriate questions to more deeply understand their values"; "I want to easily find myself probing beneath the surface to more clearly understand the psychology of others"; "I want to easily find myself consciously and accurately aware of the values, motives, and needs of those around me."

SCORPIO NORTH NODE PEOPLE ARE LEARNING TO GAIN FINANCIAL SECURITY THROUGH PARTNERSHIP

Due to past incarnations of total self-sufficiency, these folks have the idea that they must first "get their act together," and then others will value what they have built and be attracted to them. But when they try to do it on their own, they fall short of their goals. They are learning that in this lifetime, they need to partner with others in order to tap into the energy they need to accomplish their aims. Their "act" only comes together when they are making progress as a team.

Sample Wishes to Promote Financial Security Through Partnership:

"I want to easily find myself *welcoming* the energy and input of others"; "I want all restrictive fears of 'not having enough' totally lifted from me"; "I want to graciously embrace the goodness and energy of others flowing to me"; "I want the wisdom and humility to work supportively on what another is building"; "I want to consciously remember that when I am truly filling another's need, money will be a natural byproduct"; "I want to attract and begin working with the right business partner who has values I support, and with whom I can make lots of money!"

SAGITTARIUS
North Node People
and North Node in the 9th House

SAGITTARIUS NORTH NODE PEOPLE ARE LEARNING TO LISTEN BEYOND THE WORDS TO THE TRUE MEANING OF WHAT OTHERS SAY

Sagittarius North Node people have had many past incarnations in positions where they had to understand how others think for the purpose of shifting their point of view: as teachers, writers, orators, and salespeople. They have the ability to see into the mind-set of other people, so they can easily create a comfortable affinity with others. Their habit of superficial exchanges—which helps them establish this temporary mental accord—can get in the way of deeply connecting with another. They listen so closely to the specific words the other person uses that they often fail to grasp and believe the actual meaning of what is being said. Others feel they are not thoroughly heard by these folks, and Sagittarius North Node people miss the opportunity to see the other person's truth. They are learning that in order for their relationships to be lasting and fulfilling, they must be willing to go beyond logic to intuitively hear and trust what others are trying to communicate is *their truth* and what they will enact in the end.

Sample Wishes to Expand the Capacity for Deep Mental Rapport:

"In listening to others, I want to easily find myself hearing the deeper meaning behind their words"; "I want all resistance to listening profoundly totally lifted from me"; "I want the fear of boredom easily lifted from me"; "I want any attachment to staying with superficial interactions totally lifted from me"; "I want to easily find myself honoring the unique identity of others by being open to hearing what they are really saying"; "I want to easily find myself willing to deeply understand and accept what the other person is telling me without feeling that I have to shift them to my point of view."

SAGITTARIUS NORTH NODE PEOPLE ARE LEARNING TO QUIET AN OVERACTIVE MIND

Sagittarius North Node people are so accustomed to seeing everyone else's point of view that they have lost touch with their own truth. For them, decisions are difficult because they can think of so many logical reasons to go in either direction—they get confused and don't know what to do. To avoid this problem, they must not question their first feeling of "knowing," since their intuition is almost always accurate. They are learning to stop second-guessing themselves and to overcome indecision by trusting and acting on their initial, spontaneous feeling.

Sample Wishes to Help Eliminate the Habit of Second-Guessing:

"I want all excessive mental activity totally lifted from me"; "I want the habit of second-guessing myself *totally* lifted from me"; "I want the tendencies to mental indecision totally lifted from me"; "I want the self-defeating attachment to 'options' totally lifted from me"; "I want to no longer feel that I have to apply logic to every area of my life"; "I want all resistance to taking action on my inner prompting totally lifted from me"; "I want to easily find myself no longer second-guessing my own inner knowing."

SAGITTARIUS NORTH NODE PEOPLE ARE
LEARNING TO SPEAK THEIR OWN TRUTH DIRECTLY

Because they grew accustomed to "polite society" in past lives, these folks have an attachment to tact and courtesy. Sometimes their communication is so subtle and indirect that the other person doesn't really "hear" them. They are learning to speak their truth DIRECTLY and SPONTANEOUSLY, which will allow their lives to come into alignment with the greater plan for their fulfillment. As they express their true perceptions through direct communication of their inner experience, those around them will either grow closer or leave their lives, making room for those with natural affinity to enter.

Sample Wishes to Promote Speaking Directly:
"I want all self-defeating needs for social acceptance totally lifted from me"; "I want the character-weakening practice of telling 'little white lies' easily lifted from me"; "I want the habit of 'explaining myself' totally lifted from me"; "I want the idea that I have to lie to survive totally lifted from me"; "I want clear revelations showing me how telling the truth is to my advantage"; "I want to easily find myself trusting outcomes and speaking my truth clearly, directly, and spontaneously."

SAGITTARIUS NORTH NODE PEOPLE ARE LEARNING TO AVOID UNEXPECTED UPSETS BY CHOOSING SPIRITUALITY

In this incarnation, the survival and happiness of Sagittarius North Node people depends on their alignment with the spiritual life: choosing the path of morality, ethics, and high principles over social acceptance and the manipulation of others' thoughts. They are learning to trust that there is a larger picture, and if they obey their conscience they will be protected and will find the peace of mind they seek. Regular time set aside for meditation and/or prayer will promote their spiritual connection.

Sample Wishes to Gain Peace of Mind:
"I want to easily find myself taking action on the prompting of my ethical nature"; "I want to easily find myself strengthening my connection with Truth"; "I want to easily find myself acting in alignment with my conscience"; "I want to consciously and consistently experience peace of mind"; "I want to easily find myself listening to the still, small voice of my conscience and ACTING according to what that 'inner feeling' says is correct"; "I want to easily find myself relaxing into the joyous feeling of a spiritual connection."

SAGITTARIUS NORTH NODE PEOPLE ARE LEARNING TO TRUST THEIR INTUITION

Sagittarius North Node people are highly intuitive, and when they follow their intuition, they always win. After an important interaction, they "know" whether or not the result will be in their favor. But then their overactive mind replays the situation over and over and begins to question their original assessment—then they become insecure and anxious. These folks are learning to trust the voice of their intuition as the final authority of how things are progressing in their life.

Sample Wishes to Expand Trusting the Voice of Intuition:
"I want to easily find myself trusting that my intuitive knowing is showing me the correct path"; "I want to easily find myself *trusting* my initial feeing about an interaction and not second-guessing myself"; "I want to consciously experience the joy of trusting in positive outcomes in a healthy, happy way"; "I want to consciously and consistently rely on my inner feelings of certainty"; "I want to easily find myself *listening* respectfully to my voice of intuition, trusting it to lead me in the right direction"; "I want to easily find myself trusting and acting upon the guidance I receive from my intuition."

SAGITTARIUS NORTH NODE PEOPLE ARE LEARNING TO EMBRACE LIFE AS AN ADVENTURE

Due to a subconscious feeling of being dependent on society and other people for survival, these folks tend to compromise their lives. In their hearts they want to take risks and live life impulsively, but their logic often makes them fearful by showing them the possible negative consequences of every situation. They are learning to see life as an adventure, and be willing to trust that by living spontaneously, "good luck" will take care of them.

Sample Wishes to Increase Confidence in Living Spontaneously:
"I want to easily find myself living my life spontaneously, in accordance with my inner feelings and intuition and not limited by logic"; "I want to easily find myself *acting* on my motivation to take

chances"; "I want to easily find myself viewing life as an adventure!"; "I want to easily find myself taking risks and making choices in align- ment with my spontaneous impulses"; "I want to easily find myself filled with optimism and faith—pursuing directions that make me feel free"; "I want the habit of compromising my spirit of adventure totally lifted from me."

CAPRICORN
North Node People
and North Node in the 10th House

CAPRICORN NORTH NODE PEOPLE ARE
LEARNING TO TAKE CHARGE OF THEIR LIVES

Capricorn North Node people have had so many past incarnations being dependent on family for their physical survival that they subconsciously fear they are incapable of making their own way in life. They lack confidence in their ability to be responsible for themselves, let alone take responsibility for helping others to survive and thrive. In this lifetime these folks are learning to adopt an attitude of competence and self-reliance and find out that they can survive on their own.

Sample Wishes to Help Restore Self-Reliance:
    "I want all fears of being responsible for myself totally lifted from me"; "I want to easily find myself taking charge in every area of my life"; "I want to easily find myself accepting my adulthood"; "I want to experience a feeling of competency in every area of my life"; "I want to easily find myself successfully taking charge in the area of ————"; "I want to easily find myself adopting an attitude of self-reliance that leads to success in every area of my life."

CAPRICORN NORTH NODE PEOPLE ARE
LEARNING TO RISE ABOVE DIFFICULT FAMILY RELATIONSHIPS

With so many past lives spent in family environments, Capricorn North Node people developed very strong karmic ties with a few familiar souls. So in this lifetime they are often born into families with the same folks from past incarnations, and the all-too-familiar family patterns begin to play out again. This creates "difficult family karma," as these folks find themselves unconsciously being the "buffer" for the emotional upsets of those around them. In order to rise above this situation, they need to set goals outside of the family and focus on achieving self-direction in a healthy way.

Sample Wishes to Help Rise Above Family Karma:
"I want to easily find myself allowing others to be upset without feeling personally responsible for protecting them from their emotions"; "I want to easily find myself allowing others to be themselves without interference from me"; "I want to easily find myself being self-reliant and independent from family members in a way that is happy and healthy for me"; "I want to easily find myself being empathetic with others in a way that maintains my own boundaries"; "I want all negativity from my childhood totally lifted from me"; "I want to easily find myself *free* of feeling I need the support of others to accomplish my goals"; "I want to easily find myself seeing the larger worldview beyond personal family problems."

CAPRICORN NORTH NODE PEOPLE ARE CHALLENGED WITH
NOT OVERREACTING EMOTIONALLY

Due to so many past life experiences spent in protective home environments, Capricorn North Node people never developed a larger, objective worldview. They have an overly sensitive attunement to the personal side of life, becoming too focused on moods and emotions and placing an exaggerated value on feelings. To counter this tendency to emotional overreactions, these folks need to let go of the past and learn to identify a goal to aim for in every area of their life.

Sample Wishes to Prompt Letting Go of Emotional Overreactions:

"I want all tendencies to overreact emotionally totally lifted from me"; "I want to easily find myself rising above the pull of negative emotions"; "I want all self-invalidating fears totally lifted from me"; "I want all tendencies to nonconstructive mothering totally lifted from me"; "I want the habit of looking back at my past totally lifted from me"; "I want the tendency to control situations though emotional reactions totally lifted from me."

CAPRICORN NORTH NODE PEOPLE ARE DEVELOPING SELF-RESPECT

Due to past incarnations where they were "on vacation" from needing to accomplish things out in the world, Capricorn North Node people have not had experiences that helped them to recognize their own competence. They have more confidence in others' ability to achieve success than in their own, since they have never had to earn the respect of others through their own efforts. So in this lifetime they need to choose a direction and experience the feeling of self-respect that comes from passing beyond imagined personal limitations in the successful pursuit of a goal.

Sample Wishes to Help Build Self-Respect:

"I want to easily find myself making decisions that lead to feelings of self-respect"; "I want the joy of accomplishment and self-respect to enter every area of my life"; "I want to easily find myself saying no in an assertive way that leads to feelings of autonomy and self-respect"; "I want to easily find myself making sensible commitments and keeping them"; "In the troubling situation of ————, I want to see the goal I can commit to that will give me a feeling of self-respect"; "I want to easily find myself 'growing up' and accepting adult responsibilities."

CAPRICORN NORTH NODE PEOPLE ARE
LEARNING TO FOCUS ON ACHIEVING GOALS

To rise above their oversensitivity to the emotional pulls of self and others, Capricorn North Node people need a focus that is larger than their personal life. So striving toward a goal is extremely liberating for these folks. The energy created by consciously pledging themselves to a goal that is a "first value" for them lifts them above their scattering emotional tendencies.

Sample Wishes to Help Establish Goals:
"I want to easily find myself making decisions based on reaching clearly defined goals that are important to me"; "I want to easily find myself viewing problems as pointers to the next goal I need to focus on"; "I want to easily find myself aiming for small goals that are reachable on my way to achieving the larger goals I want"; "I want to easily find myself goal oriented in every area of my life"; "I want to easily find myself seeing projects through to completion"; "I want Divine Guidance to give me a clear sense of purpose and direction that will add meaning and power to my life."

CAPRICORN NORTH NODE PEOPLE ARE CHALLENGED WITH ACCEPTING THE OPPORTUNITIES THEY ARE GIVEN TO ESTABLISH LASTING SECURITY

These folks are naturally supportive and protective toward others, and so attract unusual opportunities for prosperity. Yet due to their lack of self-confidence, they hesitate to take advantage of the openings life brings them for advancement—they fear the resulting responsibility. But they undermine their own future security when they turn away from these opportunities. They are learning to ACCEPT the chances life brings for them to increase their status and financial security.

Sample Wishes to Foster Accepting Opportunities for Advancement:
"I want to easily find myself taking those risks that offer the opportunity for lasting financial security"; "I want all fears of using opportunities to my maximum advantage totally lifted from me"; "I want all feelings of insecurity totally lifted from me"; "I want all thoughts about 'not knowing what to do' totally lifted from me"; "I want all fears of success totally lifted from me"; "I want to easily find myself recognizing and accepting opportunities to advance in life."

AQUARIUS
North Node People
and North Node in the 11th House

**AQUARIUS NORTH NODE PEOPLE ARE LEARNING TO
BECOME MORE AWARE OF THE WANTS AND NEEDS OF OTHERS**

Due to various past lives as VIPs who always got their way, these folks developed a strong attachment to getting what they want, when they want it. They lost touch with the larger view that includes sensitivity to what other people want. Now they're learning that when it's feeling like their plans are obstructed, their best bet is to pull back and consider the other people involved. Does their plan take the desires of others into account so that everyone can win?

Sample Wishes to Remain Aware of Others' Wants and Needs:
"I want to consciously and consistently *listen* to what others are telling me that they want"; "I want all self-defeating pride totally lifted from me"; "I want all tendencies to expect others to put me on a pedestal totally lifted from me"; "In social situations, I want to easily find myself being interested in others, asking them questions about their lives with the intention of supporting them"; "I want to consciously promote win-win situations by also taking into account the

situations of others and what they want"; "I want to easily find myself being aware of other people's moods and life situations without taking their behavior toward me personally."

AQUARIUS NORTH NODE PEOPLE ARE CHALLENGED WITH RELAXING THEIR STRONG WILLFULNESS AND ARE LEARNING TO "GO WITH THE FLOW"

These folks have had many prior incarnations in roles requiring strength, leadership, and total self-reliance. They knew what they wanted and mustered the will and focus to make it happen. Since their "determination muscle" has been overdeveloped, they may end up resisting the natural flow of events when it is not in their best interests to do so; often their subconscious willfulness actually prevents them from getting what they want. Now they are learning to relax their self-will and trust that "going with the flow" will bring them what they need in life.

Sample Wishes to Help Relax Willfulness:
"I want all tendencies to self-sabotaging willfulness totally lifted from me"; "I want the habit of demanding things from others totally lifted from me"; "I want the need for excessive approval easily lifted from me"; "I want to easily find myself allowing the natural flow of life to bring me my good fortune, graciously accepting the Universe's bounty"; "I want all self-sabotaging desires for drama easily lifted from me"; "I want the habit of rushing to achieve results to be replaced by a willingness to go step by step and allow time to reveal the right path."

AQUARIUS NORTH NODE PEOPLE ARE CHALLENGED WITH AN OVERACTIVE EGO AND ARE LEARNING TO BE MORE OBJECTIVE

In past incarnations these folks got so personally involved in their "roles" that they lost sight of reality and began to see everything as a reflection of their glory. So in this incarnation they tend to take things very personally. When life goes well for them their ego unconsciously swells, which usually leads to a fall. They are learning the humility of being thankful when things go their way, instead of being conceited. They are learning to be more objective—not taking defeats or victories so personally, but seeing that this is just how life unfolds for everyone.

Sample Wishes to Awaken Objectivity:
"I want all feelings of superiority totally lifted from me"; "I want to easily find myself free of the obsession to gain the approval of others"; "I want to easily find myself honestly and objectively revealing myself in all life situations"; "I want to easily find myself feeling friendship with others"; "I want all fears of disapproval totally lifted from me"; "I want all role-playing totally lifted from me"; "I want to easily find myself resting in 'the Witness Position'—observing myself objectively."

AQUARIUS NORTH NODE PEOPLE ARE LEARNING TO PARTICIPATE IN HUMANITARIAN CAUSES

Aquarius North Node people have had many incarnations focused on creating personal happiness. Now they are learning to apply their creative intensity and determination to a cause that is bigger than their personal life. When contributing to the positive evolution of humankind becomes one of their priorities, they enter an arena big enough to contain and appreciate their creative force! And when they focus their energy on a larger cause, the Universe also brings the money and situations they want—and the people who can make them happy—on a personal level.

Sample Wishes to Promote Participation in Humanitarian Causes:
"I want to easily attract, recognize, and begin participating in the right humanitarian cause for me"; "I want clarity in seeing the right avenue for me to begin to contribute to the evolution of humankind"; "I want to easily find myself speaking aloud the innovative thoughts that come to me"; "I want to easily find myself being charitable toward others"; "I want all fears that it's unacceptable for me to be who I am easily lifted from me"; "I want to easily find myself consistently putting my desire for the good of others above personal wants."

AQUARIUS NORTH NODE PEOPLE ARE LEARNING TO SUCCEED IN ROMANCE BY FIRST DEVELOPING FRIENDSHIP

Due to many incarnations of dramatic creativity and passion, these folks have a tremendous attraction to the drama of romance! Subconsciously, they set themselves up for heartbreak by falling in love before they really get to know the other person. In their typical approach, they want everything NOW . . . so they don't wait for love to blossom and deepen. They are learning to slow down and create success in romance by taking the time to discover who the other person is and to become a supportive friend before beginning a sexual relationship.

Sample Wishes to Help Develop a Strong Base of Friendship in Romance:

"I want the idea that 'honestly being myself' leads to losing in love totally lifted from me"; "I want to openly communicate my feelings with my romantic partner as I would with a friend"; "I want sabotaging, overdramatic responses in romance totally lifted from me"; "In romance, I want the tendency to hide my vulnerable self totally lifted from me"; "I want to easily find myself creating closeness with my romantic partner by acknowledging our unique individuality"; "I want to easily find myself *conscious* of building strong, honest communication with ———— that hears and honors what they are saying they want in a relationship"; "When I feel attracted to someone, I want to easily find myself first exploring a happy friendship before becoming sexually involved."

AQUARIUS NORTH NODE PEOPLE ARE LEARNING TO RECEIVE LOVE

These folks learned how to give to others during their past lives, and now they have difficulty in receiving. In this lifetime, their challenge is to open to receive love from others, which means allowing others to give to them in their own unique way. These folks are used to "scripting" everything, but now it's time for them to learn to look past their own projections and accept what is actually being offered, without trying to change the content or timing of the gift. They are learning the humility of simply ALLOWING others to give to them, and to graciously and joyously receive the gift of love.

Sample Wishes to Encourage Opening to Receive Love:

"I want to easily find myself graciously receiving the love and support of others"; "I want to easily find myself *allowing others* to please me"; "I want to easily find myself allowing my heart to open—*joyously* receiving love from others"; "I want all blocks to receiving love totally lifted from me"; "I want to easily find myself accepting gifts from men (women) in a happy, healthy way"; "I want to easily find myself graciously accepting love without feeling I have to 'do something' about it"; "I want to easily find myself fully appreciating ———— being in my life."

AQUARIUS NORTH NODE PEOPLE ARE
LEARNING TO SEE THE BIGGER PICTURE

These folks are so accustomed to past lives of total self-reliance that now they inadvertently repel the help they need for success. They get trapped in their own willfulness and go rushing toward their goals without a larger view of what's going on—then they get hurt and wonder what happened! Life can seem like a total gamble to Aquarius North Node people in terms of gaining the things that they really value, until they learn that this is not a do-it-yourself lifetime. When they learn to look outside themselves to gain a clear picture of the situations around them—THEN their efforts will be successful. They can get the information they need by listening to friends for objective feedback, consulting the esoteric sciences (astrology, tarot, numerology, etc.) to see their situation more clearly, and listening to messages from their Angels.

Sample Wishes to Trigger the Habit of Gaining Needed Information Before Taking Action:
"I want to easily find myself receiving helpful messages from the positive, angelic forces around me, supporting me in successfully nav-

igating my life"; "I want to easily find myself spending a minimum of one-half hour, a minimum of ———— mornings a week, getting in touch with my Angels and seeing the larger view of my life"; "I want to easily find myself enrolling in the right ———— classes and/or reading the right books (astrology/tarot/numerology, etc.) that will give me the knowledge I need to feel empowered"; "When I hit a 'brick wall,' I want to easily find myself consulting my friends to gain a larger picture of what is occurring"; "I want to consciously and consistently find myself viewing life situations from the perspective of what is best for everyone involved"; "I want to easily and joyfully find myself accepting and cooperating with the larger picture of what is going on"; "I want to embrace the idea that this is not a do-it-yourself lifetime and graciously invite the help of others."

PISCES
North Node People
and North Node in the 12th House

PISCES NORTH NODE PEOPLE
ARE DEVELOPING HUMILITY

These folks have had past incarnations serving in the field as missionaries, nurses, nuns . . . roles with rigid rules and regulations. They
had to have impeccable behavior, since they were representing a
higher ideal, and were so accustomed to being "above reproach" that
they became overly attached to rules and regulations of behavior. So
they came into this lifetime with subconscious programming telling
them they have to be "perfect" . . . but they can never get their lives
to work flawlessly! They are learning the humility of not being perfect, and recognizing that from a larger perspective, everything IS unfolding as it should.

Sample Wishes to Help Release Attachment to "Being Perfect":
    "I want the notion that I have to 'be perfect' totally lifted from
me"; "I want the idea that I have to 'be right' totally lifted from me";
"I want the habit of blindly acting on what my mind tells me I 'should'
do totally lifted from me"; "I want to easily find myself embracing my

own imperfections"; "I want the habit of finding fault with ———— (others/myself) easily lifted from me"; "I want to easily find myself accepting my own perfection, just as I am."

PISCES NORTH NODE PEOPLE ARE LEARNING TO SURRENDER THEIR EXCESSIVE ANXIETY AND TO TRUST IN A HIGHER POWER

Pisces North Node people carry a pattern of incessant anxiety from past incarnations in their subconscious. When they don't know what's going on with a situation, their "worry habit" is triggered—they feel out of control, fear the worst, and create unnecessary problems. They are learning to TRUST in the larger picture—that everything is working toward their greatest good, and that regardless of the twists and turns in their life, a Higher Power will take care of them and bring them what they need for happiness and fulfillment.

Sample Wishes to Ease Worry and Stimulate Trust in a Higher Power:
"I want the idea that 'something is wrong' totally lifted from me"; "I want all fears of being 'engulfed' by a Higher Power totally lifted from me"; "I want to easily find myself releasing all anxieties to a Higher Power"; "When 'Plan A' fails, I want to easily find myself receptive to the emergence of 'Plan B'; "I want to easily find myself remembering that 'this is all God's job' "; "I want worry replaced by a feeling of inner serenity and knowing that 'all is well.' "

PISCES NORTH NODE PEOPLE ARE
CHALLENGED TO STOP OVERANALYZING

These folks came into this lifetime with their analytical mind in overdrive! They analyze and plan EVERYTHING . . . fearing that if they don't, their world will collapse! Whenever anything goes contrary to their plan they immediately begin examining every aspect of the situation, hoping to bring things back under their control. This creates tremendous tension for them, especially in their "belly." However, rather than trying to change the "outside," they are discovering the power of changing their own attitude and perspective, and to accept the things they cannot change.

Sample Wishes to Help Release the Habit of Overanalyzing Everything:
"I want the habit of excessive analysis totally lifted from me"; "I want all tendencies to overdetailed planning totally lifted from me"; "I want to easily find myself embracing change, knowing there is a Higher Plan at work"; "I want to easily find myself releasing the habit of 'picking everything apart'"; "I want to easily find myself surrendering anxiety to a Higher Power for resolution"; "I want to easily find myself embracing the unexpected with serenity and a sense that 'all is well.'"

PISCES NORTH NODE PEOPLE ARE LEARNING TO RELAX
STANDARDS OF PERFECTION AND TO LOVE UNCONDITIONALLY

Pisces North Node people are so accustomed to "fixing things" in past incarnations that in this life their attention automatically focuses on what is "wrong" so they can fix it! They are learning to relax their subconscious standards of perfection—for themselves and others—and to love others unconditionally. From a spiritual view, they are finding that each of us is at a different stage of learning the mastery of common lessons. In the realm of spirit, everyone already IS perfect, regardless of where we are on the physical plane.

Sample Wishes to Help Shift Judgment into Unconditional Love:
"I want my preoccupation with trying to change others' behavior totally lifted from me"; "I want to easily find myself focusing on the positive aspects of people and situations"; "I want the tendency to judge others totally lifted from me"; "I want to easily find myself treating others as I would want them to treat me"; "I want to consciously and consistently recognize that others are doing the best they can with where they are"; "I want to easily find myself experiencing Oneness with others in a mutually empowering way."

PISCES NORTH NODE PEOPLE ARE LEARNING TO RELEASE OVERCONCERN WITH PERFECTION IN THE WORKPLACE

Pisces North Node people tend to obsess about the details of what's going on, especially at work. They notice all the ways their co-workers are not doing their jobs perfectly, and are consumed with the idea that their way of doing things is the best. They fear that if others don't do their tasks in the exact Pisces North Node manner, everything will end up in crisis—and this overconcern with work can run their lives. They are learning to focus instead on the larger vision, and to let others handle getting there in their own way. If things do go wrong, reminding themselves and their co-workers of their common goal, and staying open to the ideas and input of others, will help things get back on track.

Sample Wishes to Help Release Perfectionism at Work:

"I want the habit of focusing on what others are doing wrong at work totally lifted from me"; "When mistakes occur, I want to easily find myself responding by reminding others of our shared common vision"; "I want to easily find myself receptive to others carrying out my vision in their own way"; "I want to easily find myself inviting the ideas of others on the best way to get the job done"; "I want to consciously and consistently remember that the vision is more important than the techniques people use to reach it"; "I want to easily find myself remembering that everyone is doing the best job they can with the tools they have."

PISCES NORTH NODE PEOPLE ARE LEARNING TO STAY CONNECTED WITH A HIGHER POWER

In past lives, Pisces North Node people helped others improve their lives in tangible ways. Their job was to correct people on a functional level; yet in this lifetime, when they give practical advice it is usually turned down. Now they are learning that to be of service to others they must release their focus on the tangible world and link with the world of spirit. Their job is to stay aware of a Higher Power, merging with the spiritual energy that is the source of all healing. By staying silently merged with that spiritual presence, an energy is created that automatically helps and heals others.

Sample Wishes to Promote Staying Connected to a Higher Spiritual Presence:

"I want to easily find myself meditating (praying) a minimum of ———— days a week, a minimum of ———— minutes each time"; "I want to easily find myself trusting that a Higher Power will take care of me"; "I want to easily find myself fully satisfied with the bliss and love in my own nature"; "I want to easily find myself serenely aware of the 'larger picture' in every area of my life"; "I want to easily find myself connected with a Higher Power, allowing love and trust to flow into my life"; "I want to consciously and consistently remember that a positive Higher Power is unfolding the plan for my life on a daily basis."

Part IV

Ongoing Wishes

The nature of the human spirit is to forever expand and progress. We all long to make changes that will empower us to experience the joy of life at increasingly higher levels. However, there may be issues in your life that you have unsuccessfully tried to master for many years. If an area in which you seek change is especially difficult in terms of unconscious inner resistance, it may take writing down your intention repeatedly for the energy to shift and begin to lift the layers of resistance to success in that area.

For example, when I began using the magic of New Moon Power Periods in 1980, I realized that for me, the most difficult area to change was around food and eating—that's where all of my accumulated psychological dysfunction had become rooted. It was the one area of my life where I couldn't seem to achieve mastery, and I experienced a great deal of frustration and discouragement. At the time I weighed thirty pounds more than my recommended weight (which in my mind was a consistent embarrassment and made me extremely self-conscious). So I began putting weight-loss wishes on my Power Period lists. During the first year, I discovered liquid diets and lost and gained twenty pounds three times! At the end of the first year I was back at only two pounds under my starting weight, but I was determined, and I continued to put weight-loss wishes on my lists.

Four months into the second year I joined a weight-loss group and established a plateau of ten pounds higher than my desired weight. Yet to maintain this level was a major issue and became the primary focus of my life. Then gradually the wishes on my list began to change from wanting to lose weight to wanting to be naturally attracted to foods that were low calorie, low fat, and healthy for my body. I saw that my next step was to naturally maintain my new weight without having to go on minidiets regularly.

For the first time I was gaining a sense of mastery over my weight, but it was taking a tremendous amount of vigilance. I kept making wishes in alignment with what was going on and what needed to happen next. For example, as all the old karmic and psychological issues that created resistance around changing my eating patterns came to the surface, I made wishes during the next Power Period for that specific issue to be removed from me. At one point, I even wished that "all attraction to food be totally lifted from me" . . . granted, a little radical, but in my case swinging to the opposite end of the pendulum was a way of attaining some sort of balance!

At the end of four years, I had attained my desired weight goal and have maintained it to this day. Perhaps more importantly, it is not stressful to me, since food and eating are no longer issues of concern for me. Today the foods I am attracted to naturally maintain my slimness without any form of personal deprivation or efforts at discipline, and my diet is healthier than it's ever been. I wasn't born a naturally slim person with a high metabolism, but I have become that kind of person through the power of intention, the vigilance of writing down appropriate wishes during Power Periods, and the resulting magical help of the Universe.

I have shared my example as a way of illustrating how wishes may change over time, from *attaining* your goal, to *overcoming* resistance, to *maintaining* your goal, to gratefully *accepting* the manifestation of your goal. Different wishes are appropriate at different times during the process of making your dreams come true. Trust that you alone inwardly know what your next step needs to be—what quality you need to cultivate in order for your dream to be realized.

This chapter contains sample wishes from categories that are areas of concern for many of us. They come from years of research and work with my clients. However, you may have other areas of life that are vitally important to you that are not mentioned, in which case these sample wishes can give you an idea of the most effective way to word your own personalized ongoing wishes. Keep in mind that ten wishes total are recommended each month for best results; that includes your ongoing wishes, whatever changing wishes you may choose relating to the current New Moon, and any underlying karmic wishes that you may want to be on your list.

Some of your wishes may begin to materialize almost immediately, others may take longer to come true. But if you continue writing down a wish each month, over time it WILL come true. Remember that the wording of a wish is important, so review the sample wishes provided. It is fine to allow the wording of these basic wishes to change according to the energy you feel and the wording that occurs to you on each Power Day.

ABUSE

HEALING THE BEHAVIOR OF ABUSING OTHERS

Pressure and stress prompt some of us to take out our frustrations on others. Afterward, when we see the consequences of our behavior we often feel remorseful and even helpless, in terms of knowing how to change the abusive pattern. The power of repeated wishing, when combined with a Power Day, can lift these habitual responses from our consciousness.

Wishes to Remove Abusive Tendencies:
"I want to easily find myself in charge of my emotions so that I do not verbally or physically hurt others"; "I want all tendencies to physical, verbal, or emotional abuse totally lifted from me"; "I want all damage from childhood experiences of abuse totally lifted from me"; "I want all emotional violence totally lifted from me"; "I want the habit of judging myself harshly easily lifted from me"; "I want to easily start viewing myself with compassion and love for my willingness to approach my relationships in a new way"; "I want all irritability totally lifted from me"; "I want to easily find myself seeing new solutions to the problems in my life"; "I want all tendencies to abuse myself easily lifted from me"; "I want all explosive anger totally lifted from me."

HEALING VICTIM BEHAVIOR

Sometimes due to guilt, or a feeling that we have "no way out," we may allow others to abuse us. Without realizing it, we are actually supporting the other person's habit of abuse by allowing it to occur. When we take a stand and do not allow others to abuse us, we become part of their healing and our own, rather than part of the problem.

Wishes to Remove the Habit of Being a Victim:
"I want to easily find myself saying the right words to ———— that bypass his volatility and lead to clear and loving communication between us"; "I want the idea that I can win by suffering easily lifted from me"; "I want the habit of allowing abusive people and situations into my life totally lifted from me"; "I want to see a clear way of successfully leaving the abusive situation with ———— (name)"; "I want to

easily attract, recognize, and begin working with the right counselor who successfully helps me heal abusive experiences that occurred in my childhood"; "I want all self-sabotaging patterns totally lifted from me"; "I want clear boundaries, empowering me to not allow abusive situations into my life"; "I want to easily find myself joyously establishing healthy boundaries in my relationship with ————— (name)"; "I want all habits of self-judgment totally lifted from me"; "I want to easily find myself being kind to myself."

ADDICTIONS

LIFTING COMPULSIVE ATTRACTIONS

Addictions are the result of an attraction that has become compulsive and demands satisfaction and release. Calming the element of attraction can help immensely in healing the craving.

Wishes to Free Oneself from Compulsive Attractions:
"I want all compulsive feelings surrounding ————— totally lifted from me"; "I want the attraction to ————— easily lifted from me"; "I want all cravings for ————— totally lifted from me"; "I want Divine Intervention to totally dispel my attraction to —————"; "I want to experience the sensation of satisfaction from the good things that are already in my life."

HEALING A SPECIFIC CHEMICAL ADDICTION

In the following wishes, alcohol is the example of addiction used, but you can substitute whatever chemical addiction is interfering with your life: cigarettes, drugs, coffee, junk foods, sugar, etc.

Wishes to Dispel an Existing Addiction:

"I want all desires to (drink alcohol) totally lifted from me"; "I want my Higher Power to help with my (sobriety), making it even easier for me to (stay sober) one day at a time"; "I want all feelings of awkwardness about not (drinking alcohol) totally lifted from me"; "In situations where others are (drinking), I want to easily find myself feeling totally comfortable being (a nondrinker)"; "I want to easily find myself avoiding situations where (alcohol) is served"; "I want all preoccupation with (alcohol) totally lifted from me"; "I want to easily find myself having a good time socially without (alcohol)"; "I want to easily find myself working the twelve steps of (AA) and successfully connecting with my sponsor."

RELEASING NONCHEMICAL ADDICTIONS

An escapist activity that provides a temporary psychological release from stress can become as addictive as a chemical dependency. Compulsive shopping, spending, gambling, sleeping, television, video games, and surfing the Net can be activities that postpone our facing and overcoming the problems that keep us from experiencing a balanced, happy, and fulfilling life.

Wishes to Dispel the Power of Addictive Distractions:

"I want to easily find myself willing to directly face and overcome my problem of ———— "; "I want the habit of ———— (excessive shopping) easily lifted from me"; "I want to consistently experience the feeling of healthy, complete self-confidence from within myself"; "I want the habit of trying to acquire 'more' to be happy totally lifted from me"; "I want the attraction to ———— (watching television) totally lifted from me"; "I want the habit of ———— (eating) to avoid experiencing what I'm feeling totally lifted from me."

ASSERTIVENESS

Wishes to Encourage Assertive Behavior:
"I want to easily find myself functioning independently, in a positive way"; "I want to assert myself in constructive ways that result in others wanting me to get my way"; "I want to easily find myself taking ACTION on my desires for constructive change"; "I want to easily find myself taking the initiative in a happy, playful way"; "I want to easily find myself taking those actions that are in my overall best interests."

AUTHORITY

Dealing with Authority Figures

Sometimes we may have a problem relating to authority figures (teachers, parents, supervisors at work) and would benefit from eliminating the stress we feel in those relationships.

Wishes to Release Stress with Those in Authority:
"I want all nonconstructive resistance to authority totally lifted from me"; "I want to easily find myself dealing with authority figures in ways that are in my overall best interests"; "I want all stress relative to my relationship with ———— totally lifted from me"; "I want to easily find myself cooperating with ———— (name) in a way that is happy for me."

ASSUMING AUTHORITY

Sometimes the issue may be assuming the mantle of authority ourselves and responding to others in ways that are appropriate to the responsibility of our position without creating an isolating barrier between ourselves and others.

Wishes to Properly Assume Authority:
"I want to easily find myself accepting the responsibility of my position in a way that does not alienate others"; "I want all resistance to my being an authority figure totally lifted from me"; "I want to easily find myself saying the right words to ———— that cause him to joyously release trying to control me"; "I want to easily find myself automatically taking charge in all appropriate situations"; "I want to easily find myself willing to accept responsibility for creating success in every area of my life."

BROTHERS *(see Siblings)*

BUSINESS *(also see Work)*

PARTNERSHIPS

In business, we often find ourselves in situations where we partner with others. Fine-tuning these relationships can make the difference between a successful business and one that fails. Wishes can shift our approach to others in these relationships, creating a more positive outcome.

Wishes to Facilitate Happier, More Efficient Business Partnerships:

"I want all resistance to working together as a team with ———— totally lifted from me"; "I want to easily find myself consciously and consistently aware of the beautiful bonding energy between ———— and myself, and respond to that energy in a respectful way"; "I want to easily find myself appreciating the talents that ———— is bringing to the business"; "I want to be willing to fully partner with ———— in the ———— business."

BUILDING A SUCCESSFUL BUSINESS

Sometimes subconscious resistance to success can divert us from taking the steps that are necessary to build a thriving business. Wishing reaches the subconscious and can lift such resistance and also open us to seeing the path that will lead to solid success.

Wishes to Build a Successful Business:

"I want clear ideas occurring to me, showing me the next step to take to successfully build my business"; "I want to easily find myself sharing about my business with others in a way that evokes their desire to become clients"; "I want magic to enter my life, attracting clients whom I benefit and who pay me well for my services"; "I want to easily find myself involved in social situations where I meet potential clients whom I can benefit and who will want to do business with me"; "I want to easily find myself creating opportunities to meet clients who will benefit from my ———— services"; "I want to easily find myself saying the right words to my clients that result in their recommending me to their friends"; "I want Divine Guidance to give me right ideas about speech topics that would be a contribution to the community and result in lots of new business for me."

STAYING ON TRACK

Consciously using affirmations that are time-proven for success in business can give us a clear track to run on. Wishing can help bring these formulas for success into our consciousness.

Wishes to Program Business Success into Our Thinking:
"I want to easily find myself staying focused on achieving my business goals"; "I want to easily find myself consciously remembering that if I take care of the business, the business will take care of me"; "I want to easily find myself focused on being of *service* to others with my business, knowing that the money will take care of itself"; "I want to easily find myself remembering that the more discipline I accept from within, the less I'll have to accept from without"; "I want a happy attitude toward my customers that results in their giving me lots of business!"; "I want to easily find myself seeing and taking the next step in front of me to succeed in my business"; "I want to easily find myself making success in my business a *first value* in my life"; "I want to consciously remember that if I take care of the details—the little things—in my business, the big things will take care of themselves"; "I want to easily find myself *staying in motion* to create a successful business."

CAREER *(see Work)*

CARS

Wishes to Promote Positive Car Experiences:
"I want to easily attract, recognize, and purchase the right car for me at a price I can afford and that makes me happy"; "I want to easily attract the right buyer for my car and sell it at a price I am happy

with"; "I want to easily attract and recognize a reliable mechanic who takes great care of my car at a price I am happy with"; "I want to easily find myself improving my driving skills and self-confidence behind the wheel"; "I want to be aware of my car in a way that maintains it and keeps it trouble free."

CHANGE

Wishes to Encourage Flowing with Change in a Healthy, Positive Way:
"I want to easily find myself feeling peace and serenity in the midst of change"; "I want to easily find myself growing in a happy, positive way"; "I want to easily find myself adapting to change in a positive way that is in my overall best interests"; "I want to easily find myself passing through any difficult side effects from personal growth in a healing way"; "I want to easily find myself relaxing and opening to life in a way that invites good things to come to me!"; I want to easily find myself willing to make changes that are in my best interests"; "I want to easily find myself embracing inevitable change in a way that is positive for me."

CHILDREN

INFLUENCING POSITIVE BEHAVIOR

In many ways, the mind of a child is like the hard drive on a computer—it is open to the software the environment places into it. In this way the thoughts, encouragement, and conditioning that parents feed into the mind of their child greatly influence present and future behavior. Wishing will not change a child's actions, but wishes can shift *our* behavior in a way that influences the child to change their behavior.

Sample Wishes to Encourage Healthy Habits and Behavior in a Child:

"I want to easily find myself saying the right words to ———— that result in his happily doing his homework"; "I want total clarity in seeing how I can best support ———— doing her best in school"; "I want to easily find myself saying the right words to ———— that successfully encourage him to make his dreams come true"; "I want to easily find myself saying the right words to ———— that cause her to joyously take responsibility for her life and her finances"; "When ————'s negative behavior begins, I want to easily find myself immediately initiating something constructive for him"; "I want to easily find myself saying exactly the right words that connect my child with the spiritual realm in a way that is empowering for her"; "I want to easily find myself supervising ————'s study time in a way that results in happy scholastic success for her"; "I want to easily find myself saying the right words to ———— that successfully teach him the importance of ————."

Healing Instinctive Negative Responses

If we were treated with anger, jealousy, criticism, harshness, and abuse as children, we are likely to unconsciously enact these behaviors with *our* children and pass on unhealthy family patterns. Additionally, the stresses of today's fast-paced world may build internal pressure that we unwittingly release on our children. Wishing can help us to break these habitual responses and to be the kind of parent we want to be.

Wishes to Heal Negative Reactions Toward Our Children:

"I want all unconscious negative emotional reactions toward my child totally lifted from me"; "I want the habit of yelling at ———— totally lifted from me"; "I want right ideas to guide me in exposing ———— to things that are for his highest good"; "In my relationship with my child, I want to easily find myself approaching her as a nurturing adult"; "I want to easily find myself saying the right words to my child that help him in pursuing independent activity in a happy way"; "I want to easily find myself saying the right words to ———— (child's teacher) that inspire him to give ———— (child) positive attention"; "I want to easily find myself teaching ———— about his power and strength in a happy, positive way."

BUILDING A MUTUALLY HAPPY RELATIONSHIP

Focusing on what is "right" in a relationship is more potent than trying to correct what we feel is "wrong." Building positive bonds of love and support with our child can go a long way in dissolving old responses. Through the power of wishing we can forge positive new ways of relating.

Wishes to Increase Trust, Support, and Love in Our Relationship with Our Child:

"I want to easily find myself saying the right words to my daughter that result in mutual support and friendship"; "I want right ideas to occur to me for learning more about my daughter's life in ways that she will welcome and that will be mutually beneficial"; "I want clear, accurate guidance in successfully opening the lines of communication with ————"; "I want to easily find myself bonding with ———— in ways that are healthy for both of us"; "I want to easily find myself being aware of my children in an objective way that empowers me to relate to them appropriately"; "I want to easily find myself saying the right words to my children that result in their increased happiness and well-being"; "I want to easily find myself saying the right words to ———— that encourage and support him in making positive choices for his life that he is happy with"; "I want the desire to control ————'s life totally lifted from me."

COMMUNICATION

AUTHENTIC COMMUNICATION

Sometimes it can be difficult to share with others what is really in our hearts and minds. There are many reasons we choose not to reveal ourselves, such as fears of disapproval, ridicule, or rejection. However, when we hide ourselves, we also sidestep the opportunity for others to deeply connect with us. Wishing can help to promote more self-revelation in our communication with others.

Wishes to Promote Forthright Communication:

"I want to easily find myself feeling comfortable with my ideas and sharing them with others in a way that is mutually empowering"; "I want to easily find myself using my ability with words in a constructive way"; "I want to easily find myself speaking up and letting others know what I am experiencing"; "I want to easily find myself saying the right words that allow others to really know me"; "I want to easily find myself appropriately revealing myself, with all fear of 'not knowing the "right" thing to say' totally lifted from me"; "I want to easily find myself verbally expressing the authenticity of my own being."

IMPROVING COMMUNICATION SKILLS

If the way in which we express ourselves is not understood or accepted by others, we are operating with an unnecessary handicap in our lives. Wishing can change the way we present our ideas, or the way we listen to the ideas of others, and lead to a deeper level of comfort in communicating.

Wishes to Improve Communication:

"I want to easily find myself listening and learning from others, and experiencing the pleasure of a deep mental connection and mutual understanding"; "I want to consistently ask questions that lead to my understanding others more deeply"; "I want to easily find myself feeling safe and comfortable when others communicate their perceptions of life"; "I want to easily find myself communicating my point of view to others in a way they can understand and accept"; "I want to easily find myself communicating my feelings to ———— in a non-controlling way"; "I want to consistently say the right words that tactfully allow me to leave situations if I am not comfortable"; "I want to easily find myself expressing my ideas in a lighthearted way that facilitates others understanding my point of view"; "I want to easily find myself expressing my wants and needs in a way that invites others to happily cooperate."

COMMUNICATION WITH A SIGNIFICANT OTHER

Sometimes we feel a need for special communication with someone we feel close to, and yet don't know how to establish the bond we seek. Wishing can magically lead to our saying the right words at the right time, leading to the rapport we are hoping for.

Wishes to Increase Communication Leading to Rapport:

"I want to easily find myself saying those words to ———— that increase the positive, shared communication of our thoughts and feelings"; "I want to easily find myself saying the right words to ———— that lead to our coming to terms with our current situation in a positive, constructive way"; "I want clarity in seeing the next step to take that will lead to a win-win situation for ———— and me"; "I want to easily find myself saying the right words to ———— (name) that apologize for my style of delivery on ————, without invalidating the message"; "I want to easily find myself playfully initiating positive communication between ———— and me"; "I want clarity in seizing the right moment to communicate with ———— in ways that foster closeness and mutual support"; "I want all self-defeating censorship in my relationship with ———— totally lifted from me."

CONFIDENCE (see Self-Confidence)

COURAGE

RELEASING FEAR

Sometimes unconscious fears prevent us from following our chosen path. Wishing can help remove these blocks, lifting the paralysis, instilling courage, and clearing the way for action.

Wishes to Lift the Paralysis of Unconscious Fears:

"I want all negative, judgmental thoughts and emotions around the issue of courage easily lifted from me"; "I want to experience courage and positive initiative in every area of my life"; "I want all fears of standing on my own two feet *totally* lifted from me"; "I want to easily find myself filled with the courage to love others openly in a way that is mutually empowering": "I want to easily find myself filled with courage and confidence in pursuing my goal of ————."

TAKING RISKS

Risk-taking itself evokes the excitement of potential gain versus possible loss. If we always let our fearful mind stop us from pursuing exciting paths that promise to bring us new vitality, in the end our life may be filled with regrets. Wishing can give us a "boost" in taking risks that overcome the fear that tries to discourage us.

Wishes to Inspire the Courage We Need to Take Life-Enhancing Risks:
"I want to easily find myself taking those risks that are in my best interests"; "I want to easily find myself taking risks that add vitality and joy to my life!"; "I want to consistently accept those challenges that help me to grow and make me happy!"; "I want to easily find myself completing and sending the letter I want to write to ————"; "I want plenty of courage to say what needs to be said to ———— so that honest communication is restored."

CREATIVITY

Wishes to Activate Creativity:
"I want to easily find myself experiencing happiness and pleasure through expressing my creativity"; "I want to easily find myself ———— (creative activity) a minimum of ———— days a week, and a minimum of ———— hours each time"; "I want to easily find myself expressing my creativity in ways that are appreciated by others"; "I want to experience the joy of creative self-expression in every area of

my life"; "I want to easily find myself channeling my passionate energy in creative, positive ways"; "I want all blocks that prevent me from using my imagination completely lifted from me"; "I want to easily find myself taking a class that helps me develop my talents in the area of ————"; "When others are watching television, I want to easily find myself spending time in my room doing creative projects"; "I want to easily find myself expressing through my ———— (art/painting/writing/dancing, etc.) in the most brilliant way."

DEPRESSION

Depression is often accompanied by negative thoughts beating upon us repetitively. Sometimes we are aware of these thoughts and sometimes they are buried deep in our subconscious minds, feeding us negativity about ourselves or our situations. Wishing can magically bring these beliefs to the surface, release them, and free us from thought-induced depression.

Wishes to Eliminate Common Symptoms of Depression:
"I want all depression totally lifted from me"; "I want all thoughts of suicide *totally* lifted from me"; "I want to easily find myself using positive assertion to dispel negative thoughts"; "I want all feelings of being victimized and defeated totally lifted from me"; "I want all feelings of helplessness totally lifted from me"; "I want all negative impulses totally lifted from me"; "I want all self-hatred *totally* removed from me"; "I want all feelings of desperation easily lifted from me."

Wishes to Shift Tendencies That Invite Depression:
"I want all tendencies toward giving up magically transformed into renewed energy for success and happiness"; "I want all negativity

from my childhood totally lifted from me"; "I want the habit of looking back at my past totally lifted from me"; "I want the habit of blaming others for my circumstances easily lifted from me"; "I want the
idea that 'I am trapped' totally lifted from me"; "I want the sensation
of despair easily lifted out of my body and my consciousness"; "I want
all emotional pain and sadness totally lifted from me"; "I want new
ideas entering my consciousness, showing me the next step for a constructive, happy direction in my life."

DISCIPLINE

HEALING THE HABIT OF PROCRASTINATION

For some of us, procrastination can be a major stumbling block to
achieving our goals. The power of wishing can, bit by bit, eliminate
this habit from our consciousness. If this is a major issue, it's fine to
write several wishes for procrastination to be lifted on your wish list,
worded in slightly different ways.

Wishes to Eliminate the Habit of Procrastination:
"I want all tendencies to procrastination easily lifted from me"; "I
want the habit of procrastinating totally lifted from me"; "I want the
response of procrastinating taking action totally lifted from me"; "I
want to easily find myself using time to my advantage in a way that
makes me feel good about myself and the direction my life is going";
"I want to easily find myself moving forward into completion in every
area of my life."

ENCOURAGING SELF-DISCIPLINE

The quality of self-discipline is inherent in each of us. Wishing can stimulate this trait and bring it to the surface, where we can apply it to important areas of our lives.

Wishes to Enhance Self-Discipline:

"I want to easily find myself taking action on my ideas—seeing the next step and doing it"; "I want to easily find myself bringing projects to completion"; "I want to easily find myself taking immediate *action* on ideas for creating clarity and order in my life"; "I want all resistance to the idea of self-discipline totally lifted from me"; "I want to easily find myself making wise decisions in terms of my timing and my actions"; "I want to easily find myself using positive visualization in every area of my life."

EXERCISE

CULTIVATING POSITIVE ATTITUDES TOWARD EXERCISE

Although we may wish to include regular exercise in our lives, resisting thoughts may be interfering. It can be difficult to follow up good intentions with resolute action! Wishing can help change our attitude toward exercise, making it easier to plan and perform those routines that will be best for us.

Wishes to Instill a Positive Attitude Toward Exercise:

"I want to easily find myself maintaining an exercise program that is happy and invigorating"; "I want to easily attract, recognize, purchase, and use the right dependable exercise equipment for me"; "I want to easily find myself looking forward to my regular exercise routine with joy and enthusiasm"; "I want to be willing to do aerobic exercise on a regular basis"; "I want to easily attract information leading to my doing the correct exercise program for my metabolism and body type."

Wishes to Help Put Exercise Plans into Practice:
"I want to easily find myself exercising at the gym a minimum of ———— minutes a day, at least ———— days a week"; "I want to easily find myself doing yoga postures at home a minimum of ———— times a week"; "I want to easily find myself responding to agitation by taking brisk walks"; "I want to easily find myself doing aerobic exercises at least ———— days a week, a minimum of ———— minutes each time"; "I want to easily find myself doing stretching and breathing exercises at work a minimum of ———— times every day"; "I want to easily find myself joining the right gym for me so it is a pleasure for me to go on a regular basis"; "I want to easily find myself walking/running on the treadmill a minimum of ———— days a week for at least ———— minutes each time"; "I want to easily find myself taking those steps that result in a strong, toned, healthy body."

FATHER *(see Parents)*

FEAR

Each of us has experienced the sensation of fear, and yet different circumstances stimulate this response in each of us, and we all react to fear in different ways.

ANGER

Fear can translate into anger in less than a heartbeat, and often rage is actually a substitute for acknowledging that one is afraid. These reactions can become so ingrained that they are habitual, but wishing can lift them from our consciousness, giving us the space to make new decisions about handling situations where we feel inadequate or fearful.

Wishes to Diffuse Fear-Triggering Anger:
"I want all rage totally and easily lifted from me in a happy way"; "I want all emotional violence totally lifted from me"; "I want all frustration *totally* lifted from me"; "I want the instinctive reaction of anger totally lifted from me."

REPRESSION

Sometimes we respond to fear by repressing our own natural instincts. For example, rather than communicate when we are upset or when our feelings are hurt, we may simply "be quiet" for fear of the other person's reaction. However, this represses the outward flow of our energy and inhibits our instinctive responses, which may be just what is needed to heal a situation. Wishing can help to lift these habits of repression.

Wishes to Release Repression:
"I want the habit of controlling and restricting my natural life force totally lifted from me"; "I want all excessive seriousness totally lifted from me"; "I want all guilt totally lifted from me"; "When fear arises, I want the habit of withdrawing or changing the subject totally lifted from me"; "I want the burden of being distracted by others'

thoughts—and what they think about me—easily lifted from me"; "I want the habit of self-suppression easily lifted from me."

PHOBIAS

Phobias are specific circumstances that evoke panic or paralyzing fear. Common phobias include the fear of heights, fear of small spaces, fear of flying, and fear of leaving the house. Phobias can rule our lives, causing us to go out of our way to avoid the situations or objects that trigger them. Wishing can help to dissipate these phobic thoughts and lift them from our consciousness.

Wishes to Release Phobias:
"I want all terror around ———— (being in crowds/flying/heights, etc.) totally lifted from me"; "I want the feeling that I'm 'running from something' easily lifted from me"; "I want the phobia of ———— totally lifted from me."

PANIC RESPONSES

Panic is a phenomenon that is becoming more widespread. Stemming initially from free-floating anxiety, panic can take us over and render us helpless to deal in a "normal" fashion. Wishing can help to reduce the power of a panic response, and over time (with consistent Power Day wishing) dissipate it altogether.

Wishes to Deactivate the Panic Response:
"I want the idea that 'something is wrong' totally lifted from me"; "I want all panic attacks totally lifted from me"; "I want all debilitating panic totally lifted from me"; "I want all anxiety totally lifted from me"; "I want all ideas about 'not knowing what to do' *totally* lifted

from me"; "I want all fear totally lifted from me"; "I want the fear that I am dying totally lifted from me"; "I want to easily find myself consciously trusting that the Universe (God/a Higher Power) is in charge and is taking care of me."

ENCOURAGING POSITIVE RESPONSES TO FEAR

When viewed accurately, fear can actually prompt us to operate at a higher and more exciting level in the situation where it arises. Fear heightens our senses and makes us more aware of the here and now. By cultivating positive responses, fear becomes less an enemy and more a stimulus to growth.

Wishes to Promote Positive Responses to Fear:

"I want to experience patience in every area of my life in a happy way"; "I want to easily find myself recognizing and releasing upsetting feelings"; "I want to easily find myself open to other people's energy in a way that is validating for me"; "I want to easily find myself acknowledging fear in a way that is empowering for me"; "I want to easily find myself taking those risks that result in personal freedom and fearlessness."

FOOD

COOKING

Cooking is a key to maintaining a healthy diet. Wishing can open the way to a more positive view of cooking, improving results and removing any unconscious resistance.

Wishes to Encourage Cooking:

"I want to easily find myself joyously cooking healthy meals for myself and ————"; "I want to easily find myself happily putting the necessary effort into preparing healthy meals"; "I want all resistance to cooking totally lifted from me"; "I want to easily find myself enjoying the process of cooking"; "I want to easily find myself preparing tasty, healthy meals."

DISCRIMINATION IN CHOOSING A HEALTHY DIET

Sometimes eating convenience foods can result in choices that are not in our best interests. Wishing can magically shift us into becoming conscious of our food choices in an empowering way.

Wishes to Establish a Healthier Diet:

"I want to easily find myself attracted to and consuming only those foods that are healthy for my body"; "I want all attraction to junk foods and convenience foods totally lifted from me"; "I want all attraction to fattening bakery goods totally lifted from me"; "I want all attraction to fatty, greasy foods totally lifted from me"; I want to easily find myself being totally conscious around food, making those choices that result in my feeling a positive sense of self-worth."

ATTITUDES TOWARD FOOD

Food can be used as a substitute for other types of nurturing: love, security, emotional well-being, etc. Consistent wishing can stop the habitual response of eating as a "quick-fix remedy" for emotional needs, empowering us to take charge of our food intake.

Wishes to Stop Using Food to Satisfy Emotional Needs:

"I want all unconsciousness around food totally lifted from me"; "I want to easily find myself no longer using eating to suppress my feelings"; "I want all addiction to food totally lifted from me"; "I want the habit of associating food with emotional well-being totally lifted from me"; "I want the practice of eating after ————P.M., *totally* lifted from me."

FRIENDS

Friends are an essential part of a balanced and joyful life. In our fast-paced world where we often experience not having enough time, we may tend to focus on our immediate personal lives—our job and family. It's all too easy to lose track of our friends, and long times apart can erode the closeness of these bonds. Friends provide a "broader view" of life that is very important. They offer fresh insights, support, and the satisfaction of relating to a peer with common interests and having a bond of caring that is not a "requirement" in our lives. Friends remind us of the importance of expanding our horizons beyond strictly personal interests.

INITIATING FRIENDSHIP

We may find ourselves in a situation where we have a sense of being a "kindred spirit" with a person we meet, yet lack the confidence to initiate a friendship with them. Wishing can help us rise above these inhibitions and free us to initiate a friendship when we feel a connection with someone.

Wishes to Promote Our Ability to Initiate Friendships:

"I want to easily find myself socializing with others in healthy, happy ways"; "I want to easily find myself participating in those activities that attract happy, healthy friendships"; "I want to become genuinely interested in others in a way that evokes a feeling of mutual rapport and friendship"; "I want to easily find myself initiating positive conversations that create healthy friendships"; "I want to easily begin lots of happy new friendships with people who have similar values and interests"; "I want to easily find myself successfully initiating friendships and doing things with those I am interested in spending more time with."

ATTRACTING MORE FRIENDS

Sometimes we want more friends in our life but may not know how to go about finding them. The solution may be in attending activities (social, cultural, or recreational) we enjoy to meet those with similar interests, or we may simply need to be more open to the possibility of friendship with the people we meet in our day-to-day lives.

Wishes to Attract More Friends:

"I want to easily attract and begin happy friendships with people who can share mutual interests, support, and caring"; "I want lots of new friends!"; "I want to easily attract healthy, happy, mutually empowering friendships with the right people for me"; "I want to easily attract and begin new friendships with peers who have similar interests to mine and are compatible with me"; "I want to attract a nurturing, happy group of friends"; "I want the barriers that keep me from finding nurturing, mutually empowering friendships totally lifted from me"; "I want to easily find myself creating lasting friendships"; "I want all self-defeating resistance to friendship totally lifted from me."

IMPROVING FRIENDSHIP SKILLS

Attracting and creating happy friendships has a lot to do with our own attitudes and knowing how to treat friends in a way that nurtures the relationship. This has to do with developing the habit of being genuinely interested in others with no motive other than wanting to support them in attaining their hearts' desires.

Wishes to Improve Friendship Skills:
"I want to begin listening to others in a way that establishes a natural feeling of friendship with them"; "I want to easily find myself relating to others in friendly, helpful ways that evoke friendship"; "I want to easily find myself actively participating with others in a happy way"; "I want all fears of interacting in group situations totally lifted from me"; "I want Divine Guidance to give me the wisdom to see clearly how to relate to my friends in a way that promotes mutual caring and support"; "I want to easily find myself interested in knowing and understanding others in a way that is helpful to them and not threatening to me"; "I want to easily find myself open to accepting and appreciating the support of others"; "I want to easily find myself creating lasting friendships."

BUILDING CLOSER BONDS WITH ESTABLISHED FRIENDS

We may have a friend whom we value, and yet feel we are not as close to them as we would like. Wishing can help us in taking those actions that lead to closer bonds of friendship.

Wishes to Promote Closeness with Our Friends:

"I want a total healing to occur in my relationships with —————, resulting in mutual support and goodwill"; "I want to easily find myself saying the right words to ————— (name) that lead to feelings of mutual affection, support, and respect in our relationship"; "I want to easily find myself spending time with one of my friends at least ————— times a week"; "I want right ideas to occur to me, showing me how to become closer to ————— in a happy, healthy way"; "I want to easily find myself initiating mutually fun, happy activities with my friend, ————— (name)."

FUN

Having fun is the way we take a break from the seriousness of life, and results from experiencing activities we enjoy. As we participate, the spirit of fun, play, and pleasure are activated. The flame of fun is also kindled by taking a playful approach to our daily routines, and by consciously experiencing the pleasure of the delicious sensuality of our life experience as it unfolds. In the following wishes, the example of dancing is used, but substitute whatever activity makes *you* happy.

EXPERIENCING PLEASURE AND FUN

The most beautiful day won't cheer us up if we aren't receptive to it. Life, love, and enjoyment can be happening all around us, and yet we only experience the benefits when we are open to them. Wishing can magically release us to experience the pleasure and fun in our lives.

Wishes to Expand Our Awareness of Fun and Pleasure:

"I want to easily find myself allowing my childlike nature to guide me into happy, pleasant activities and new ways of having fun"; "I want a total healing to occur, opening me to the fun and pleasure of life!"; "I want to easily find myself living my life in an exciting, adventurous, healthy way"; "I want to experience the ecstasy of pleasure in healthy, happy ways"; "I want to easily find myself letting go of repressive inhibitions"; "I want to easily find myself willing to include the element of fun in my life"; "I want to easily find myself having fun and enjoying my life."

MAKING TIME FOR PLEASURABLE ACTIVITIES

A strong work ethic can tempt us to discount the value of having fun and how important it is in our lives. Through the power of wishing it's possible to help the mind "remember" to allot time to having fun.

Wishes to Remind Us to Make Time for Activities That Are Pleasurable and Fun:

"I want to easily find myself traveling in environments that liberate me and bring me joy"; "I want to easily find myself saying the right words to ———— that result in our ———— (taking dancing lessons) together joyfully"; "I want to easily find myself enrolling in ———— (dance lessons) and having a wonderful time"; "I want to easily find myself attending fun ———— (dancing) events on a regular basis"; "I want to easily find myself creating goals in my life that are fun for me"; "I want to easily find myself experiencing an activity that is fun for me a minimum of ———— times a month, a minimum of ———— hours each time"; "I want to easily find myself remembering to schedule time for fun in my daily life!"; "I want to easily find myself using my retirement in a fun way that is in my best interests."

HABITS, BAD

Habitual negative ways of thinking or counterproductive behaviors prevent us from having the things that we desire in life. Without even realizing it, we continue unconscious patterns that work against our best interests. Releasing these habits through the power of wishing opens the way for our dreams to begin coming true.

LIFTING HABITUAL NEGATIVE THOUGHT PATTERNS

Negative thinking can be one of our greatest enemies, actually repelling the very things in life that we want the most. For example, if our thoughts fill us with guilt, we will subconsciously feel unworthy to have happy life experiences and sabotage situations that could lead to satisfaction. In this case, for us to be open to happiness, the thought patterns producing guilt must be eliminated.

Wishes to Eliminate Negative Thought Patterns:
"I want worry and anxiety totally lifted from me"; "I want all guilt totally lifted from me"; "I want any resistance to happiness totally lifted from me"; "I want the tendency to take things personally easily lifted from me"; "I want all negative judgment of myself and others totally lifted from me"; "I want all internal blocks that prevent me from going after what I want totally lifted from me"; "I want all self-hate *totally* removed from me"; "I want the habit of self-sabotage totally lifted from me"; "I want all sadness easily lifted from me"; "I want the habit of remorse replaced by recognizing that I'm doing the best that I can."

Lifting Habitual Negative Behavior Patterns

Habitual negative responses to our environment—anger, impatience, criticism, and moodiness—pull negative reactions to us from others. Wishing can break the unconscious pattern around such reactions and help us eliminate behaviors that bring us pain.

Wishes to Shift Negative Behavior Patterns:
"I want to easily find myself handling anger in a constructive way"; "I want all self-defeating stubbornness totally lifted from me"; "I want the habit of gossiping totally lifted from me"; "I want all impatience totally lifted from me"; "I want the habit of controlling situations through emotional upheaval totally lifted from me"; "I want the habit of ————— (complaining/nagging) easily lifted from me"; "I want the habit of responding as a ————— (curmudgeon/pessimist, etc.) totally lifted from me"; "I want to easily find myself offering suggestions in noncritical ways."

Creating New Positive Habits

Focusing on the positive result that we DO want in our lives is another way to change behavior. Use the approach that feels the most potent and empowering for you, and substitute the subjects that are important to you in the following wishes.

Wishes to Create New Habitual Responses:
"I want to easily find myself losing interest in ————— (watching television, surfing the Net, etc.) and using my time in ways that make me feel good about myself"; "I want to easily find myself identifying with being a ————— (nonsmoker, nondrinker, etc.)"; "I want to easily find myself putting off the habit of ————— (having a cigarette,

arguing with my husband) on a permanent basis"; "In the matter of
——— (drinking, sleeping too much, biting my nails, etc.), I want to
easily find myself responding by ———."

HAPPINESS

Ultimately, happiness is what we are all seeking. Sometimes we
think it will come to us through external circumstances—material
possessions, wealth, fame, or an ideal relationship. Sometimes we follow an inner path to connect with happiness through prayer, meditation, or selfless service.

DIRECTLY EXPERIENCING INNER HAPPINESS

The flow of happiness is constantly pulsating within us, whether
we are aware of it or not. Consciously focusing on this inner flow
strengthens our connection to it and makes happiness a more consistent experience in our daily lives.

Wishes to Increase Our Conscious Awareness of Happiness:
"I want to consciously and consistently experience my own inner
happiness"; "I want to continue waking up to consciously enjoying the
delight of my own being"; "In the midst of chaos, I want to easily find myself consciously aware of the feeling of peace and joy inside myself"; "I
want to know, feel, and experience that God (Life/the Universe) loves
me"; "I want to easily find myself consciously experiencing an open and
joyful heart"; "I want to easily find myself consciously and consistently
viewing life in a way that creates laughter and ease for me."

APPRECIATION

Thankfulness and appreciation slow down the active mind and open us to an awareness of the abundance that is already ours. Sometimes even when we attract situations that bring us joy, we don't really allow the love and happiness to soothe us and give us more than temporary pleasure. This may be because we fear that if we allow ourselves to fully experience the joy, pain will follow; or we may be in a "more/better/different" mode that prevents something from giving us happiness over time. Appreciating what we already have creates an immediate experience of happiness and love.

Wishes to Increase Appreciation:

"I want to easily find myself consciously and consistently appreciating the abundance in my life"; "I want to easily find myself consciously aware of the beauty of the Earth and Mother Nature"; "I want to easily find myself appreciating the good things that are already in my life"; "I want to consciously, consistently remember to be thankful"; "I want to easily find myself being thankful for the people in my life"; "I want to consciously, consistently experience a feeling of appreciation."

CREATING HAPPINESS

Because each of us is unique, the activities that bring us pleasure and delight may be different from what brings joy to others. We can do our part to create more happiness in our lives by honoring the things that bring us personal satisfaction—and spending time doing them! Wishing can help shift us in consciously using our time to include activities we enjoy.

Wishes to Help Us Make Time for Pleasurable Activities:

"I want to easily find myself taking risks that lead to my greatest happiness"; "I want to easily find myself experiencing joy and elation in expressing my creativity"; "I want to easily find myself allotting at least ———— day(s) a ———— (week/month) to enjoy my hobby of ————"; "I want to easily find myself consciously allotting time for those activities that I enjoy"; "I want to easily find myself being in those environments that satisfy my passion for ———— (learning/dancing/self-improvement/friends)"; "I want to easily find myself taking steps that lead to having a happy life."

HEALTH *(also see Exercise)*

REGAINING GOOD HEALTH

If there is an area of your body that needs special attention and healing, wishing can be a powerful tool for attracting effective help as well as lifting some of the symptoms.

Wishes to Regain Good Health:

"I want to be totally open to Divine Intervention performing a complete healing in the area of my ————"; "I want to easily find myself using positive imagery in a way that restores my body to perfect health"; "I want to easily attract, recognize, and accept those healers/remedies that will lift the pain associated with my ———— (periods, back pain, etc.)"; "I want all PMS totally lifted from me!"; "I want to easily attract, recognize, and begin working with the right healer(s) for me, who restores my body to perfect, vibrant health"; "I want all tendencies to the health condition of ———— totally and easily lifted from me"; "I want to easily find myself going through the operation on my ——— with strength and grace"; "I want all resistance to healing totally and easily lifted from me."

Wishes to Increase Physical Strength:

"I want vibrant health flowing through my body consistently"; "I want to easily attract, recognize, and begin using those nutritional supplements that restore my perfect health and vitality"; "I want to find myself filled with solid reserves of energy"; "I want to easily find myself making choices that lead to increasing my physical strength"; "I want the white light of healing energy to restore my body to total, perfect health"; "I want all barriers to allowing healing energy to flow through me totally lifted from me."

MAINTAINING GOOD HEALTH

Maintaining good health is not only the best prevention against future disease, but also enhances the quality of our daily lives now. Good health habits are often a matter of discipline at the beginning, and wishing can help us get started.

Wishes to Maintain Good Health:

"I want total clarity in following the right routine for me—one that includes time for exercise, quiet time, work, family time, having fun, and ———"; "I want the energy of love, healing, and appreciation to enter every area of my life"; "I want to easily find myself viewing my body with acceptance, appreciation, and love"; "I want to easily find myself breathing fully in a healthy, life-enhancing way"; "I want to consistently experience healthy high energy and enthusiasm"; "I want to easily find myself taking those substances and following those routines that successfully restore my youthful vigor in a happy, healthy way!"; "I want to easily find myself taking care of myself in ways that lead to maintaining optimum health."

HEALING OTHERS

Wishing for others directly during New Moon cycles doesn't work, although the power of our good intentions for them is certainly a helpful and healing influence at any time. However, we can wish for ourselves to be open as a channel through which a healing influence takes place for the other person.

Wishes to Become an Influence That Heals Another:
"I want to easily find myself a channel, providing information that will help ——— (name) with (his/her) health"; "I want to be a vehicle for healing energy for my son, ——— (name)"; "I want to easily attract and share specific health remedies with ——— that will restore her to perfect health"; "I want to easily find myself saying the right words to ——— (name) that lovingly prompt him to begin a healthy ——— (diet/exercise routine/doctor checkup, etc.)"; "I want to easily attract and share information with ——— that restores him to perfect health."

HOME/REAL ESTATE

HOME IMPROVEMENT

Many of us spend a great deal of time at home. Improving its atmosphere so that it is a place of respite and regeneration is certainly a worthwhile endeavor.

Wishes to Improve Our Home Environment:
"I want to easily find myself successfully creating a beautiful environment in my home"; "On a daily basis, I want to easily find myself

maintaining order and cleanliness in my home"; "I want to easily attract, recognize, and begin working with the right ——— (land-
scaper/decorator/painter) for me, who will do a job that I am totally
pleased with at a price I can easily afford"; "I want Divine Guidance to
intervene on the refinancing of my home for renovation, showing me
the exact steps to take that are in my best overall financial interests";
"I want to easily find myself reorganizing my home in a way that makes
me happy and serene"; "I want to easily find myself going through my
possessions and discarding everything that is no longer useful to me";
"I want to easily find myself creating an aura of peace, serenity, and
beauty in my home."

MOVING

Moving is on the "top ten" list of stressful situations. The following wishes can pave the way for moving to be easier and less stressful.

Wishes to Ease the Stress of Moving:
"I want all nonconstructive stress around moving totally lifted
from me"; "I want total mental clarity and ease surrounding my
move"; "I want Divine Intervention to enter the situation of my moving, creating a happy stress-free move"; "I want to easily attract and
work with the right moving people for me, who do a job I am pleased
with at a price I can afford"; "In my upcoming move, I want total clarity in discarding those possessions that are not helpful to my present
and future."

BUYING OR SELLING A HOME

This can be a difficult process. In buying, we may have an unclear
picture of the type of new home that would make us happy, or have
requirements that, in reality, act against our best interests. In selling,

we may encounter subconscious resistance to letting go of a home we have lived in for years, even if we feel happy about the future situation. Wishing can help eliminate these inner resistances to buying or selling a home.

Wishes to Support Buying a Home:
   "I want total accurate guidance showing me those steps to take regarding housing that are in my best interests"; "I want to fully claim the self-respect that comes from my experience of owning my own home"; "I want to consistently make enough money to easily afford living in the home of my choice"; "I want to attract, recognize, and purchase the right happy home for me at a price I can easily afford"; Regarding the right place for me to live, I want Divine Guidance to show me the location and situation in which I would be happiest."

Wishes to Support Selling a Home:
   "I want Divine Intervention showing me the correct path to take to sell my house immediately at a price I am happy with"; "I want all attachment to my house in ——— totally lifted from me"; "I want to attract the right buyer to my home, selling it easily at a price I am happy with"; "I want to easily attract, recognize, and begin working with the right realtor for me who promptly sells my home at a price I am happy with"; "I want to easily find myself saying the right words to my realtor that cause her (him) to have a successful mind-set of completion relative to the house in ———"; "I want to easily find myself fully appreciating the goodness that has come to me from my old home, and then letting it go"; "I want to easily find myself listing my home at exactly the right time that results in an easy sale"; "I want to easily find myself recognizing the sale of my house as a step of accomplishment and completion for me."

HONESTY *(see Integrity)*

INTEGRITY/AUTHENTICITY

Integrity has to do with living our lives in accordance with what we really consider valuable: our ethics, morals, principles, ideals, and dreams. Maintaining integrity may include taking an unpopular stand because it is a true reflection of how we personally feel about something. However, our desire for authenticity—expressing ourselves in a way that is a true reflection of our individuality—can be all too easily undermined by conflicting desires: money, social conformity, status, and acceptance by those we love. Wishing can support us in staying in touch with our integrity, as well as sparking the courage to give a voice to what is truly important to us.

Wishes to Encourage Openness and Integrity in Our Communications with Others:

"I want to easily find myself revealing my true nature to others in a healthy, happy way"; "I want to easily find myself following the prompting of my inner nature"; "I want to easily find myself communicating with others in a way that is a true reflection of my inner self"; "I want all fears of being honestly myself totally lifted from me"; "I want to easily find myself speaking and acting in alignment with my conscience"; "I want to easily find myself authentically letting others know where I truly stand."

JOB *(see Work)*

LEGAL ISSUES

DIRECT COMMUNICATION

Sometimes a lawsuit can best be resolved through personal communication with our "opponent." If this is an option, wishing can help us to communicate in a way that creates a win-win situation for both parties.

Wishes to Enhance Effective Communication:
"I want to easily find myself saying the right words to ———— that lead to our working out a mutually beneficial solution that empowers both of us to go on with our lives"; "I want to easily find myself saying the right words to ———— that cause him (her) to immediately want to get on with his (her) own life, and complete the papers relating to the divorce"; "I want to easily find myself saying the right words to ———— that cause him (her) to complete the divorce papers in a way that is fair for both of us"; "I want right ideas to occur to me that show me the best approach to take with ———— that will result in a win-win resolution."

ATTORNEY RELATIONSHIPS

Finding an expert attorney for the specific type of legal situation in which you are involved is paramount. Additionally, there is the need to take responsibility for handling the relationship in a way that doesn't result in an unfair distribution of monies in favor of the attorney! To prevent ending up as a "trusting victim," it is necessary to stay conscious and responsible about the process as it unfolds—both by knowing the expenses being accrued and in authorizing how the attorney's time is to be spent.

Wishes to Promote a Healthy Relationship with Your Attorney:

"I want to easily attract, recognize, and hire an attorney who is an *expert* in the kind of lawsuit I'm involved in"; "I want clear guidance in seeing *exactly* how to relate with my attorney in a way that is in my overall best interests"; "I want to easily find myself saying the right words to my attorney that result in his (her) giving me a clear, accurate appraisal of the money I will be spending as we go along"; "I want to easily attract, recognize, and begin working with the right attorney who will do a *great* job representing me on a percentage basis"; "I want to easily find myself saying the right words to my attorney that result in her (his) representing me in a way I feel good about."

LAWSUITS

The adversarial nature of lawsuits can distract us from focusing on the other parts of our lives. Should we find ourselves enmeshed in a lawsuit, holding on to the larger picture of what we want to do with our lives is a good way to facilitate the legal process and avoid being swallowed up by it.

Wishes to Expedite a Lawsuit:

"I want total brilliance in handling the legal case with ———— in a way that is in my ultimate best interests"; "I want all pain related to actively pursuing and winning the court case with ———— totally lifted from me"; "I want all resistance to creating successful results in my lawsuit with ———— totally lifted from me"; "I want to be conscious of Divine Guidance showing me when—and if—it is in my best interests to settle this legal issue and move on with my life"; "I want clear, positive, accurate intuition, followed by resolute action, in seeing exactly what steps I should take in the lawsuit with ———— that serve my best interests"; "I want to easily find myself taking those actions that lead to a speedy out-of-court settlement that makes me happy in my lawsuit with ————."

LOVE *(also see Romance)*

Giving and receiving love is certainly one of the sweetest sensations possible to feel as human beings. Love, in one form or another, is constantly offered all around us, but sometimes we are not able to recognize it. Wishing can help open us to experiencing the love that is already available in our daily lives.

Wishes to Increase Our Experience of Love:
"I want to easily find myself viewing my life in a way that leads to forgiveness and unconditional love"; "I want to easily find myself consciously and consistently experiencing love in all my relationships"; "I want to easily find myself consciously and consistently aware of feelings of love within my own being"; "I want all feelings of isolation totally lifted from me"; "I want to consciously and consistently experience thankfulness as I walk through my daily life"; "I want full realization of my potential to experience love"; "I want the sensation of sadness to transform into feelings of love."

ALLOWING OTHERS TO LOVE US

Sometimes those around us are showering us with love and we are simply not letting it in. We may acknowledge the love outwardly, but we don't really let it reach our hearts. Allowing ourselves to fully experience others loving us is a huge step in realizing the abundance and joy of life as a human being.

Wishes to Open Ourselves to Fully Experience Others Loving Us:

"I want to easily find myself TOTALLY RECEPTIVE when others express their feelings of closeness with me"; "I want to easily find myself taking those actions that result in my feeling loved in a happy, healthy way"; "I want all resistance to experiencing love from others easily lifted from me"; "I want to easily find myself appreciating and acknowledging the gifts that others give me"; "I want to easily find myself experiencing all the love flowing from others toward me"; "I want to consciously experience feeling loved by others"; "I want to easily find myself consciously and consistently aware of—and nurtured by—the love I receive from others."

LOVING OTHERS

As we extend ourselves to love others—through kind words, a caring phone call, a thoughtful gift, or supportive interest in their lives—we simultaneously open ourselves to receive more love. Wishing can help us put our instincts to love others into action.

Wishes to Help Us to Actively Extend Love to Others:

"I want to easily find myself feeling loving acceptance when I am with others"; "I want to easily find myself consciously and consistently loving and supporting others in the way that they need to feel loved"; "I want to easily find myself saying the right words to the people around me that cause them to feel loved"; "I want all resistance to giving love to others easily lifted from me"; "I want all resistance to experiencing the exchange of healthy love with others easily lifted from me"; "I want all fears around healthy loving easily lifted from me"; "I want to easily find myself consistently validating ———'s healthy sense of self-worth."

MANAGEMENT *(see Work)*

MARRIAGE/SIGNIFICANT OTHER
(also see Relationships and Communication)

Creating a successful and happy marriage is certainly among the greatest of challenges for many of us. It requires the wisdom to choose a compatible partner with similar life goals and values, then it takes constant vigilance to not take the relationship for granted. A primary challenge is remaining aware of the other person's needs and consistently planting positive seeds that keep the specialness of the relationship vital, loving, and mutually supportive.

ATTRACTING THE RIGHT MARRIAGE PARTNER

For a successful, happy, and lasting marriage, the first step is choosing an appropriate partner. Beyond passion is the necessity of selecting someone whom we truly like and respect as a human being, a person whom we can trust to open our heart in a lasting way.

Wishes to Attract an Appropriate Marriage Partner:
"I want to easily attract the right marriage partner for me, an available ———— (man/woman) who also wants ———— (a home and children), with whom I can build a stable, happy relationship"; "I want accurate wisdom illuminating what is best for me in terms of marriage"; "I want to easily attract, recognize, and begin a happy romantic relationship with the right, available mate for me, leading to marriage"; "I want all resistance to having a happy marriage totally lifted from me"; "I want total clarity leading me to make right decisions surrounding my wedding with ————, leading to a closer,

more loving relationship"; "I want the wisdom to recognize the appropriate mate for me and to easily find myself entering into successful courtship with him/her"; "I want Divine Guidance to lead me to being in the right place at the right time that results in my meeting my proper life mate."

REVITALIZING AN EXISTING MARRIAGE

Sometimes we are in a marriage that has lasted for years and yet has lost its spark. The challenge may be to provide a catalyst so that vital, loving energy can be restimulated in the bond. Wishing can help us add new ingredients to the relationship that rekindle the connection.

Wishes to Bring New Vitality to an Existing Relationship:
"I want to easily find myself successfully initiating activities with my ———— (husband/wife/partner) that are fun for both of us"; "I want to easily find myself communicating with ———— (partner) in a way that is mutually empowering, exciting, and fun"; "I want to easily attract, recognize, and begin interacting with couples that are compatible and fun for both ———— (partner) and myself to socialize with"; "I want to easily find myself cooperating with ————'s desire for ———— (less/more time together) in a way that is also healthy and happy for me"; "I want total clarity regarding my marriage, leading me to take those actions that restore the fun for all concerned"; "I want to easily find myself being authentic with my husband/wife in a way that encourages happy friendship and deeper emotional rapport in our relationship."

Wishes to Add Closeness in an Existing Relationship:
"I want to easily find myself having those perceptions that empower me to love and trust ———— (my mate) in a healthy, happy

way"; "I want to easily find myself responding to ———— in a way that creates mutual emotional fulfillment"; "I want all tendencies to try to change my partner totally lifted from me"; "I want to easily find myself lovingly accepting my partner for who he/she is"; "I want to easily find myself saying the right words to ———— that encourage him/her to actively participate in building a full and happy relationship with me"; "I want to easily find myself listening to my husband in a way that successfully encourages him to ————"; "I want to easily find myself saying the right words to ———— that result in his/her going to marriage counseling with me"; "I want to easily attract, recognize, and begin working with the right marriage counselor that restores positive communication between ———— and me."

Wishes to Prompt New Responses in an Existing Relationship:
　　"I want to easily find myself communicating with ———— (partner) in a way that joyously results in him/her being totally supportive of me"; "I want to easily find myself joyously responding to ————'s needs in a way that does not discount my own needs"; "I want the habit of taking ———— for granted totally lifted from me"; "I want to easily find myself saying the right words to ———— that cause him (her) to cease taking me for granted and to appreciate me in positive, loving ways"; "I want all anger toward ———— totally lifted from me"; "In my relationship with ———— (partner), I want total accurate wisdom in seeing how to conduct myself in a way that is in my overall best interests"; "I want to easily find myself listening to and acting in accordance with my own inner wisdom when I am with ———— (partner)"; "I want to *stay conscious* in my relationship with ————, leading to my shifting the relationship into a mutually positive interaction."

Conjugal Sexual Relationship

Sometimes in a long-term marriage, the sexual intimacy may diminish for a variety of reasons: job, money concerns, children, etc. In this case, rekindling sexual interest and the desire for physical intimacy may be an important issue in creating a greater experience of bonding in the marriage.

Wishes to Rekindle Sexual Intimacy:

"I want right ideas to occur to me showing me how to expand my sexual relationship with ———— in a way that creates mutual pleasure and enjoyment"; "I want to easily find myself acting on right ideas that rekindle the happy romance between me and my mate"; "I want total clarity in seeing and following the correct path that results in a joyous, consistent, sex life with ————"; "I want to easily find myself stimulating ———— in a way that causes him/her to become sexually excited in a mutually empowering way"; "I want to easily find myself saying the right words to ———— that cause him/her to want to seduce me!"; "I want to easily find myself taking the initiative in my sexual relationship with ———— in a way that is mutually stimulating, exciting, and fun!"; "I want to easily find myself aware of ———— in a way that increases my ability to stimulate the sexual aspect of our relationship."

Bonding

Bonding is a byproduct of becoming vulnerable to another and opening our hearts on a very personal level. It can be among the most precious of experiences, requiring trust and commitment on the part of both partners not to hurt each other by damaging the bond.

Wishes to Encourage Trust and Bonding:

"I want to easily find myself saying those words to ———— that give him/her more confidence in our relationship and lead to a deeper bond of mutual trust, love, and support"; "I want to easily find myself consciously and successfully creating a happy relationship with deep, loving intimacy with ————"; "I want to easily find myself saying the right words to ———— that cause him/her to feel confident and supported by me"; "I want to easily find myself consciously and consistently spending moments being fully 'there' with and for ————"; "I want to easily find myself becoming open and vulnerable with ———— in a healthy, happy way"; "I want to be consciously, consistently aware of nurturing the precious loving bond between me and ————."

MEDITATION/PRAYER

Wishes to Enhance Meditation:

"I want to easily find myself approaching life from a position of being grounded and serene within myself"; "I want to easily find myself experiencing emotional reassurance and spiritual bliss through meditation"; "I want to easily find myself surrendering stress through a form of meditation that is correct for me"; "I want to easily find myself taking 'quiet time' to center myself for the day every morning, a minimum of ———— mornings a week, a minimum of ———— minutes each time"; "I want to easily find myself experiencing peace through meditation"; "I want to easily attract, recognize, and work with the right technique and meditation teacher for me"; "I want to consistently, consciously be in touch with high spiritual guidance during my meditations, leading to revelations that clearly and accurately guide my life to the happiest place!"

Wishes to Enhance Prayer:

"I want to easily find myself actively praying a minimum of ———— times a week"; "I want clarity in seeing how to pray to get the answers I want and need"; "I want to easily find myself feeling close and deeply connected to the positive Higher Power I am praying to"; "I want to easily find myself consistently spending a minimum of ———— days a week, a minimum of ———— minutes each day, in prayer or other self-renewing spiritual activity."

MONEY

Mastering the use of money in our lives requires knowing how to attract money, to spend it wisely, and to invest it in ways that ensure future financial security. If money does not seem to come to us, we may be inadvertently blocking the flow through subconscious resistance to our own abundance. Wishing can help to release these blocks, as well as bring us the wisdom to use money in ways that allow it to multiply.

BECOMING A MONEY MAGNET

The power to attract money largely depends on our maintaining a calm and confident attitude that money is entering our lives. Writing down wishes for more money on a Power Day focuses the mind in a way that can increase our receptivity to money being attracted to us.

Wishes to Attract Money to Us:

"I want the money I need for ———— (spiritual work/college/painting classes/a new car, etc.) to abundantly flow into my life"; "I want lots of money in a happy way"; "I want to easily find myself filled with right ideas resulting in my making money in a happy way"; "I want prosperity to enter into every area of my life"; "I want to easily find myself making choices around money that lead to financial prosperity for me"; "I want total clarity in seeing the correct path that will lead to my making money in a way that is in my overall best interests"; "I want to easily find myself taking those actions that will joyously increase my salary to a *minimum* of $——— each year"; "I want all resistance to attracting lots of money into my life totally lifted from me."

SPENDING HABITS

If our spending habits are out of control, no matter how much money is coming to us it will just pass "through" us. We may be attracting money into our lives, and still feel anxious because there is "not enough" for us to feel secure. If this is the case, we may be subconsciously wanting to keep ourselves feeling poor.

Wishes to Prevent Spending Habits from Undermining Our Prosperity:
"I want Divine Intervention to show me the right way to eliminate all financial debt"; "I want to easily find myself filled with total clarity around the issue of money, leading to my spending money in a way that is in my best interests"; "I want to easily find myself becoming debt free in a happy way"; "I want to easily find myself paying off all my credit cards"; "I want the habit of compulsive ——— (clothes/toys, etc.) shopping totally lifted from me"; "I want to easily find myself saving ———% of *every* paycheck"; "I want intelligence and awareness to consistently govern my spending of money."

LIFTING NEGATIVE THOUGHTS AROUND MONEY

Sometimes we may consciously want to have a great deal more money in our lives, but our negativity or anxiety around the issue of money may actually push money away from us. Wishing can lift these negative thoughts and allow the money we desire to arrive in our hands!

Wishes to Eliminate Negative Thinking Around Money:
"I want all financial worry lifted from me in a happy, healthy way"; "I want all fears of poverty totally lifted from me"; "I want all feelings of scarcity—the idea that if someone is getting more, I am getting less—easily lifted from me"; "I want all tendencies toward greed totally lifted from me"; "I want to have good, happy feelings about money"; "I want all self-sabotaging thoughts around money easily lifted from me"; "I want all feelings of inadequacy around money totally lifted from my consciousness"; "I want all thoughts that 'I don't know what to do with money' totally lifted from me"; "I want all fears about amassing tremendous amounts of money totally lifted from me."

GOOD INVESTMENTS

Making good investments assures financial ease and comfort in the future. Wishing can draw opportunities to us and give us the wisdom to discriminate and invest in ways that will be to our maximum advantage.

Wishes to Attract Good Investments:
"I want to easily find myself attracting, recognizing, and investing in opportunities that bring me huge financial returns"; "I want to eas-

ily attract, recognize, and purchase the right real estate investment for me that leads to substantial profits in a happy way"; "I want to easily find myself becoming CONSCIOUS around money in a way that leads to financial prosperity and security for me"; "I want Divine Intervention, giving me accurate insight about how to handle my money in a way that is to my maximum advantage"; "I want to be filled with accurate wisdom leading to my using and investing my money in ways that I am totally happy with over the long run"; "I want to easily find myself taking advantage of financial opportunities that are in my overall best interests"; "I want to easily attract, recognize, and begin working with a financial advisor who helps me become wealthy"; "I want Divine Intervention to give me the wisdom to use my resources in ways that create financial abundance."

ABUNDANCE CONSCIOUSNESS

The way we handle and distribute our money greatly influences our power to attract more. Money loves to circulate. When we allow it to freely pass through our lives—using and investing it wisely—money becomes an ally we can count on.

Wishes to Create a Consciousness of Abundance:

"I want clarity regarding money, leading to my handling it with wisdom and balance, and in ways that are in my best interests"; "I want all compulsions about money totally lifted from me"; "I want all resistance to receiving money easily lifted from me"; "I want to easily find myself graciously receiving money and gifts from others in a happy, healthy way"; "I want to easily find myself taking charge of my money in ways that result in joyous abundance and financial prosperity"; "I want to consciously and consistently enjoy my wealth"; "I want to easily find myself regularly tithing a minimum of ——% of my income to ———"; "I want clear thinking regarding money, leading to my handling my resources in ways that empower me to make changes when I am ready for them."

MOTHER (see Parents)

ORGANIZATION

Organizing time and space gives us a measure of control over our lives. We all have an inner sense of what we want to do during our lifetime—the talents we would like to explore and the experiences we would like to have. Conscious planning of how we use our time is the key to fulfilling our own purposes.

ORGANIZING OUR ENVIRONMENT

Our environment is either a constant help or hindrance to our progress in life. Regardless of our circumstance, an orderly, clean environment is an influence that furthers success and advancement. Wishing can help to remove subconscious blocks to creating order and aid us in surrounding ourselves with a supportive environment.

Wishes to Aid in Creating an Orderly Environment:
"I want Divine Intervention to enter into the situation of my apartment/house, showing me how to organize it in a way that will be fully supportive and empowering for me"; "I want to easily find myself restoring my home to order and cleanliness"; "I want all resistance to maintaining an orderly, clean home totally lifted from me"; "I want accurate discrimination, followed by action, in ridding myself of those

material possessions that are no longer useful to me"; "I want the habit of 'clutter' totally lifted from me."

LIFE PLANNING/ROUTINES

It's all too easy to get "swept up" in life—our energy consumed by repetitive daily responsibilities, old habit patterns, and the moment-to-moment needs of those around us. Years can go by without our consciously *using* time for those things that are important to us. Wishing can make us conscious of how we are spending our time, and support us in directing our lives in ways that are truly valuable to us.

Wishes to Increase Awareness of How I Use Time, and the Willingness to Make Changes That Are in My Best Interests:
"I want to easily find myself restoring balance in my life by establishing order and a healthy routine"; "I want to easily find myself filled with ideas about exactly the right routine for me"; "I want to easily find myself making time for those activities that are important to me"; "I want to easily find myself perceiving time in a way that allows me to use it to my best advantage"; "I want to easily find myself fully enjoying, appreciating, and making the best use of my time alone, and my time with ———— (spouse, child, etc.)"; "I want to easily find myself simplifying my life in a happy, healthy way"; "I want to easily find myself creating a healthy balance between my home life and my needs for spending time in the world."

LIFTING NEGATIVE THOUGHTS AROUND ORGANIZATION

Sometimes we may see the value of creating order in our lives, but feel a subconscious resistance that blocks us from taking the necessary steps. Wishing can help release these blocks and free us to take action that is in our best interests.

Wishes to Eliminate Blocks Around Organization:
"I want to easily attract, recognize, and begin working with people who totally support me in constructively taking care of all the details in my life"; "I want to easily find myself associating routine with freedom and happiness"; "I want all anxiety around organizing my life totally lifted from me"; "I want to find myself easily and consistently creating positive organization in every area of my life"; "I want to easily attract and begin working with books and/or classes that empower me to organize my life."

PAPERWORK

Disorganization in terms of paperwork—filing, taxes, magazines we've saved—can cause tension that prevents us from fully enjoying our lives. Wishing can help eliminate any subconscious obstructions to handling paperwork in a way that supports order.

Wishes to Promote Handling Paperwork Efficiently:
"I want to easily find myself organizing and completing all the necessary paperwork to present to ————, clearly and effortlessly"; "I want to easily find myself organizing my life in a way that leads to financial security and happiness"; "I want to easily find myself *discarding* all magazines and newspapers from the past"; "I want to easily find myself completing and filing my taxes on time"; "I want to easily find myself ———— (cleaning up my files and discarding outdated information, filing the unorganized paperwork in my environment, etc.)."

PARENTS

Our relationship with our parents is one of the most important in our lives. Regardless of any estrangement that may have resulted from miscommunication or misunderstanding, the opportunity to reestablish the closeness of the initial bond in that primary relationship is always present.

IMPROVING RELATIONSHIPS WITH OUR PARENTS

At any point, we can take charge in this primary relationship and begin to actively shift the negative patterns that we may be enacting with our parents. Love is a powerful force—turning on even a small light immediately dispels the darkness in a room. Through the power of consistently wishing for positive results, habitual negative patterns in the relationship begin to break up and dissolve.

Wishes to Support Healing the Relationship with Our Parents:
"I want to easily find myself saying the right words to my mother/father that evoke feelings of love, harmony, and mutual support"; "I want to easily find myself viewing my mother with love, understanding, and forgiveness"; "I want to easily find myself successfully taking the initiative in building a strong bond of friendship and mutual support with my parents"; "I want to easily find myself saying the right words to my father that empower him to support the decisions I make for my own life"; "I want to easily find myself saying the right words to my mother/father that evoke mutual feelings of equality and friendship"; "I want to easily find myself saying the right words to my mother that successfully facilitate her healing."

RELEASING THE PAST

All of us are learning and growing, and parents are seldom perfect. In a moment of frustration, the parent may behave in a way that results in psychological damage to the child. Or negative family patterns from one or both parents' families (or unpleasant family conditioning that one of the parents experienced as a child) may be unconsciously passed on to their child. Through the power of wishing, these psychological patterns that may be hindering us can be healed.

Wishes to Aid in Releasing the Past:
    "I want all damage from childhood experiences totally lifted from me"; "I want to be filled with total clarity, giving me right insights about how to become independent from my mother in a way that is healthy and happy for me"; "I want to easily find myself saying the right words to my mother that permit her to happily support my needs for personal space and an independent life"; "I want to easily find myself saying the right words to my ———— (mother/father) that prompt ———— (her/him) to respond to me with psychological support and unconditional love"; "I want to *cease* acting out my ———— (mother's/father's) behavior of ————."

PARTNERSHIPS (see Relationships)

PEACE OF MIND

These days it is easy for stress to become a chronic pattern, as we adapt to the fast pace of an age filled with new technology. It will help if we remember that, as we walk through our lives, we have a choice about where we focus our attention. If our minds are focused on the constant input of new information, even a trip to the supermarket can be exhausting. But if we consciously focus on staying in a peaceful place inwardly, we can emerge from the supermarket—and many of life's other side trips—with our serenity intact.

PEACE OF MIND THROUGH SURRENDER

Trusting that a Higher Power is ultimately in charge of our lives allows us to release the tension of trying to control outcomes. The path to serenity then becomes one of consciously surrendering upsets and problems to a Higher Power for resolution, and continuing to move forward, taking life "one day at a time."

Wishes to Encourage Surrendering Stress to a Higher Power:
"I want the habit of second-guessing myself totally lifted from me"; "I want the habit of second-guessing others totally lifted from me"; "I want inspired clarity in seeing life from a perspective that leads to understanding, forgiveness, and love"; "I want all the negative voices in my mind totally lifted from me"; "I want all feelings of anger toward———— totally lifted from me"; "I want to easily find myself allowing other people to be negative without taking it personally"; "I want to easily find myself surrendering negative situations to a Higher Power for protection and resolution."

PEACE OF MIND THROUGH TAKING CHARGE OF YOUR THOUGHTS

Conscious alchemy—the blending of two energies to create a third thing—is another path to peace of mind. The power of wishing can shift habitual negative thinking into more positive directions.

Wishes to Encourage Positive Thought Patterns:

"I want all anxiety around ———— transformed into a powerful force of healing energy"; "I want to easily find myself consciously recognizing that life loves me"; "I want to easily find myself actively participating in creating my world the way I want it to be"; "I want to consciously and consistently be aware of the presence of a positive Higher Power moving in every area of my life"; "I want all fear of 'having something taken away' totally lifted from me."

PETS

Wishes to Enhance Our Relationship with Our Pets:

"I want to easily find myself doing the right things to successfully heal my ———— (horse's) injury/illness"; "I want to easily find myself successfully training my dog to ————"; "I want to easily find myself organizing my life in a way that my home and pets are cared for and that also gives me freedom"; "I want to easily attract, recognize, and begin working with the right person to take care of my ———— (dogs/cats)"; "I want to easily attract, recognize, and purchase the right pet for me that creates a deep sense of love and happiness in my life"; "I want to easily begin to understand situations from my animal companion's point of view, resulting in my increasing ability to be sensitive to his/her needs, and generally enhancing the quality of our relationship."

PHOBIAS *(see Fear)*

PLAY *(see Fun)*

PRAYER *(see Meditation / Prayer)*

PROCRASTINATION *(see Discipline)*

PROFESSION *(see Work)*

RELATIONSHIPS

It is fairly easy to feel serene when we are by ourselves; it is when we relate to others that we often face the challenge of maintaining our inner harmony. To fully enjoy our relationships with others, there may be specific issues to work with at different stages of our lives.

PARTNERSHIPS

Partnership is a relationship where two or more people work together to attain a common goal. For success, it is necessary to attract the right person (or people) to partner with, and then to establish positive patterns of relating that lead to happiness within the relationship, as well as a successful worldly outcome.

Wishes to Aid in Forming Positive Partnerships:
"I want to easily attract, recognize, and begin working with the right business partner for me that will result in happy mutual abundance!"; "I want to intuitively recognize those people who have

integrity, whom I will enjoy working with, and with whom I will make lots of money"; "I want to easily attract and begin working with the right partner to manifest my dream of ————— in a way that creates a win-win situation for everyone concerned"; "I want to easily find myself saying the right words to ————— that evoke cooperation and mutual support in our partnership"; "I want to easily find my best qualities emerging in my partnership with —————"; "I want to easily find myself saying the right words to ————— that allow our partnership to be productive, cooperative, brilliant, and fun."

RELEASING THE PAST

To create happy relationships in the present, sometimes it is beneficial to work on releasing bad memories of hurtful experiences from our past. As the burden of the past is lifted, we are free to create what we truly want to experience.

Wishes to Encourage Releasing the Past:
"I want to easily find myself releasing all blocks resulting from past unhappy relationships"; "I want negative beliefs about relationships easily lifted from me"; "I want any inner resistance to having happy relationships totally lifted from me"; "I want all bad memories about past relationships totally lifted from me"; "I want all self-limiting fears in relationships easily lifted from me."

BUILDING POSITIVE PATTERNS OF RELATING

Successful relating has to do with establishing habits of positive approaches and responses. Shifting our attitude toward relationships changes the outcome we will experience.

Wishes to Prompt Positive Patterns of Relating:

"I want to experience a feeling of healthy, happy self-confidence in all my relationships"; "I want to easily find myself empathetically receptive to —————— (name) and aware of his/her needs in a nurturing and supportive way"; "I want to easily find my heart opening to the prospect of a happy relationship with ——————"; "I want to easily find myself viewing others in a way that creates healthy, happy feelings of unconditional love"; "I want to easily find myself involved in constructive relationships with others"; "I want to easily find myself attuned to other people's needs and desires before speaking, so that my words reinforce positive, win-win energy"; "I want to easily find myself consciously approaching relationships and life from the perspective of lightheartedness and mutual enjoyment"; "I want to approach relationships that carry emotional baggage in a fresh, honest, healing way"; "I want to easily find myself saying the right words to —————— that further his/her feeling loved by me."

MAINTAINING HEALTHY BOUNDARIES

The element of carelessness enters relationships when we forget to be aware of our boundaries or respect the other person's boundaries. By remaining conscious of the fact that relationships are based on a true exchange of energies between the individuals involved, we are more likely to maintain our boundaries and approach others without unconscious expectations.

Wishes to Increase Awareness of Healthy Boundaries:

"I want to easily find myself maintaining moral and ethical boundaries that cause me to feel good about myself"; "I want to easily find myself aware of—and communicating—my boundaries to others"; "I want to easily find myself aware—and supportive—of the boundaries of others"; "I want to easily find myself accurately weighing situations, and then initiating action in a way that is accepted by others"; "I want to easily find myself being aware of ———'s drama, without being swept up in it"; "I want to easily find myself being aware of ———'s emotional state before speaking"; "I want to be filled with right ideas showing me the way to bring my relationship with ——— to closure."

SPECIFIC RELATIONSHIPS

Sometimes there are specific relationships in our lives where we want to experience a positive shift.

Wishes to Promote Change in Specific Relationships:
"I want to be totally centered, in a positive way, when I am with ———, resulting in constructive changes in our relationship"; "I want to easily find myself filled with right ideas and saying the right words that allow healing in my relationship with ———"; "I want to easily find myself saying the right words to ——— that lovingly help her become aware of her counterproductive behavior"; "I want to easily attract, recognize, and begin healthy, happy relationships with my spiritual family"; "I want to easily find myself sending ——— positive thoughts and energy that support ——— in getting a positive new direction for his (her) life"; "I want to easily find myself saying the right words to ——— that allow him (her) to trust me"; "I want to easily find myself saying the right words to ——— that encourage him to openly, joyfully communicate with me"; "I want to easily find myself free of the desire to change ——— (name)."

REPUTATION *(see Social Status)*

ROMANCE

Different stages and situations in our lives may require work in very distinct areas in order to experience romantic satisfaction. For example, the issue may be attracting a new romantic partner, changing our attitudes so that romance can flourish, or rekindling romance in an existing relationship.

SEEKING A NEW ROMANCE

People who are single and not currently involved in a satisfying love relationship may desire someone new in their lives with whom they can experience the joys of romance.

Wishes to Attract a New Romantic Partner:
"I want to easily attract, recognize, and find myself dating the right ———— (woman/man) with whom I share romantic energy and have happy, healthy experiences"; "I want to begin dating ———— (men/women) who are ———— (secure, solid, confident within themselves, etc.)"; "I want to easily follow information that leads me to go to the place where I meet the ———— (woman/man) of my dreams"; "I want to fall in love in a happy, healthy way"; "I want to experience a happy, healthy romantic relationship that is comfortable, enduring, and satisfying for both myself and my partner"; "I want to easily attract, recognize, and begin a happy, healthy romantic relationship with one of my positive soul mates"; "I want to easily attract, recognize, and begin a happy, healthy romantic relationship with a

———— (man/woman) I am at ease with, who's fun, who wants to grow, and with whom I share similar interests."

Wishes to Enhance Personal Attractiveness:
"I want to easily find myself receptive to experiencing a happy, healthy romance in my life"; "I want to easily find myself feeling comfortable with (women/men), approaching even the most desirable with the energy of friendship and genuine interest in them as individuals"; "I want lots of charisma in my relationships with ———— (men/women), leading to happy, healthy experiences"; "I want to easily find myself saying the right things that make me romantically attractive to (men/women) in a happy, healthy way"; "I want to enjoy the energy of flirtation in an easy, fun way"; "I want to easily find myself accepting love from others and from life in a healthy, happy way"; "I want to easily find myself handling romance in a way that is in my overall best interests"; "I want to be fully aware of the opportunities for romance in my life, and easily find myself graciously accepting those that are happy, healthy, and nurturing."

HEALING INNER RESISTANCE

Sometimes the barrier to romance is actually our own inner resistance to believing that it is truly possible for us. In this case, the first challenge is to heal this subconscious resistance so that we can attract the happiness and fulfillment we seek.

Wishes to Help Heal Inner Resistance to Romance:
"I want total clarity regarding the area of romantic attraction, leading to a healing of any unconscious resistance to experiencing personal love"; "I want to easily release all obstructions to my experiencing the joy and playfulness of romance"; "I want all resistance to being happy in a romantic relationship totally lifted from me"; "I want all

self-defeating tension and fear around experiencing happiness in romance totally lifted from me"; "I want all self-sabotaging patterns in
romantic relationships totally lifted from me"; "I want all resistance to
experiencing the healing of a healthy, happy romantic relationship in
my life totally lifted from me"; "I want to be willing to be open to creating a successful romantic relationship that brings me joy."

INCREASING SELF-CONFIDENCE IN ROMANCE

It may be that the most important work initially will focus on feeling better about ourselves and creating more self-confidence in approaching a romantic relationship.

Wishes to Increase Self-Confidence:
"I want to easily find myself filled with healthy self-confidence relative to the arena of dating"; "I want to be filled with lots of self-
confidence in approaching those (women/men) that I feel attracted
to, and saying the right words that will easily initiate a conversation";
"I want to be filled with healthy self-confidence about how attractive
I am!"; "I want to easily find myself filled with right ideas about how
to successfully court and win the (lady/man) I want"; "I want to be
filled with ease in romantic relationships, conversing naturally, and
genuinely taking an interest in the other person and getting to know
them."

DEVELOPING SUCCESSFUL PATTERNS OF ROMANTIC RELATING

When someone with whom there is the potential for a healthy romantic relationship enters our lives, sometimes personality habits that
repel, rather than attract, the other person begin to express themselves. Developing successful patterns of relating allows for the possibility of a positive outcome when a romantic opportunity arises.

Wishes to Develop Positive Patterns of Relating in Romance:

"I want total clarity in romance, empowering me to discriminate which issues are whose"; "I want to easily find myself responding to romantic attraction by taking the relationship slowly, allowing the process of getting to know one another to flourish"; "In developing a romance, I want to easily find myself giving the relationship quality time and helping to create a sense of joy and adventure"; "I want to easily find myself successfully adding the sexual component to romance when the time is right and I feel comfortable"; "I want to easily find myself really getting to know those I am attracted to, and communicating my honest feelings before becoming romantically involved with them"; "I want the habit of 'passive dating behavior' totally lifted from me."

REKINDLING ROMANCE IN AN EXISTING RELATIONSHIP

Sometimes we find ourselves in an ongoing relationship that is satisfying in many ways, but lacks the romantic spark we would like for maximum enjoyment. In this case, one of the following wishes may help to renew a sense of romance.

Wishes to Help Rekindle Romance:

"I want all inner resistance to experiencing happiness and romance in my relationship with ———— easily lifted from me"; "I want to easily find myself saying the right words to ———— that evoke feelings of love in our relationship"; "I want total clarity in my relationship with ————, leading to my taking steps that result in greater happiness and love between us"; "I want to easily find myself communicating with my romantic partner in a way that creates mutual understanding, accord, and happy cooperation"; "I want to easily find myself interacting with my romantic partner in a way that keeps the love between us alive, happy, and fun!"; "I want to easily find myself successfully adding the ingredient of romance to my relationship with ————."

SCHOOL

Wishes to Successfully Locate and Enroll in a New School:

"I want clear insight in seeing which school/university has the best program for me"; "I want to easily find myself taking those steps that lead to my being accepted into the ———— program at ———— (school)"; "I want total clarity in seeing and attending that school that is in my best overall interests"; "I want to easily attract and successfully gain those monies from scholarships that will bring ease to my process of going to school"; "I want to easily find myself recognizing and learning from those teachers who will give me the education I need to do my life's work."

Wishes to Succeed at a Current School:

"I want the habit of procrastinating with my homework easily lifted from me"; "I want total mental clarity in my ———— class, leading to my easily grasping and retaining the subject matter"; "I want all emotional resistance to understanding and completing my schoolwork easily lifted from me"; "I want to easily find myself studying in exactly the right way that leads to my getting high grades in my ———— class"; "While in school, I want to easily find myself filled with mental clarity leading to successfully passing tests with a minimum of stress"; "I want to easily find myself feeling comfortable and at ease with my schoolmates"; "I want to attract and establish a good friendship with a schoolmate for fun and mutual support"; "I want to easily find myself doing those things that lead to my being successful and happy at school"; "I want to easily find myself studying in the right way that leads to my getting a *minimum* grade of ———— on my tests."

SECURITY *(see Self-Confidence)*

SELF-CONFIDENCE

Wishes to Free Us from Insecurity:

"I want all thoughts and feelings of being ———— (old, matronly, powerless, unattractive, etc.) totally lifted from me"; "I want to easily find myself filled with a happy, healthy sense of security"; "I want all feelings of insecurity totally lifted from me"; "I want all self-consciousness about ———— totally lifted from me"; "I want the crippling fear of being hurt totally lifted from me."

Wishes to Promote Self-Confidence:

"I want to easily find myself experiencing a solid sense of healthy self-confidence and self-worth in all life situations"; "I want to easily find myself asking for things in a way that empowers other people to give me what I need and gives me confidence in myself"; "I want to easily find myself filled with feelings of self-confidence and competency"; "I want to easily find myself staying present in the here and now in a way that increases my self-assurance and self-confidence"; "I want to feel happy and self-confident at ———— (work/school/dating/my bridge group, etc.)"; "I want to easily find myself taking those risks that result in my consciously accepting my power"; "I want to easily find myself taking those actions that lead to a solid sense of security and self-confidence in all areas of my life."

SELF-CONTROL *(see Discipline)*

SELF-ESTEEM

RELEASING SELF-NEGATING THOUGHTS

Sometimes the key to healthy self-esteem can simply be letting go of the habit of putting ourselves down. Self-negating thoughts can just keep running through our minds, without our even being aware of how much damage they are doing. Wishing can help to remove dark thoughts from our consciousness, opening the way for happier experiences coming into our lives.

Wishes to Release Self-Negating Thoughts:
"I want the habit of self-judgment totally lifted from me"; "I want all feelings of worthlessness easily lifted from me"; "I want all ideas that I am 'unlovable' totally lifted from me"; "I want the idea that 'death is better than life' totally lifted from me"; "I want all thoughts of being a 'bad person' totally lifted from me"; "I want to easily find myself releasing the habit of putting myself down"; "I want all self-critical thoughts totally lifted from me."

BUILDING SELF-ESTEEM AND SELF-RESPECT

Without a strong and healthy sense of self—seeing ourselves as a good person doing the very best we can—it can be difficult to make successful progress toward our goals. Wishing can increase positive thoughts about ourselves that begin to bolster self-esteem and self-respect.

Wishes to Promote a Positive Self-Image:

"I want to easily find myself surrendering to a new, empowering, positive image of myself"; "I want to easily find myself consistently validating myself in a healthy, happy way"; "I want to easily find myself treating my body with care, respect, and love"; "I want to easily find myself taking those actions that cause me to feel good about myself"; "I want to easily find myself placing a high value on my own time and energy"; "I want to easily find myself embracing spiritual values that increase self-esteem and peace in my life"; "I want to easily find myself interacting with others in a way that enhances my self-respect."

INCREASING SELF-WORTH

If, on an unconscious level, we don't feel worthy of receiving life's bounty, we may work very hard to earn rewards and then at the last minute sabotage ourselves so that the prize passes us by. Self-worth is a byproduct of validating ourselves—noticing what is "right," worthy, and good about ourselves.

Wishes to Promote a Sense of Self-Worth:

"I want total clarity in seeing what is valuable to me"; "I want to easily find myself being true to those values that give me a sense of self-worth"; "I want to easily find myself taking actions that lead to a solid sense of my own self-worth"; "I want to easily find myself appreciating and valuing myself"; "I want to easily find myself experiencing a healthy, happy sense of self-worth in all life situations"; "I want to easily find myself noticing and appreciating the beauty and goodness within me."

SELF-RESPECT *(see Self-Esteem)*

SELF-WORTH *(see Self-Esteem)*

SEX

Building a Satisfying Sexual Relationship

We cannot expect to have a fully satisfying sexual relationship that lasts over the years without putting forth the effort to help create it. Wishing can lift internal blocks, opening the way for us to take action to successfully maintain such a relationship.

Wishes to Enhance Sexual Receptivity:

"I want to easily find myself fully receptive to ————'s initiating sexual contact in ways that create a happy, satisfying romantic relationship for both of us"; "I want to easily find myself totally aware and cooperating with the positive flow of oneness between ———— and myself"; "I want to experience increased fun, joy, and pleasure in my sexual relationship with ————"; "I want all barriers to my fully enjoying sexual pleasure with ———— joyously lifted from me"; "I want to easily find myself successfully communicating and letting ———— know what pleases me sexually, leading to enhanced mutual pleasure and joy"; "I want the pressure of 'goals' totally lifted from me in sexual interaction, leading to my fully enjoying the pleasure of sensual intimacy by being present in the moment."

Wishes to Support Successful Sexual Initiation:

"I want to easily find myself pleasing my partner in ways that enhance our love and sexual intimacy"; "I want to easily find myself initiating sexually in a way that is joyously received and enjoyed by my partner"; "I want to easily find myself successfully creating private, satisfying romantic time with ———— at least ———— times a week"; "I want to easily find myself touching ———— sexually in ways to which (he/she) is most receptive"; "I want to easily find myself saying the right words to ———— that cause (her/him) to share my interest in us building a sensual, satisfying sex life"; "I want to easily find myself discovering from my partner sexual secrets that are really exciting for (him/her)."

RELEASING SEXUAL FEARS

Sometimes subconscious fears surrounding sex keep us from fully experiencing the pleasure and closeness that is possible with our partner. Wishing is an incredibly potent technique for releasing these hidden anxieties.

Wishes to Help in Releasing Sexual Fears:
"I want all sexual fears stemming from early abuse easily lifted from me"; "I want to easily find myself communicating my fears surrounding sex to my partner in a way that evokes support and a willingness to work together for successful intimacy"; "I want to easily find my consciousness joyously staying in my body and enjoying the 'now' moment during sexual intimacy"; "I want the habit of invalidating or suppressing my sexual feelings easily lifted from me"; "I want all fears of rejection around sex totally lifted from me"; "I want all fears around sexuality totally lifted from me"; "I want to easily attract, recognize, and begin working with those healers who facilitate my successfully releasing sexual fears"; "I want all self-defeating inhibitions surrounding sex easily lifted from me"; "I want all fears of ———— (frigidity/impotence) totally lifted from me"; "I want to easily find myself trusting and following the joy of my own sexual impulses."

INCREASING SEXUAL ATTRACTIVENESS

Positive feedback from the males or females we want to attract definitely enhances self-confidence in this area! Attractiveness is an energy that can be greatly enhanced through the power of wishing.

Wishes to Enhance Sexual Attractiveness:
"I want lots of healthy, happy charisma in my relationships with (men/women)"; "I want to easily find myself saying the right words to ————— that rekindle his sexual desire for me in a mutually healthy, happy way"; "I want to easily find myself aware of my own beauty"; "I want to easily find myself radiating the energy that is pleasing to those I want to attract"; "I want to easily find myself dressing in a way that is appealing to the mate I want to attract"; "I want all behaviors that repel others totally lifted from me."

SIBLINGS

Wishes to Improve Relationships with Brothers and Sisters:
"I want a total healing to occur in my relationship with my brother, —————"; "I want to easily find myself spending quality time with ————— so that we can get to know one another better"; "I want to easily find myself relating to ————— in a way that builds mutual trust, support, and love"; "I want all negative memories associated with ————— totally lifted from me"; "I want to easily find myself saying the right words to ————— that open the door to a positive rebuilding of our relationship"; "I want to easily find myself joyfully writing a letter to my sister that creates mutual understanding, support, and love"; "I want to easily find myself saying the right words to ————— that lead to him joyously supporting me in a way that truly meets my needs."

SISTERS *(see Siblings)*

SLEEP

Wishes to Help Heal Insomnia:

"I want to easily find myself connected with a sense of reassurance at night so that I go to bed peacefully, feeling unconditional love and healthy surrender"; "I want all symptoms of insomnia totally lifted from me"; "I want all disturbing dreams totally lifted from me"; "I want all connections to disturbing, negative astral fields during sleep totally lifted from me"; "When my head touches the pillow each night, I want to easily find my entire body and mind relaxing into a healthy sleep within the first half hour"; "I want to easily find myself sleeping through an ————— (8) hour night"; "At night, I want to easily find myself trusting my Angels to take care of me and protect me"; "I want all anxieties that keep me from sleeping peacefully through the night easily lifted from me."

Wishes to Help Eliminate Excessive Sleeping:

"I want all tendencies to escapism through excessive sleeping totally lifted from me"; "I want to easily find my body and mind fully restored and refreshed after ————— hours' sleep each night"; "I want to easily find myself rising and energetically beginning my day after ————— hours' sleep."

Wishes to Aid in Establishing Healthy Sleep Patterns:

"I want to easily find myself consistently recharged and refreshed after a full, healthy night's sleep"; "I want to easily find myself establishing regular, healthy sleep patterns"; "I want to easily find myself joyously getting out of bed at ————— A.M., five days a week, after a restful night's sleep"; "I want to easily find myself going to bed each night no later than ———— (P.M./A.M.)."

SOCIAL STATUS

Wishes to Enhance Status:

"I want to easily find myself making a contribution in my current position that I am proud of"; "I want to easily find myself constructively behaving in ways that increase my status in the eyes of others and myself"; "I want to cease the habit of judging myself as higher or lower than others"; "I want to fully appreciate myself and the status I have achieved thus far in my life."

Wishes to Improve Reputation:

"I want to consistently develop my character in a way that results in an honorable reputation"; "I want to easily find myself demonstrating the competency that improves my reputation"; "I want all anxiety surrounding my reputation totally lifted from me"; "I want to easily find myself following right ideas for improving my reputation in a way that is happy for me"; "I want to easily find myself being of service to others in a way that creates a model reputation."

SPIRITUAL HELP

Spiritual help can come to us in many forms. Sometimes it comes through another person, including help from counselors, mentors, and spiritual masters. Sometimes it comes through a direct, intuitive link with our Higher Power.

COUNSELING

Sometimes it becomes necessary to better understand our "inner wiring" in order to heal personality patterns that block us from experiencing the things in life that we desire. At such times we may seek the help of a counselor or mentor, and it is crucial to attract someone who understands us and can truly help us gain healing and harmony.

Wishes to Help Attract an Appropriate Counselor/Mentor:
"I want to easily attract, recognize, and begin working with the right ——— (counselor/mentor) for me who helps me overcome my problem of ———"; "I want clarity, empowering me to get the most out of my counseling experiences"; "I want to easily attract, recognize, and begin working with the right mentor for me who successfully guides me into ———"; "I want to easily attract, recognize, and begin working with the right spiritual channel who gives me accurate information from my Guides about the path I now need to take in my life"; "I want to easily find myself recognizing the right mentor for me to learn from and actualize my own completion."

SPIRITUAL GUIDANCE

At times we may want spiritual help, through guidance or intuition, to show us the next step to take that will be best for us. In this case, we may seek a closer conscious connection with our Guides, Angels, or other specific spiritual concepts or entities that are personally meaningful for us.

Wishes to Strengthen Our Ability to Receive Spiritual Guidance:
"I want to easily find myself being fully receptive to my Guides leading me to ——— (a happy love relationship/the right job for me, etc.)"; "I want to easily find myself fully tuned in to Truth in a way

that adds joy and clarity to every area of my life"; "I want to easily find myself recognizing the Divine Order in a way that empowers me to act on my desires constructively"; "I want to easily find myself consciously connected to my Angels and being positively guided by their insights"; "Instead of holding back, I want to easily find myself expressing what my intuition tells me is the right thing to say"; "I want a strong connection with my Spiritual Guides, easily seeing the next step to take on my own path."

SPIRITUAL AWARENESS

We may feel the desire to become more cooperative with the spiritual flow that is operating in our lives. In this case, we may want to strengthen our awareness of being "the Witness"—the objective observer of the opportunities for growth that continually come into our life.

Wishes to Enhance Our Experience of "the Witness":
"I want to easily find myself aware of 'right timing,' alerting me to take maximum advantage of the opportunities life brings to me"; "I want to consciously and consistently be aware of the Flow of Life bringing me what I need, moment by moment, to make my life complete"; "I want to easily find myself turning to my Angels for positive suggestions and insights about my life"; "I want conscious clarity regarding every area of my life"; "I want to clearly understand and express my soul's true purpose"; "I want to easily find myself experiencing feelings of awe in an empowering way."

SPIRITUAL INTERVENTION

In some areas of our lives we may feel helpless to create success on our own, and need to "call on our Angels" for an extra boost! Wishing can help us evoke the support of positive spiritual forces to help us.

Wishes to Evoke Positive Spiritual Intervention:

"I want Divine Intervention to fill me with right ideas, leading me to trust that life is naturally unfolding to my advantage"; "I want my Higher Power to enter into the situation of ———— (my sobriety), making it easier for me to ———— (stay sober one day at a time)"; "I want to easily find myself consciously and consistently relying on a Higher Power that successfully lifts me out of feelings of limitation"; "I want to easily find myself 'letting go and letting God'—releasing my problems to a Higher Power"; "I want Divine Guidance to intervene in the ———— situation, magically showing me how to create the best outcome"; "I want to easily find myself ACTING on the correct ———— (relationship/job/financial, etc.) guidance my Guides and Angels are giving me."

STRESS

The issue of stress is a huge factor in twenty-first-century daily living. New technologies fill the air with a bombardment of electromagnetic fields, and combine with widespread pollution to clog the atmosphere. These and other environmental and personal factors, along with a kind of "speeding up" of time, create a need for us to cope with the constant stress in our lives. However, if handled correctly, stress can actually be a springboard propelling us to go to a higher, more peaceful place of consciousness in our daily lives.

Wishes to Help Us Constructively Cope with Stress:

"I want all stress totally lifted from me"; "I want the habit of taking life too seriously totally lifted from me"; "I want all tendencies to take myself too seriously totally lifted from me"; "I want to easily find myself joyously handling the ———— situation without stress"; "I want to easily find myself involved in meditation practices that allow me to walk through my life without stress"; "I want to easily attract those spiritual ways of viewing life that empower me to rise above stress"; "I want to easily find myself responding to stress by ———— (walking/going on my treadmill, etc.)"; "I want to easily find myself embracing spiritual values that enhance peace in my life."

SUCCESS

PROGRAMMING FOR SUCCESS

If our minds are creatively focused on success, accomplishment will come to us easily and repeatedly. Sometimes the first step is clearing any thoughts or feelings that resist success so that we are fully open to receive it.

Wishes to Help Program Our Minds for Success:
"I want my mind to automatically think in terms of creating success in every situation"; "I want to easily find myself taking charge in every area of my life"; "I want to feel comfortable about taking responsibility for creating success in the area of ————"; "I want total clarity in setting appropriate goals in those areas of my life in which I seek success"; "I want total clarity leading me to create a success in the area of ————"; "I want to easily find myself joyfully embracing the aim of creating success in every area of my life."

Wishes to Be Open for New, Success-Producing Ideas:
"I want the habit of resisting new ideas totally lifted from me"; "I want to be filled with new, innovative ideas for successfully making my

dreams come true"; "I want to easily find myself fully receptive to all of my wishes coming true"; "I want all feelings of inadequacy totally lifted from me"; "I want all fears of success totally lifted from me"; "I want all fear of failure totally lifted from me."

FOLLOWING UP IDEAS WITH ACTION

The desire for success must be followed by appropriate action in order to create the results we are seeking. Wishing can help us initiate the actions that lead to success.

Wishes to Promote Action Leading to Success:
"I want to easily find myself taking those actions that lead to success in the area of —————"; "I want to easily find myself taking action to get what I want in a healthy, happy way"; "I want to easily find myself extending myself and successfully creating results in my life that make me happy"; "I want to easily find myself accomplishing goals that are important to me"; "I want to easily find myself taking action in alignment with the prompting of my inner being"; "I want to easily find myself taking appropriate ACTION in making my dreams come true!"; "I want to easily find myself handling the pressures of success in a positive way."

USING OPPORTUNITY

Success is dependent upon recognizing opportunities that, if responded to appropriately, will allow the results we seek to manifest. For example, if we are focused on buying a home, people around us may begin mentioning houses that are for sale, people who are moving, etc. If we are seeking an assistant, people who could fill that role may begin coming into our lives. RECOGNIZING—and acting on—

opportunities when they present themselves is one of the important keys to success.

Wishes to Increase Our Awareness of Appropriate Opportunities:

"I want to easily find myself aware of 'right timing,' taking advantage of the opportunities life brings me as they arise"; "I want to successfully realize my goals by taking one step at a time, not rushing to the next step until the step in front of me has been taken"; "I want to easily find myself conscious in daily life situations, leading to managing my life successfully"; "I want to easily attract, recognize, and begin working with those people who will help me successfully reach my goals"; "I want to easily find myself focusing on 'what can I *do*' rather than 'what can I get'"; "I want total clarity, leading me to take advantage of appropriate opportunities in a way that is happy for all concerned."

THOUGHTS

The mind has enormous power to create the external circumstances of our lives by focusing on positive or negative thoughts. When we hold positive thoughts, we automatically see the pathways that will create success in the areas that are important to us. If we allow negative thoughts to clog our minds, we look for the "down side" and inadvertently create circumstances that make us sad or disappointed. Wishing can help discipline the mind to focus only on positive thoughts that actually attract the things in life that we want and need.

Wishes to Discard Negative Thinking:

"I want all feelings of being 'trapped' totally lifted from me"; "I want all resentment totally lifted from me"; "I want all thoughts that diminish me or others totally lifted from me"; "I want the habit of blaming myself replaced by seeing the value of the lessons I have learned from my experiences"; "I want all negative thoughts totally lifted from me"; "I want all thoughts of ———— totally lifted from me"; "I want all indecision totally lifted from me"; "I want the habit of compulsive thinking totally lifted from me."

Wishes to Enhance Positive Thinking:

"I want true, constructive intelligence to enter every area of my life"; "I want to easily find myself accepting the mind-set of humility in a healthy, happy way"; "I want to easily find myself viewing life in a way that encourages me to move in positive directions"; "I want to easily find myself using my mind to my advantage in a happy, relaxed way"; "I want to easily find myself adopting a positive mind-set to watch, observe, and then take appropriate action"; "I want to consciously, consistently be aware that everything that occurs in my life is somehow working toward my highest good"; "I want to easily find myself seeing the silver lining behind the clouds that occur in my life"; "When unexpected changes occur, I want to easily find myself seeing the hidden opportunity for advancement"; "I want to easily find myself holding only positive thoughts about ————."

TRAVEL

Wishes to Attract Travel Experiences:

"I want to easily find myself enjoying travel for business needs, personal recreation, and spiritual renewal"; "I want to easily find myself taking a great, healing vacation at a price I can afford"; "I want to find myself joyfully taking my dream vacation in a way I can afford"; "I want to easily find myself taking a trip to —————— at a price I can easily afford."

TRUST

Trust can make a huge difference in how we view—and deal with—the upsetting events in our lives. If we have a basic sense of trust that a higher spiritual power is ultimately in charge, then we can view all events, no matter how painful they may be, as somehow working to our ultimate good. This allows our responses to change to become less resistant and therefore less distressful. Cultivating trust in a Higher Power can be a potent way to reduce personal suffering.

Wishes to Enhance Optimism and Trust:
"I want to easily find myself transforming anxiety into faith in positive outcomes"; "I want to easily find myself consciously and consistently trusting my inner spirit and intuition"; "I want all self-doubt easily lifted from me"; "I want to accurately see which people and situations in my life I can trust to support me"; "I want to easily find myself trusting that every situation in my life will somehow work out to my advantage"; "I want to easily find myself consistently remembering that 'God is in charge' and that everything that happens is somehow working to my highest good."

VITALITY

Wishes to Enhance Vitality:

"I want to easily find myself filled with a vital sense of enjoying life!"; "I want to consistently experience vitality and high energy in every area of my life"; "I want to easily find myself making decisions that lead to increased vitality, excitement, and happiness in my life"; "I want to easily find myself channeling my creative energies into healthy directions that lead to increased vitality and joy"; "I want to easily keep my fire and passion burning, fueling everything I do in a steady, dependable way."

WEIGHT LOSS (also see Exercise)

In achieving your optimum weight, different wishes may be appropriate at different stages of the process. As external goals are achieved (losing weight and changing eating and exercise habits), accepting and incorporating a new self-image on an inner level must also be addressed for a full healing to occur. At any given time, wishes from one or more of these categories may apply and can be used at the same time.

ACHIEVING YOUR DESIRED WEIGHT

Achieving your desired body weight certainly goes hand in hand with lifting inner resistance and changing eating habits and exercise habits, so repeating wishes stating the desired result throughout the process is beneficial.

Wishes to Help Achieve Your Desired Weight:

"I want to easily establish my weight at ———— pounds in a healthy way that is beautifying for my body"; "I want to be filled with accurate, positive thinking regarding my weight-loss program, leading to easily achieving successful results"; "I want to easily find myself establishing and maintaining my weight at a level that makes me feel good about myself: light, free, and beautiful!"; "I want to easily find myself taking those steps that result in a strong, slender, toned, healthy body"; "I want to easily find myself taking those steps that result in a muscular, trim, and healthy body"; "I want the connection between anxiety and eating totally lifted from me"; "I want to easily find myself responding to stress by breathing deeply, or taking a walk to relieve the tension."

DROPPING ADDICTIONS

One of the biggest obstacles to achieving your desired weight may be an addiction to foods that are counterproductive to having a slim body (sweets, high-fat, starchy, or salty foods). In this case, lifting the addiction to that type of food is an essential step in achieving and maintaining your goal.

Wishes to Drop Addictions:

"I want all tendencies to overeating totally lifted from me"; "I want the habit of binge eating totally lifted from me"; "I want all attraction to sugar totally lifted from me"; "I want the addiction to ———— (type of food) totally lifted from me"; "I want all cravings for fatty, greasy foods totally lifted from me"; "I want the habit of eating at night totally lifted from me"; "When I am eating, I want to easily find myself *fully conscious* of what I am doing and the foods I am eating."

DROPPING RESISTANCE

Sometimes psychological fears can prevent us from achieving our weight-loss goals: fear of being too attractive to the opposite sex; of having to cope with sexual advances; of being expected to reach things that are not important to us. In this case, releasing our inner resistance to weight loss may be the first practical step.

Wishes to Release Resistance:
"I want to easily find myself releasing all inner resistance to losing weight"; "I want all resistance to exercise and being physically trim and fit totally lifted from me"; "I want all resistance to following my diet plan totally lifted from me"; "I want to easily find myself embracing new eating habits that support a healthy body and a positive self-image"; "I want all fears of restoring my body to a slim and beautiful form totally lifted from me"; "I want to easily find myself embracing the idea of my enhanced level of manipulation when I am slim, knowing that I will use this gift in a positive way."

DEVELOPING AN ATTRACTION TO HEALTHY FOODS

The key to maintaining a slim body without constant dieting or exercise is to eat low-calorie, low-fat foods. However, if we are not attracted to these foods, it's all too easy to slip back to our old eating habits. So making a change in our subconscious regarding the foods we are attracted to can go a long way toward helping to maintain our ideal weight.

Wishes to Develop Attractions to Healthy Foods:
"I want to easily find myself attracted to and consuming only those foods that are naturally low calorie, low fat, and healthy for my body"; "I want to find myself naturally attracted to eating lots of fresh fruits

and vegetables"; "I want to easily find myself fully conscious about food choices—naturally eating those foods that maintain my desired weight"; "I want to easily find myself fully satisfied from eating small portions of food"; "I want to easily find myself joyously cooking healthy meals."

WORK

Work is a major factor in our lives. A lack of work and routine can lead to boredom and depression. Too much work can lead to neglecting the other parts of our lives that would bring balance and joy. Being in a job we don't enjoy or in a difficult work environment can produce so much stress that it undermines the other parts of our lives. Taking time to make our work enjoyable is important if we are to experience full and complete lives.

Getting a New Job

Wishing can help to clarify which occupation would be best for us. We can also use the power of wishes to attract appropriate job opportunities, and to see how best to respond in interviews in order to get the position we want.

Wishes to Get a New Job:
"I want an inflow of Divine Wisdom regarding my career, leading me to make those choices that are in my overall best interests"; "I want to be employed by a company that holds values I believe in and can support"; "I want to easily find myself working in the right job, resulting in happiness in my everyday life"; "I want to easily find myself saying exactly the right words that lead to my being hired into a creative

work situation that I enjoy"; "I want to easily find myself making exactly the right moves that result in landing a happy job situation"; "I want to easily attract, recognize, and find myself working in the right job for me that includes ———— (international travel)"; "In my negotiations with ————, I want to easily find myself initiating in a way that is in my overall best interests"; "I want to easily find myself saying the right words to ———— that cause them to joyously hire me with a win-win contract."

IMPROVING CURRENT WORK CONDITIONS

Sometimes we are aware of changes that need to be made at work, but feel powerless to do anything about it. Wishing can prompt us to speak up and help to positively shift our job environment in ways that benefit all concerned.

Wishes to Help Us Improve Conditions at Work:
"Relative to my work situation, I want Divine Guidance showing me exactly what steps to take that will be in my overall best interests"; "I want all feelings of being 'beaten up' and defeated at work totally lifted from me"; "I want to find myself efficiently prioritizing my work so that I get it done with a minimum amount of stress"; "I want to easily find myself filled with right ideas leading to actions that move my career to a higher level that is happy, prosperous, and fulfilling for me"; "I want to easily find myself developing my career in a way that also supports my emotional life and my happiness"; "I want to easily find myself assimilating the technical knowledge I need for optimum success at work"; "I want to easily find myself saying the right words to ———— that show them the advantage of giving me a commission/bonus in addition to my salary"; "I want to easily attract, recognize, and find myself working with the right clients who will result in mutual empowerment and prosperity."

RELATIONSHIPS WITH CO-WORKERS

Many of us spend eight hours (or more) a day, five days a week, in the workplace. Given the amount of time we spend with co-workers, having harmonious relationships with the people surrounding us becomes worth cultivating. To accomplish "getting the job done" in a way that is fun and enlivening is largely dependent upon the helpful and supportive interactions of those who are participating in projects of which we are a part.

Wishes to Improve Relationships with Co-Workers:
"I want to easily find myself behaving toward my co-workers in ways that I want them to behave toward me"; "I want to easily find myself interacting with my co-workers in ways that validate productive behaviors"; "I want to easily find myself saying the right words to _____ that constructively point out to her (him) her (his) counterproductive behavior"; "I want to develop the habit of being open to suggestions from my co-workers that facilitate interacting with them to get the job done more easily"; "I want to cooperate with my co-workers in ways that lead to our supporting each other in getting the job done"; "I want to easily find myself saying the right words to _____ that harmoniously resolve past misunderstandings."

IMPROVING MANAGEMENT SKILLS

A good manager must have a clear picture of the common objective that all are working toward, as well as the ability to effectively communicate that goal to others in an inspiring way. Their own positive attitude and energy must set the example that helps others stay on track. The best managers have the sensitivity and awareness to empower their employees to do their best without suppressing their spirits.

Wishes to Improve Management Skills:

"I want to easily find myself demonstrating to others the way to get the job done"; "I want to easily find myself treating those who work for me in a way that evokes their loyalty and support"; "I want to easily find myself emitting an energy at work that inspires others to want to create the same positive energy in their jobs"; "I want to easily find myself creating an atmosphere for my employees where they can flourish and are free to use their talents creatively to reach our common goal"; "I want to develop the habit of telling my employees what they are doing right before I tell them what needs to be changed"; "I want to easily find myself expressing my appreciation to my employees in a way that shows them I care about them"; "I want to easily find myself consciously and consistently being grateful for the support of the people who work for me."

WORK PROJECTS

If the work we do is task oriented, our attitude toward the project can greatly influence not only the outcome, but also the enjoyment we feel while on the job. A "begrudging" attitude toward work can rob us of the vitality that is generated by rising to the occasion and getting the job done.

Wishes to Encourage a Positive Attitude Toward Work Projects:

"I want to easily find myself consistently taking those steps that make my ——— (video) project a success"; "I want to easily attract, recognize, and begin working with the right people on the ——— (Web page design) project, producing excellent results I am happy with"; "I want to easily find myself joyously putting together presentations that are an accurate and potent portrayal of my ideas"; "I want to easily find myself developing a ——— (fax, e-mail, newsletter) system that communicates to a wide range of people and results in lots of new business!"; "I want all resistance to doing ———— (the newsletter) totally lifted from me"; "I want to easily find myself viewing the ———— project as fun, and working on it joyfully!"

WORLD PEACE

The idea of world peace is no longer an idealistic hope, but a practical key to survival and the enrichment of our lives. In an age of high stress and fast-paced living, we are propelled to rise to a new level of peace—inwardly and outwardly in the world—in order to have the serenity to navigate our lives in a way that includes room for a sense of connectedness and enjoyment.

Personal Cooperation with World Peace

One thing each of us can do to bring about world peace is to become more peaceful within ourselves. By changing our own inner attitudes, thoughts, and responses to life, we alter the effect we have on others. This creates a chain reaction that affects the whole world.

Wishes to Experience More Peace Within Ourselves:
"I want to easily find myself consciously feeling more peaceful in my daily life"; "I want to easily find myself viewing people all over the world as my brothers and sisters, an extension of myself"; "I want all feelings of threat and separation between myself and others totally lifted from me"; "I want to consciously recognize the Oneness between myself and the brothers and sisters who come across my path"; "I want to be filled with love and caring for my sisters and brothers all over the world."

BEHAVIOR THAT PROMOTES WORLD PEACE

Our response to outer stimuli greatly affects the people around us, and thus affects the vibration of the whole world. Habitual reactions of impatience, irritation, judgment, intolerance, criticism, pessimism, or bigotry perpetuate the pattern of feeling "greater or lesser" and promotes our feeling of isolation and the need for battle. By consciously being more loving in our responses to external stimuli, we shift the impact we have on others, and begin to actively promote world peace right where we are.

Wishes to Shift Our Habitual Responses:

"I want all tendencies to destructive attitudes totally lifted from me"; "I want to easily find myself behaving toward others in a way that directly promotes world peace"; "I want to easily find myself promoting world peace through my own example of peacefulness"; "I want to easily find myself taking actions that promote world peace"; "When others promote war, I want to easily find myself saying those words that cause them to be open to the idea of peace"; "I want all fears of 'speaking up' regarding world peace totally lifted from me"; "I want to easily see through war provocations and see the alternative, peaceful solution that is possible."

WORLD PEACE PROJECTS

We may feel called to actively participate in a project that promotes world peace on a local or global level. Wishing can help attract those opportunities that best suit our talents and temperament, as well as inspire us to take the first step and connect with an organization that is actively promoting world peace.

Wishes to Begin Active Participation in Humanitarian Projects:

"I want all procrastination to doing my part to promote world peace totally lifted from me"; "I want total clarity in seeing the part I can play that will successfully promote world peace"; "I want to easily find myself playing an active role in telling my government my feelings about world peace"; "I want to easily find myself doing my part to end hunger in the world"; "I want to find myself involved with groups and activities that actively support bringing world peace into manifestation"; "I want to easily find myself involved in community-service activities that promote ideals I believe in."

---

*In looking at the sample wishes from the category you want to work on, you will find that some of the wishes are appropriate to your situation and goals, and some are not. For example, in the Self-Confidence/Security category: "I want to feel secure and confident in all life situations" is very different from "I want to easily find myself taking those actions that lead to a solid sense of security." Choose the wishes you resonate with and that are in alignment with what you truly want to manifest in your life. You can also change the wording slightly so that you feel comfortable with it.

Part V

Conclusion:
Living at a New Level

Actively using New Moon Power Periods will add magic to your life. When you take a pen in hand and write down your wishes during a Power Period, you are saying to the Universe: "Okay—I'm in charge. This is *my* life and I've decided I'm going to be happy! AND, *this* is what I need. . . ."

At that moment of taking responsibility and consciously deciding to *have* the things you want in your life, the power shifts and the entire game changes. The only reason you don't already have the things you will be wishing for is that, up until now, your life has been created from your subconscious mind. In your subconscious are all the negative tapes from your past lives, your early childhood, and the society you live in—all the voices that say: "You can't have this"; "You don't deserve to have that"; "You can't have BOTH this and that." This is what has been dictating what is currently manifesting in your life. Using Power Periods releases these negative beliefs from the subconscious mind. You have the power to release these tapes and create the life you truly want to live.

The main message of this book is "Above all, pursue your dreams!" If fulfilling your desire doesn't come easily, don't second-guess the dream, but be open to new approaches for manifesting it. The wishes of your heart are sacred; they would not be in your heart if they were not something you were meant to have. In pursuing your dreams, a tremendous growth of character is acquired. This is the invitation that is depicted in all the ancient fairy tales and myths: the prince/princess must go through frightening tests (confronting monsters, going on perilous journeys, etc.) in order to win the hand of the princess/prince and inherit the kingdom.

In the process of actually attaining what you most want, you will be forced to grow beyond the barriers—inner and outer—that you most fear. Your inner inhibitions will be transcended, released, and dissolved forever. So press past the obstacles and the inertia and take the risks. Although it may temporarily terrify you, be willing to leave what is familiar (and often stagnant) for a path of renewed vitality and growth. The Universe has arranged it so that what you most desire is exactly what you must pursue in order to experience true personal happiness.

About the Author

JAN SPILLER is known throughout the world as a trusted and perceptive leader in astrology. She contributes monthly columns to *Dell Horoscope*, the largest-circulation astrology magazine in the world. She teaches regularly at New Age and astrology conferences and is a highly sought-after radio and television guest. She was a contributing editor for the anthology *Astrology for Women*, and she has written *Spiritual Astrology* (with Karen McCoy) and *Astrology for the Soul*. To date, her books have been translated into ten languages. Her website is www.cosmicpath.com, and she lives in New York City, and Santa Fe, New Mexico.